# The Behavioural Finance Revolution

# BEHAVIOURAL FINANCIAL REGULATION AND POLICY (BEFAIRLY) SERIES

**Series Editors:** Barbara Alemanni, *University of Genoa, Italy*, Umberto Filotto, *University of Rome "Tor Vergata", Italy*, Shabnam Mousavi, *Johns Hopkins University Carey Business School, USA and Max Planck Institute for Human Development, Germany* and Riccardo Viale, *University of Milano-Bicocca, Italy, and Herbert Simon Society*

Promoted by the Herbert Simon Society in collaboration with the Bank of Italy and the Max Planck Institute for Human Development, BEFAIRLY's mission is employing, interpreting, and translating the behavioural finance and economic discourse to enhance the design of financial regulations. By encouraging direct exchange between members of academia, industry, and government in the form of academic papers, policy proposals, and industry case studies, the aim is multi-channel propagation and dissemination of knowledge. The Behavioural Financial Regulation and Policy (BEFAIRLY) book series is an important outlet to achieve this goal.

# The Behavioural Finance Revolution

## A New Approach to Financial Policies and Regulations

*Edited by*

Riccardo Viale

*University of Milano-Bicocca, Italy and Herbert Simon Society (Series Senior Editor)*

Shabnam Mousavi

*Johns Hopkins University Carey Business School, USA and Max Planck Institute for Human Development, Germany (2018 Edition Associate Senior Editor)*

Barbara Alemanni

*University of Genoa, Italy*

Umberto Filotto

*University of Rome "Tor Vergata", Italy*

BEHAVIOURAL FINANCIAL REGULATION AND POLICY (BEFAIRLY) SERIES

Edward Elgar
PUBLISHING

Cheltenham, UK • Northampton, MA, USA

Published by
Edward Elgar Publishing Limited
The Lypiatts
15 Lansdown Road
Cheltenham
Glos GL50 2JA
UK

Edward Elgar Publishing, Inc.
William Pratt House
9 Dewey Court
Northampton
Massachusetts 01060
USA

A catalogue record for this book
is available from the British Library

Library of Congress Control Number: 2018954371

This book is available electronically in the **Elgar**online
Economics subject collection
DOI 10.4337/9781788973069

ISBN 978 1 78897 305 2 (cased)
ISBN 978 1 78897 306 9 (eBook)

Typeset by Servis Filmsetting Ltd, Stockport, Cheshire
Printed and bound in Great Britain by TJ International Ltd, Padstow

# Contents

## PART 1   THE MANY FACES OF FINANCE IN ACADEMIA

# Figures

# Tables

# Contributors

**Barbara Alemanni**, The University of Genoa, Italy

**Caroline Attia**, University of Toulouse, France

**Magda Bianco**, Bank of Italy, Italy

**Giampio Bracchi**, Politecnico Milano University, Italy

**Enrico Maria Cervellati**, Ca' Foscari University of Venice, Italy

**Caterina Cruciani**, Ca' Foscari University of Venice, Italy

**Gregorio De Felice**, Chief Economist Intesa Sanpaolo, Italy

**Massimo Egidi**, LUISS Guido Carli University, Italy

**Umberto Filotto**, University of Rome Tor Vergata, Italy

**Francesco Franceschi**, Bank of Italy, Italy

**Gloria Gardenal**, Ca' Foscari University of Venice, Italy

**Gerd Gigerenzer**, Harding Center for Risk Literacy, Max Planck Institute for Human Development, Germany

**Cristina Giorgiantonio**, Bank of Italy Research Department, Italy

**Denis Hilton**, University of Toulouse, France

**Nadia Linciano**, Consob, Italy

**Adriana Lojschova**, European Central Bank

**Donato Masciandaro**, BAFFI CAREFIN Centre, Bocconi University Milan and SUERF

**Benoit Mojon**, Banque de France, France

**Paolo Mottura**, Bocconi University Milan, Italy

**Shabnam Mousavi**, Johns Hopkins University Carey Business School, USA and Max Planck Institute for Human Development, Germany

**Adrian Penalver**, Banque de France, France

**Lorenzo Portelli**, Head of Cross Asset Research Amundi, Deputy Head of Macroeconomics and Strategy Research – Amundi Italy

**Ugo Rigoni**, Ca' Foscari University of Venice, Italy

**Salvatore Rossi**, Senior Deputy Governor Bank of Italy and President of IVASS, Italy

**Zeno Rotondi**, UniCredit, Italy

**Giacomo Sillari**, LUISS Guido Carli University, Italy

**Alessandro Varaldo**, Deputy CEO of Amundi SGR and University of Turin, Italy

**Riccardo Viale**, University of Milano-Bicocca, Italy and Herbert Simon Society

**Giordano Zevi**, Bank of Italy, Italy

# Foreword

## Salvatore Rossi[*]

The legitimacy of including behavioral economics in mainstream economic thinking has sharply increased in the last few years.[1]

Behavioral-based books are in the best-seller list in many countries; behavioral analyses are part of the standard curriculum in most graduate schools; most recently, the Nobel Prize committee attributed this year's prize to Richard Thaler, for "integrating economics with psychology".[2]

But we must go further. There is a widely perceived need for economic studies that explore real human behavior, especially after the global financial crisis hit the world ten years ago.[3] The simplifying assumption of a rational and self-interested agent has proved insufficient to explain the systematic deviations that have contributed to the crisis.[4]

Of course there is a long tradition of studies on individual behavior, tracking back to Simon's seminal 1955 contribution and his 1957 book aptly named *Models of Man*.[5] Allais, Ellsberg and others[6] detected the fundamental limits of the economists' particular model of man. But for many years the economic discipline, while fully accepting those insights, considered them as just a useful warning that economics does not deal with real human beings but with simplified representations.

We now believe that economic models, especially when used to inform policy making, should also be robust regarding real human beings' behavioral traits. Limited ability to process information, aversion to losses, endowment effects, and social preferences could all imply that policies deemed sub-optimal in standard neoclassical settings are in fact the most

---

[*]   Senior Deputy Governor of the Bank of Italy and President of IVASS.
[1]   See DellaVigna (2009) for a survey of academic literature; Driscoll and Holden (2014) for a discussion on how the behavioral findings have informed macroeconomic modeling; Lunn (2014) and OECD (2017a) for wide-ranging examples and analyses on the application of behavioral insights to public policies.
[2]   The Committee for the Prize in Economic Sciences in Memory of Alfred Nobel (2017).
[3]   See for example Hendry and Muellbauer (2017) and the literature quoted there.
[4]   See the account in Gorton (2010).
[5]   Simon (1955; 1957).
[6]   Allais (1953) and Ellsberg (1961).

appropriate. This could be true also when recognizing the richness and flexibility of the fully rational agents-based theories.[7]

Behavioral economics has also entered the core business of central banks: monetary policy. As Janet Yellen put it some years ago: "Individuals have money illusion, follow heuristic rules of thumb, and care about issues like fairness and equity. . .. theories built on behavioral foundations have strikingly different implications from those predictions that follow from more standard theories".[8] Importantly, behavioral considerations have also become part of the general discussion on the role of expectations in economic theory, especially in times of high uncertainty.[9] Recently De Grauwe and Ji have proposed macroeconomic models where agents are not sophisticated enough to formulate rational expectations, and are therefore forced to adopt simpler heuristics to forecast the future.[10]

Depending on a range of parameters, the policy trade-offs faced by central banks can be actually different from those based on standard models.

Finance is an obvious field in which to apply behavioral insights. Financial services are in fact often complex, involve trade-offs between the present and the future, require an assessment of risk and uncertainty, and the decisions are sometimes not repeatable, so that people cannot learn from their own past experience.

The "behavioral finance revolution", as it has been labeled, has opened the way to a more integrated approach to the analysis of economic phenomena.

Consider households' financial decisions. Heuristic thinking, which is people's tendency to use simplistic rules to make complex decisions, has emerged as one of the main explanations for why people concentrate their investments in a few assets (portfolio under-diversification)[11] or why many households over-pay for their bank accounts, keeping old and expensive tariffs when their bank has made cheaper options available to them.[12] The predisposition to simplify decisions can also explain the propensity to over-borrow, to under-save and to favor shorter debt maturities, phenomena all observed in households' borrowing decisions.[13]

Financial intermediaries may have an incentive to exploit consumers' biases. Let me give you an example, referring to the US subprime mortgage market. In the run-up to the crisis, advertisement "framing" was used by many banks to increase their business: low initial interest rates were

---

[7]   See for example the discussion in Gul and Pesendorfer (2008).
[8]   Yellen (2009).
[9]   Visco (2009).
[10]  De Grauwe and Ji (2017).
[11]  Benartzi and Thaler (2001).
[12]  Stango and Zinman (2009a); Branzoli (2016).
[13]  Stango and Zinman (2009b).

frequently publicized with much more prominence than the higher rates that would inevitably follow.[14] The rational *homo economicus* would not have been tricked by such strategies, while the main man in the street was.[15]

A deeper understanding of how investment and saving decisions are made and why people make predictable mistakes when choosing financial services is therefore crucial in order to achieve effective financial consumer protection.

The financial industry, the banking industry in particular, is rooted in trust: financial intermediaries have to be trusted by the millions and millions of individual savers giving money to them. Trust is based on the stability and transparency of financial intermediaries: because people's trust is a public good, public authorities have to protect savers on both fronts. I do not want to enter here into the debate about whether a single supervisory authority should be charged with both missions, or whether we need two. What the economic literature and international experience have shown is that laws and rules are not enough.[16] There is more. Savers do not usually have the knowledge to really understand the characteristics of the financial products they buy, even when they are clearly explained to them. But also when they do, their decisions might not be fully rational.

Financial education is key in both respects.

The initiatives of financial education, for students and for adults, promoted by the Bank of Italy now take behavioral considerations more into account. We try to increase savers' basic concepts and at the same time help them make rational choices in accordance with their true needs. For instance, this year we involved about one hundred teenagers in a role play whose aim was to make them aware of their mistakes and irrational behavior.

It is hard to estimate precisely how pervasive behavioral biases are in the population, but we have some evidence suggesting that they are actually quite common.[17] A survey conducted recently by the Bank of Italy shows that almost a quarter of the Italian adult population are overconfident, which means they overestimate their actual knowledge of basic financial concepts.[18]

In other developed countries this percentage is even higher. Overconfident savers face a significantly higher risk of making bad investments, and overconfidence is just one of the relevant biases!

---

[14] For a general overview of how the presence of biased consumers may affect firms' pricing decisions, see Grubb (2015).

[15] Gurun et al. (2016).

[16] OECD (2017a).

[17] See DellaVigna (2009).

[18] Banca d'Italia (2017).

New technologies can affect those biases. On the one hand, they bring risks that are not yet completely understood. For instance, being able to buy a financial product with a single click on my smartphone may exacerbate my short-termism, self-control problems and confirmatory bias.[19] On the other hand new technologies offer an opportunity: for instance, digital practices may lead savers to take "good" actions, through automated reminders to save or to pay back a loan, or a better price/product comparison.

Anyway, laws and regulations must be an important part of the picture. We may think of many: nudges, default options, framing disclosure, cooling off periods, and also restrictions to consumer choices. Such interventions entail an increasing degree of intrusiveness and they have different welfare implications. Nudges, defaults and disclosure requirements usually benefit not-so-rational consumers without imposing costs to rational agents: they in fact help the former to make the right choice, for instance overcoming the framing effect, but they do not change the actual decision of the latter. Restrictions to consumer choices, such as limitations to product selling, imply a trade-off between the protection of vulnerable savers and the costs imposed to rational ones.[20] But there could be circumstances that justify these costs, with well-founded reasons.

Let me conclude. Economic theory is a simplified representation of the world and it should be considered as a tool to increase human welfare, offering good predictions and supporting the decisions of policy makers.

During more than three decades of fierce debate, behavioral economics has influenced the way we think about real-world phenomena and how we design economic policies. It still has some opponents.

However, the question is not whether behavioral finance should replace the standard theory, but whether the debate between behavioral and "traditional" economists improves our understanding of the real world, and provides policy makers with more effective tools.

## REFERENCES

Allais, M. (1953). Le Comportement de l'Homme Rationnel devant le Risque: Critique des Postulats et Axiomes de l'Ecole Americaine. *Econometrica* **21**, 503–46.

Banca d'Italia (2017). Annual Report for 2016, pp. 84–7.

Benartzi, S. and Thaler, R. (2001). Naive diversification strategies in defined contribution savings plans. *American Economic Review* **91**, 79–98.

---

[19]  See OECD (2017b).
[20]  Campbell (2016).

Branzoli, N. (2016). Price dispersion and consumer inattention: evidence from the market of bank accounts. Bank of Italy Working Paper No. 1082.

Campbell, J.Y. (2016). Restoring rational choice: the challenge of consumer financial regulation. *American Economic Review* **106**(5), 1–30.

Committee for the Prize in Economic Sciences in Memory of Alfred Nobel (2017). Richard H. Thaler: Integrating Economics with Psychology, Scientific Background on the Sveriges Riksbank Prize.

De Grauwe, P. and Ji, Y. (2017). Structural reforms and monetary policies in a behavioural macroeconomic model. CEPR Discussion Paper No. 12336.

DellaVigna, S. (2009). Psychology and economics: evidence from the field. *Journal of Economic Literature* **47**, 315–72.

Driscoll, J.C. and Holden, S. (2014). Behavioral economics and macroeconomic models. *Journal of Macroeconomics* **41**, 133–47.

Ellsberg, D. (1961). Risk, ambiguity, and the savage axioms. *Quarterly Journal of Economics* **75**(4), 643–69.

Gorton, G.B. (2010). *Slapped by the Invisible Hand: The Panic of 2007*. Oxford: Oxford University Press.

Grubb, M. (2015). Failing to choose the best price: theory evidence and policy. *Review of Industrial Organization* **47**(3), 303–40.

Gul, F. and Pesendorfer, W. (2008). The case for mindless economics, in Caplin, A. and Schotter, A. (eds), *The Foundations of Positive and Normative Economics*. Oxford: Oxford University Press.

Gurun, H.G., Matvos, G. and Seru, A. (2016). Advertising expensive mortgages. *The Journal of Finance* **71**(5), 2371–416.

Hendry, D. and Muellbauer, J. (2017). The future of macroeconomics: macro theory and models at the Bank of England. Economics Series Working Papers No. 832, University of Oxford.

Lunn, P. (2014). *Regulatory Policy and Behavioural Economics*. Paris: OECD Publishing.

OECD (2017a). *Behavioural Insights and Public Policy. Lessons from Around the World*. Paris: OECD Publishing.

OECD (2017b). *G20/OECD INFE Report Ensuring Financial Education and Consumer Protection for All in the Digital Age*. Paris: OECD Publishing.

Simon, H.A. (1955). A behavioral model of rational choice. *Quarterly Journal of Economics* **69**, 99–118.

Simon, H.A. (1957). *Models of Man, Social and Rational: Mathematical Essays on Rational Human Behavior in a Social Setting*. New York: John Wiley.

Stango, V. and Zinman, J. (2009a). What do consumers really pay on their checking and credit card accounts? Explicit, implicit, and avoidable costs. *American Economic Review Papers and Proceedings* **99**(2), 424–9.

Stango, V. and Zinman, J. (2009b). Exponential growth bias and household finance. *The Journal of Finance* **64**(6), 2806–49.

Visco, I. (2009). On the role of expectations in Keynesian and today's economics (and economies). Paper presented at the International Conference on "Gli economisti postkeynesiani di Cambridge e l'Italia", Accademia Nazionale dei Lincei. Rome.

Yellen, J.L. (2009). Implications of behavioral economics for monetary policy, in Foote, C.L., Goette, L. and Meier, S. (eds), *Policymaking Insights from Behavioral Economics*. Boston, MA: Federal Reserve Bank of Boston.

# Preface

Economics has a history of drawing on other sciences that are helpful for understanding markets, most obviously mathematics and statistics, and arguably physics. Drawing on cognitive sciences to improve analysis of demand and supply, namely, behavioural finance, is a natural supplementary step. The behavioural approach is not limited to psychology. Increasingly, scholars promote the use of cognitive anthropology, neuroscience and Artificial Intelligence in socioeconomic sciences.

The regulators' mandate involves improving financial markets' efficiency and functionality, while protecting people from exploitation by financial institutions. To this end, the regulator needs to understand the drivers of the observed equilibria, which arise from the processes that generate decisions of firms, consumers and of course, of regulators themselves. Behavioural economics can help this pursuit by shedding light on how people make choices and why they might make choices that are not in their best interest or in line with their goals. Such insights allow both firms and regulators to detect behaviourally rooted problems in the markets and to design and test ways to deal with them. In particular, financial consumers are vulnerable in the face of many financial products that are credence or experience services. Sophisticated suppliers can and do observe consumers' decision biases by observing decisions under different conditions, then use these biases to design exploitative marketing strategies. A behavioural approach to the design of regulations enables the government to employ psychology and other sciences to sort out relevant from irrelevant elements towards increasing the efficiency of both market and non-market mechanisms, while reducing the possibility of exploitative practices.

The behavioural approach that we advocate does not retire the existing body of knowledge but seeks to expand and enrich it. We believe that behavioural and traditional analysis can complement each other to generate more comprehensive insights that adequately acknowledge and meaningfully combine the roles played by specific market structures, competitive dynamics, information access, culture, values, emotions, beliefs, regulators' licence to operate, compliance vs. non-compliance conditions, contract design, law of contract, law of tort, consumers' general rights, consumer advocacy bodies, marketing by firms, institutional structures such as courts and so forth. Many of these aspects of behavioural finance are discussed in different chapters of the current book. Focusing on improving regulations, a variety of topics are examined from multiple aspects: What are the right criteria for intervention in the markets? Do we mean to improve total welfare or the welfare of specific groups? Or is welfare altogether the wrong metric? Which remedies work best for which problems? What is the optimal combination of regulatory tools? And how does this differ by regulatory goals? What is the right unit of account for designing interventions? Are regulators to interfere with property rights?

A multidisciplinary behavioural-based approach to economics is not limited to the development of more comprehensive financial market regulations. All macroeconomic actions – monetary, fiscal or regulatory – are ultimately intended to influence behaviour. For instance, monetary policy changes interest rates in order to affect people's preference to hold or spend money. Fiscal stimulus increases aggregate demand, giving people more income in the short term, which is hoped they will spend, and thus directly brings unemployed resources back into use by paying them to work. Regulatory changes restrict or encourage some behaviour more directly than others, but generally aim to channel the behaviour of consumers by directly restricting the actions of financial institutions (or more properly, their staff). Although aiming at changing behaviour, almost all approaches to managing the economy share a common but fallacious assumption: that people, on the whole, respond rationally to price incentives. By adopting a behavioural view, regulators can thus benefit from going beyond the dominant but unrealistic hypothesis of full rationality in their search for the roots of the observed behaviour and for designing rules to tame the unwanted. There is much to be done in this area. While many tools have been experimentally tested at the micro level the extensions to macroeconomics are severely limited. Price anchoring, framing, endowment effects, confirmation bias and various social and peer effects all demonstrably allow us to influence behaviour in market transactions; however, their direct and significant applications to what we might call "macro-rationality" are much less explored. Macroeconomics needs to significantly engage other disciplines both to define analytical metrics and to generate decision aids. The current book offers some recommendations towards this goal.

This book is part of a larger project that commenced on 6 December 2017 as an initiative by Herbert Simon Society in collaboration with the Bank of Italy and the Max Planck Institute for Human Development. Behavioural Financial Regulation and Policy Initiative (BEFAIRLY)'s mission is to employ, interpret and translate the behavioural finance and economic discourse to improve financial regulatory decision-making and outcomes. This mission is fulfilled by creating a forum for direct exchange between members of academia, industry and government presenting and discussing academic papers, policy proposals and industry case studies followed by multichannel propagation of the generated knowledge. The initiative is a non-profit project, whose venues and operations are funded by sponsorships. The initiative operates under a steering committee composed of the chairman Riccardo Viale of the University of Milano-Bicocca and the Herbert Simon Society, and members Barbara Alemanni of the University of Genoa, Umberto Filotto of the University of Rome "Tor Vergata", and Shabnam Mousavi of Johns Hopkins University and the Max Planck Institute. All administrative and operational tasks, including those related to the publication of the current volume, are overseen by Giovanni De Rosa of the Herbert Simon Society.

The steering committee is advised by an international scientific committee (being currently shaped) envisioned to be European oriented with a balanced mix of 10 to 14 members from central bankers, regulators, practitioners and academics. The scientific committee convenes annually to provide guidelines and suggestions for speakers, to evaluate and approve themes and topics proposed by the steering committee, and thereafter to disseminate the topic and invitations among its community and network to attract contributions and papers of the highest possible quality. Furthermore, to promote the cause of this initiative, an annual award will be granted to a young researcher for a publication in behavioural sciences with application to financial regulations and policies.

Our ultimate goal is making meaningful and sustainable contributions to the well-being of society. By upholding a behavioural and cognitive approach to financial regulations and policy, we employ a wholesome view of people that acknowledges human beings simply as they are. By bringing together academics and practitioners, we build a platform for combining wisdom from both sources. The BEFAIRLY initiative translates this rich combination into recommendations and recipes for financial regulators towards increasing stability and security of the people. This volume is our first delivery in print, which we hope to be found useful by the reader. We welcome and encourage inputs and contributions from you, the reader, and invite you to join our cause for making the financial world a safer place for everyone.

This book is part of the programme BEFAIRLY (Behavioural Financial Regulation and Policy) promoted by the Herbert Simon Society in collaboration with the Bank of Italy and the Max Planck Institute for

Human Development with the support of Compagnia di San Paolo, Intesa Sanpaolo, Allianz and Amundi.

BEFAIRLY Steering Committee,
Barbara Alemanni, Umberto Filotto, Shabnam Mousavi
and Riccardo Viale

# PART 1

# The many faces of finance in academia

# 1. Understanding financial behaviour for better policy making: an introduction[1]

## Riccardo Viale

We must develop a theory of what he intends, simultaneously giving content to his attitudes and his words. Because we need to give meaning to his words, we will propose a theory that recognizes him as a coherent person, who believes in truth and loves good.

Davidson (1970, p. 253)

## 1. INTRODUCTION

In 1994, *The Economist* asked members of four groups, four former finance ministers from OECD countries, four chairmen of multinational companies, four students of economics at Oxford University, and four London dustmen to provide their forecasts for four items: the average growth rate of OECD countries, average inflation, the price of petrol in the coming year, and the year when Singapore's GDP would overtake Australia's. Who made the worst forecasts? Not the dustmen, but the former finance ministers. The dustmen and the company managers actually identified the most accurate scenarios.

The results of these tests, and those of many others, should certainly make us sit up. Our savings, and the economic policies of governments and large companies depend on analyses and forecasts that prove unreliable. Goldman Sachs, Credit Suisse, UBS, Citigroup, Morgan Stanley, JPMorgan Chase, Deutsche Bank, Bank of America and numerous other institutions in the world employ hoards of analysts to predict the future, who are systematically proven wrong by reality. We can take some recent examples. In 2009, Morgan Stanley predicted that inflation would be low in China, and instead it reached a peak of 5 per cent in 2010. Goldman

[1] The current chapter represents a modification of Viale (2012, chapter 11). I thank Shabnam Mousavi for her precious editorial support and Barbara Alemanni and Umberto Filotto for their interesting advice.

Sachs guaranteed that China would grow by just 6 per cent in 2009, and instead it reached 9.3 per cent. For the United States, low interest rates were forecast for 2011, as an effect of quantitative easing, that is, the increased money supply decided by the Fed. Instead, so far this very measure has brought an increase in the rates of 10-year bonds of 2.5 to 3.5 per cent.

What is more striking about the incorrect forecasts is the impudent way that analysts glibly adjust their mistakes after the event, as if nothing has happened. In October 2010 Goldman Sachs forecast that the American economy would slow down from a growth rate of 2.6 to 1.8 per cent. In December 2010, they had already changed their estimate, increasing it by 40 per cent, predicting that the United States will grow by 2.5 per cent at the beginning of the coming year, and can go up to an average for the year of 4 per cent. Financial forecasts as such seem to be absolutely useless.[2] Philip Tetlock (2005)[3], a psychologist at Berkeley, analysed 82 361 forecasts by 284 professional analysts. The forecasts contained in this study were so inadequate that they were surpassed by the casual forecasts made by "dart-throwing monkeys", that is, by the darts thrown at a blackboard by a group of monkeys.

---

[2]  We must ask ourselves one question: what are financial forecasts for if, as we have shown, they are not generally reliable? We suspect that their role may be to create that imitative behaviour that is gradually transformed into herd behaviour from which careful speculators can make enormous profits. Many years ago George Soros, in a private conversation, told me that when he invests he does not look at analysts' numbers, but tries to empathetically interpret what the other small, medium and large investors who read those numbers will do. Interpreting what the herd is thinking, trusting analysts' estimates and being prone to fall into the many cognitive traps, has enabled smart financiers like George Soros to make their fortunes. By empirically anticipating the hypotheses of behavioural finance!

[3]  An important and underreported conclusion of that study was that some experts do have real foresight, and Tetlock has spent the past decade trying to figure out why. What makes some people so good? And can this talent be taught? In *Superforecasting*, Tetlock and co-author Dan Gardner (2015) offer a masterwork on prediction, drawing on decades of research and the results of a massive, government-funded forecasting tournament. The Good Judgment Project involves tens of thousands of ordinary people – including a Brooklyn filmmaker, a retired pipe installer and a former ballroom dancer – who set out to forecast global events. Some of the volunteers have turned out to be astonishingly good. They've beaten other benchmarks, competitors, gurus, and prediction markets. They've even beaten the collective judgement of intelligence analysts with access to classified information. They are "superforecasters". Tetlock and Gardner show that good forecasting doesn't require powerful computers or arcane methods. It involves gathering evidence from a variety of sources, thinking probabilistically, working in teams, keeping score, and being willing to admit error and change course.

## 2.   SEMANTIC AND PRAGMATIC ANCHORING

Social reality is too complex; there are too many initial conditions to take into consideration and, above all, it is the kingdom of ontological uncertainty, that is, there is never any regularity in the phenomena. So all "forecasters" can do is to extrapolate arbitrary regularities from contingent trends, relying only on small samples,[4] and project them into the future. This is what financial analysts do all the time, cloaking their products behind the label of scientific analysis. The forecasts mentioned are the product of this fallacious methodology.

But the error is magnified if we consider a recurring bias that forecasters fall into systematically. When they select the data on which to base their projections, they are unconsciously conditioned by what is known as the anchoring and adjustment heuristic. This describes the individual's tendency to perform a numerical estimate in two steps. First he anchors himself to some initial value, which is then corrected in the most plausible direction, up or down. This heuristic produces a chain reaction: the saver is anchored to the forecasts of the bank analysts, who are themselves influenced by the news from economic journalists, who are conditioned by the numbers of the analysts of the large merchant banks, which are influenced by the forecasts of the rating agencies or the assessments of international financial institutions, themselves anchored to present and immediately past stock values and prices. The anchoring effect is produced very subtly and unconsciously. Some experiments have shown that even non-pertinent data such as a telephone number or social security number can influence the numerical evaluations of completely different topics like the evaluation of a house or a consumer product.

What is more, the way the data are presented also has a powerful effect.[5] Tversky and Kahneman (1974) asked two questions about the trend of the Dow Jones Index which were semantically the same but differed in the manner of their presentation, and obtained different results. The framing of the second question, which contained numerical information, acted as an anchor which automatically influenced the reply, hooking onto the numbers read. This phenomenon emerges in many financial decisions, such as the choice of a form of financing or insurance cover, because most financial and welfare products focus attention on specific threshold values.

---

[4]   Small samples that are not representative of the financial phenomena and that therefore cause variance.

[5]   One of this effects is called priming. Priming is a psychological phenomenon whereby exposure to one stimulus influences a response to a subsequent stimulus, without conscious guidance or intention. Priming can be perceptual, semantic or conceptual.

Another phenomenon studied in recent years that influences anchoring is the order in which data are presented. Generally speaking, it seems that the first data have greater weight in terms of the formulation of a judgement (priority effect) while the last are remembered better (recency effect). But it appears that in some cases the recency effect prevails as an anchorage. The problem is that the prevalence of one of the two effects seems to depend on the complexity of the task, the amount of information provided and when the opinion is formulated (if it is formulated after the data are communicated or gradually as they are presented).

In general, when faced with a range of information, the individual follows conversational and epistemological maxims of interpretation. *Conversational maxims* were introduced some time ago in 1993 in the studies of Paul Grice (1989) and subsequently developed by other scholars like Dan Sperber and Deirdre Wilson. One of the basic principles is that of cooperation. When one speaks elliptically, omitting some passages and leaving areas of shadow, the listener will complete the semantic gaps with inferences known as *conversational implicatures*. For example, if one person says: "The Monsanto share is growing strongly, but it is a technological share", the listener will assume from the "but" that the speaker intends to underline that in these times of financial crisis and recession, the fact that it is a share in a company with a high intensity of biotechnological research, may make it more fragile compared to shares in less cyclic or more stable sectors like foods. Apart from these pragmatic conversational maxims, according to some epistemologists like Donald Davidson (1970, 1980, 1984) and Daniel Dennett (1981, 1987), we apply other logical and epistemological principles to our interpretation. For example, we try to give *logical consistency* when we are faced with muddled and disjointed expressions, phrases and texts. We also assume, if there is no evidence to the contrary, that whoever is speaking to us is telling the *truth* when he makes statements that at first sight appear unrealistic.

Conversational maxims and principles of consistency and truth help us to construct a story with causal links to the text that we are reading or that is communicated to us. Recent research shows that constructing a consistent and comprehensive story is necessary to take decisions. The problem is that the individual is not always able to make a complete reconstruction and sometimes remains anchored to the way information is presented. For example, if two different presentations are made of a company – one orderly and historical from the past to the latest results, and the other muddled – and a sample is asked to predict its performance on the Stock Exchange, only the first report allows the important element of performance to be fully used. In the case of the muddled reconstruction the individual is more influenced by variables other than the results. What does this tell us? That if one tries to anticipate the actions of investors, analysts and savers, it is not enough to know what information they have but also how this was communicated to them, and therefore the "story model" that they have constructed mentally. Depending on the model, some variables are more important in determining an opinion and the consequent decision.

## 2.1   Loss versus Gain

The importance of the order in which information is presented, and the pragmatic dimension of communication are linked to another powerful effect connected to the way data are presented. Classic experiments carried out by Kahneman and Tversky (1979a) have highlighted the fact that in tests that present the same monetary value of the stakes, if the question is posed as a gain, the answer tends to present an aversion to risk, whereas if the question is perceived as a loss, the individual decides with a propensity to risk. This phenomenon, known as the *framing effect*, leads to an inversion of the preferences when the same problem is framed differently. This inversion, called the *reflection effect*, proves to be a very powerful phenomenon in economic behaviour. People decidedly increase their propensity to risk when they interpret the situation in terms of loss, while they are averse to risk if the situation is presented as a gain.

As Fyodor Mikhailovich Dostoevsky asked in *The Gambler*, when is the irrational escalation behaviour that takes a gambler to bankruptcy manifested? Towards the end of the evening, when the gambler perceives that the day is closing at a loss and he wants to overturn the result by increasingly risky behaviour. The same attitude was noted in a series of studies of the banking and financial world of Wall Street and other international stock markets. When the Stock Exchange adds up the gains and losses at the end of the day, there will be a greater trend on the part of traders to take risky decisions if negotiations have not gone well during the day. The same also happens when the Stock Market opens the following day; focusing on the losses and overlooking the gains will also generate risky investment behaviour.

The different psychological impact of a loss as opposed to a gain is represented by *prospect theory* (Kahneman and Tversky, 1979b). The value function of this theory abstracts this aversion to loss. The value of this coefficient is equal to two: in other words, to put it simply, one has to gain approximately 2000 euros to compensate for the annoyance of having lost 1000.[6] This value function, which differs from that of neoclassical economics which presumes a coefficient of one, explains much economic

---

[6]   David Gal and Donald Rucker (forthcoming) publish in the *Journal of Consumer Psychology* a critical review on loss aversion that aims to prove that it is a fallacy. That is,

behaviour that violates the forecasts of economic theory. First of all, it explains the difficulties of negotiation between the purchaser and the buyer: the seller who deprives himself of an asset, values it much more highly than his counterpart who purchases it, who must deprive himself of his money. In addition to this, each of the parties perceives the concession made to the other as a loss, thus attributing greater weight to it than to a potential gain.

An *aversion to loss* also produces the well-known *disposition effect*, that is, the tendency to sell shares too soon whose prices have risen, but to hold on to shares that have lost value. In some analyses by American and Israeli fund managers, we can note a systematic tendency to the *disposition effect*, which damages their performance. The best managers are those that have shown the greatest ability to realize losses. Is it only aversion to loss that is responsible for this behaviour? No, various studies seem to show that *anticipated regret* for the loss of possible future earnings prevails, determining the disposition effect. In other words, as often happens in our decision-making processes, we usually reason counterfactually, asking ourselves what could or should have happened if we had taken a different decision. In this case, the alternative hypothesis that a share sold at a loss might regain value triggers regret that prompts us not to sell. Anticipated regret for a possible loss has a value several times higher than the annoyance due to an actual loss caused by remaining inactive.

## 2.2 Affect, Emotions and Heuristics

The regret illustrated in the previous example opens the discussion of an increasingly important chapter of economic psychology and behavioural finance: the role of affect and emotion in judgement, choice and decision (Gigerenzer, 2007). The issue has been overlooked for many years by cognitive psychology due to the methodological difficulties of studying it. Today, on the other hand, it is becoming central in most fields of psychology. Daniel Kahneman himself, in his Nobel Lecture of 2002, clearly underlines that it is important to refer to two types of cognitive processes. There is System 1 – or the emotional and intuitive mind – which thinks rapidly, without effort, in an associative, tacit, automatic and parallel manner, while System 2 – or the reasoning mind – thinks more slowly, in a serial, conscious way, expending energy and respecting the rules (Kahneman, 2011).[7]

---

that there is no general cognitive bias that leads people to avoid losses more vigorously than to pursue gains.

[7]   There is a growing critique to the dual model of mind. Many psychological and neural data seem to show that it is unlikely that the mind should be divided in two systems

The so-called System 1 is proving increasingly to be the submerged part of the iceberg. Its "pervasiveness" is expressed in all aspects of human behaviour and even more so of economic and financial behaviour. If we wish to conventionally break down the components of behaviour into judgement, decision and action, we can see that many past hypotheses in the explanation in each of these stages have been revised in the light of the affect and emotion variable. This has led some people, like Paul Slovic, to introduce the concept of an "affect heuristic" (Slovic et al., 2001) and Antonio Damasio (1994) to talk of "somatic markers" in decision-making. For example, affect plays a role in the value function (utility) and the pondering of probabilities. Subjective probabilities are not independent of the affective nature of outcomes. A 1 per cent probability is greater when the outcome has a significant affective component rather than a poor affective component. The subjective perception of probability depends on the affective value that the individual associates with the expected results. While the theory of utility maintains that utility and probability are independent, the results of some research show that they are not. The low probabilities have a greater weight when the expected positive or negative results trigger sentiments of hope or fear. This phenomenon has obvious consequences for the judgement that lies at the basis of one's economic and financial choices, between options with different probabilities and expected utilities. As we have seen earlier, even loss aversion, regret and the *endowment effect* (that is, attributing greater value to an asset when one owns it) have a strong affective base. This is displeasure, the negative emotion of losing or of depriving oneself of an asset which conditions the value function, increasing the utility of the asset itself.

Another effect of affect on judgement is linked to the relationship between risk and utility. Generally speaking, in economic theory there is a direct link between the two variables: the more a choice embodies risks, the greater the apparent utility of the outcome. On financial markets, the riskier the share, the greater the premium paid as a result; we can think of the bonds of risky countries like Argentina and Greece compared to those of Germany and the United States. Obviously in everyday life, reality is often different. There are large risks that have no utility, except that of

---

or in two type of processes (Viale, under review). The mind seems to be better represented by a unified model, that is by a single account of mental processes. The two main anti-dualistic approaches are that of the "cognitive continuum" put forward by Hammond (1996), Cleeremans and Jimenez (2002) and Osman (2004) and the "rule-based processing unified theory of decision making" argued by Kruglanski and Gigerenzer (2011). In this chapter my use of System 1 and 2 language is instrumental to describe the mental phenomena that are responsible for biases and errors according to mainstream behavioural economics.

having run them. I can walk for no reason on the cornice outside my flat on the twentieth floor just to show everyone how brave I am. Or I can drive at top speed when I am drunk just to entertain my friends. In these cases large risks are associated with low utility. In fact, at a psychological level, we tend to apply a trade-off between risk and affective evaluation. For example, when we positively value a share for its past history, for the company's good communicative image, for its pleasant managing director and so on, we are attributing a low risk of negative outcomes to it. Take the effect on investors of adding ".com" to the name of shares, at the peak of the Internet bubble, between June 1998 and July 1999. In a study undertaken a few years ago (Cooper et al., 2001) out of 95 shares analysed, the "dotcom effect" caused their value to increase by an average of 74 per cent in the 10 days following the announcement of the name change. Financial bubbles seem to owe a great deal to the value of the affect component in judgement.

The affect component is crucial in the representativeness and availability heuristics, and the emotional salience of an example is the basis for the generalization for an entire category. The error of extrapolation made by investors, when they tend to consider that the past performance of a share is representative of its future performance, is typical. And the emotionally more salient events are those recalled most easily at a mnemonic level. According to many authors, it is thanks to this mechanism that in periods of expansion many financial institutions relax the risk standards and make gross forecasting errors. As Galbraith said in 1954, it is our mnemonic skills that make us forget past crises and only remember present successes, which takes us gradually towards a new crisis. *Prototype heuristics* (Kahneman, 2003) have been developed recently to introduce emotional salience into various types of judgement. For example, various experiments carried out in the past have shown that it is the emotional accessibility of a prototype (for example, a share in a sector that has enjoyed strong growth on the Stock Market, promoted in all the media) that determines the judgement of the entire category (for example a growth forecast for the entire sector).

There is another way that the so-called System 1 of the mind affects judgement. If we go back to the initial example of *The Economist*, it does not seem that the quantity of data and analyses is a guarantee of analytical and forecasting success. Often too many data reduce our capacity to judge. As Gigerenzer underlined successfully (2007), intuitive, gut feelings are often better than elaborately structured judgements. The less-is-more principle is the compass in uncertain environments. In tasks characterized by uncertainty various simple and frugal heuristics give better decision-making results than those achieved with the algorithms of economic rationality (Gigerenzer et al., 1999).

And finally, affectivity comes into play not only at the judgement stage, but also at the downstream stage of decision-making and action. As neuroeconomics has shown (Camerer et al., 2005), affective components, conveyed by cortical and subcortical structures like the amygdala or the insula, underpin risk behaviour and the perception of trust in one's own actions and those of others.

## 3.    INSIDE THE HUMAN BRAIN

Early in the 1990s, Giacomo Rizzolatti and his colleagues in a neuroscience laboratory at Parma University made a revolutionary discovery which many scientists claim was as important for our understanding of the brain as DNA was for the cell. They identified the "mirror neuron", a particular type of motor neuron of the brain that has a dual function, being responsible both for our actions and for our understanding of other people's actions (Rizzolatti et al., 2001). The discovery is a classic case of serendipity (a term coined by British diplomat Horace Walpole in 1754, who referred to a Persian fairy tale in which three princes from the kingdom of Serendip – the Arab name for Sri Lanka – made unexpected and lucky discoveries). In the laboratory where Rizzolatti's group were studying the motor neurons of macaque monkeys, there were some peanuts:

> Sometimes the monkeys used them to perform tasks, and at other times they were the reward for a task performed with another object. But everyone liked the peanuts, not only the primates. And at a certain point, between recordings, someone watching the experiments "stole" some from the container prepared for the animals. When one of these "thefts" occurred, just as the researcher on duty was putting a handful of nuts into his mouth, the oscilloscope recording the monkey's neuron activity let out a very strange tac-tac-tac sound. The monkey had stopped and was not interacting with any other object. (Rizzolatti and Vozza, 2008, pp. 30–31)

The very neurons that were activated when the macaque took the peanuts were stimulated when the monkey saw the researcher do the same thing. These neurons have the ability to be activated to reflect the actions of others, as well as permitting our own.

This is an important discovery. For the first time we understand the brain mechanisms that allow the individual to understand the behaviour of others. In experiments also carried out successfully on humans, it has been shown that, to understand someone else's action, when we observe it, it needs to be reproduced by the network of neurons that is active when we perform the same action ourselves. The amazing fact is that mirror neurons are differentiated for the purpose of the action taken. Neurons that are activated when we grasp something are different from those excited when we hold or drop or tear something, and so on.

The gradual opening of the black box of the brain will provide more surprises that will help to change the old concepts of human science. Neuroeconomic research is changing the way economic research is performed. First of all, it is a powerful aid to cognitive and experimental research into decision-making models and economic action. Secondly, it poses new problems and issues, like those of the prevalence of automatic affective processes, which will profoundly change the same economic concepts. One example of the overpowering force of neuroscience, which digresses a little but is particularly intriguing, is the redefinition of the concept of free will in the light of some data obtained from EEG recordings of brain activity. As we know, free will is a theological expression, introduced by St Augustine in the fifth century and the subject of his bitter disputes with Pelagius and subsequently of the violent clashes between Luther and Erasmus in the sixteenth and seventeenth centuries. It basically represents the freedom of choice and human will. There are very well articulated philosophical arguments that develop and define the concept. One of these is the deterministic argument, which starts from the assumption that every event in nature is determined by its causal precedents and that it is therefore impossible for human choice not to follow the same rule. This negative vision is questioned not only by great philosophers like Kant, but also by our common psychological experience. At the moment that we choose, we have the feeling that nothing has prompted our choice. It seems that there is an infinitesimal moment that generates our decision, but that it is not caused by anything at all. Neuroscience seems to explain this sensation today with a structural characteristic of the human brain, the cognitive inaccessibility of much of its activity. The brain works and produces psychic activity and we do not realize it. For example, through research with EEG, it has been demonstrated (Libet, 1985) that the moment when we have a feeling that we are about to take a decision is preceded by 300 milliseconds by the wave of brain activity associated with that decision. After another 200 milliseconds from the moment in which we feel that we are about to decide, the behavioural response manifests itself. So the brain has already started to act before we have the sensation that we want to act. Because this brain activity is not accessible to us on a cognitive level, we have the feeling that we have decided freely, that no cause has preceded our decision, but that is not the case. What is more, this sensation of free will is reinforced by the awareness that our previous decision has produced our subsequent behaviour. The issue is a complex one and there could be many objections: for example, that free will anticipates the first wave of brain activity. This is not the time or place to go into this problem in detail. What I wanted to underline is the impact that neuroscientific studies have on problems that are apparently a long way from the goals of neuroscience.

## 4. THE EMERGING TOPIC OF FINANCIAL ORGANIZATIONS

Until recently the main field of behavioural finance was the financial market and consumer behaviour. Few studies were done about financial organizations and institutions. In contrast, nowadays, according to Thaler (1999), the emergent topic is behavioural financial organization and in particular behavioural corporate finance and banking (Sheffrin, 2005). Financial policy makers need to understand better the behaviour of financial organizations in order to establish sound financial regulations and policy. Important questions should be answered: what are the decision-making processes of bankers? What kind of rationality do they use? What are their institutional constraints, that is, the bundle of cognitive features, beliefs, mental models, routines and heuristics? One way to deal with this new emerging field is to rely on the tools of mainstream behavioural economics and in particular with Heuristics and Biases programmes. An alternative preferred way is to follow the Simonian tradition of science of administration (March and Simon, 1958) and the post-Schumpeterian tradition of the theory of the firm (for example Dosi et al., 2017), empowered by the new programme of ecological rationality and simple heuristics (Artinger et al., 2014; Loock and Hinnen, 2015).[8] The study of simple heuristics took place mainly at the individual level or at most "in the wild" (used for example by professional figures or employees in bureaucratic organizations) (Gigerenzer et al., 2011). To date, there has been little empirical analysis of how this type of heuristics can be effective in an organizational context as a bank or a financial institution. In the first place it will be interesting to investigate what kind of heuristics are used at the level of individual organizations and whether there are "local" heuristics, that is, specific and idiosyncratic that depend on the organizational context, or whether there are the same simple general heuristics that are used in different contexts. It is a question of understanding, ultimately, whether or not the same heuris-

---

[8] The preference relies mainly on the critique to the normative model of rationality, that of neoclassical economics, used by behavioural economists to assess biases and errors of human decision making. Conversely, under uncertainty only an adaptive and ecological approach to rationality seems to be justified (Berg and Gigerenzer, 2010). Moreover, the main models of behavioural economics seem to be descriptively unsound. In contrast, simple heuristics theory seems to fulfil better the desiderata of a realist theory of decision making.

tics identified at the individual level are valid, in which decision contexts they are rational, and how they relate to the other cognitive and decisional aspects of the organization (Bingham and Eisenhardt, 2011).

Many empirical questions are relevant: are heuristic decisions favoured in the normality of daily management or are they preferred in situations of risk to survival or at least of stress as in the event of a warning about the performance of the company? If the heuristics seem rational at the ecological level in turbulent environments are they also stable? Which portfolio of heuristics defines organizational identity? And can there be a heuristic identity not only at the level of a single company, but at that of industrial sectors? If a new company in emerging markets does not have the time and financial resources for complex analysis and extensive information gathering, can heuristics be the strategic solution to reduce the cost and time of this collection and analysis? In particular, when it comes to predictions and decisions in conditions of ontic or epistemic uncertainty, can heuristics be the solution? Which is the external context in which simple heuristics can assert themselves at the expense of organizational routines?

The more the environment is uncertain, unpredictable and turbulent (as in the case of fin-tech companies or those of investment banking, private equity and venture capital), the greater the possibility that a company finds the use of heuristic decisions profitable (Oliver and Ross, 2005). When simple heuristics are shared, they allow greater coordination (easier to understand each other), improvement in the accuracy/effort ratio (good accuracy with little effort), more ability to improvise in dynamic contexts (given their elasticity), more time saving (in fact they are fast), and more resources for attention (not needing "need for cognition"). Simplicity improves the dissemination and sharing of heuristics. This type of heuristics, especially the one-reason based, may be suitable for semi-structured environments where organizational flexibility is needed because the context is very competitive, dynamic and mutant.

When the external environment becomes turbulent, as in the example of the abrupt variation of the market by new products of competing companies, it seems, therefore, that the principle "less is more" is preferable. In particular, if we analyse the memory of a company,[9] characterized by beliefs and background knowledge, that is, by cognitive reading keys to categorize external and internal states (Dosi, et al., 2017; Balconi et al., 2007) and by automatic decision-making procedures (routines and

---

[9]  Organizational memory may be represented by a cognitive and a procedural component. The first includes beliefs, values and cognitive rules to categorize the world: tacit and explicit knowledge. The second includes decision-making procedures (routines, algorithms and heuristics) and skills.

automatic heuristics) and not (aware heuristics and algorithms) its divergent role between stationary and unstable states can be highlighted.

> Broadly speaking, in simple and stable environments memory does not matter, provided it satisfies some minimal requirements. In more complex and gradually changing ones, having more memory provides an advantage. However, there is some critical level of environmental instability above which forgetfulness is evolutionarily superior from the point of view of long-term performance. (Dosi et al., 2017)

In sum, when the situation changes radically, and the scenarios become characterized by uncertainty (epistemic or ontic), it seems that it is not advantageous to consume resources of time and calculation to retrieve information from the organizational memory. The information refers to effective action patterns in different market contexts and cannot be a valid basis for decisions in the new competitive context. Therefore it becomes less rational and adaptive to rely on a massive information retrieval from the organizational memory to elaborate complex decisions, while it seems more adaptive to forget part of this "traditional" memory (especially linked to the forms of expert categorization of the external environment), and to base decisions on a small amount of information and to use simple recognition heuristics (such as individual ones of non-experts) or heuristics based on few reasons. The questions to be answered are numerous: in the case of external states, the market in particular, it is important to understand which cognitive tool replaces the previous categorization and how much the choice of this tool is connected to the situation of uncertainty that has emerged. With regard, instead, to the memory of decision procedures, it seems interesting to identify what organizations tend to forget: the routine procedures (in relation to the change in the external environment), the algorithmic ones, or both, since they are no longer adaptive in relation to the situation of uncertainty and to the lack of meaningful information that is required to draw reliable inferences (without the risk of variance). It will then be verified whether these elements of forgetfulness are an element in favour of the financial company's competitiveness.

## 5. CONCLUSION: THE BEHAVIOURAL SCIENCES TO BETTER PREDICT AND REGULATE THE FINANCIAL MARKETS AND ORGANIZATIONS

What is surprising after the various financial crises or scandals that have involved several industrial giants, is that they have not taken into consideration the explanations and possible remedies that behavioural and cognitive economics has for years been proposing to decision-makers to avoid or attenuate these disasters (Bazerman, 2009; Hilton, 2001; Attia and Hilton, 2011). Take the case of the LTCM (Long Term Capital Management), a hedge fund created in 1994 which was increasingly successful until its disastrous collapse in 1998. It adopted "brilliant" models to price shares and measure risks, elaborated by brilliant economists and mathematicians like Fisher Black, Myron Scholes and Robert Merton, who won the Nobel Prize for Economics in 1997 (after Black's premature death in 1995). In the first two years the fund doubled its capital. It had assets of $125 billion and off-balance sheet positions of $1250 billion (the United States budget!). These resources were the result of the uninhibited use of the leverage between indebtedness and capital. While most hedge funds had leverage of 2:1, the LTCM leverage was as high as 50:1 and in some cases 250:1. The entire system was based on supposed risk management that made it possible to establish a given value for the shares and was based on a hypothesis of normality (as if the fluctuations and risks followed a Gaussian curve). For example, it envisaged that the maximum loss in one day could not exceed $35 million. We know what happened. The managers were unable to correct the estimates, even if since 1997 they had seen many signs of anomalous turbulence on the Asian and South American markets. At the peak of the Russian crisis, daily losses amounted to $553 million, which forced the Fed to intervene to bail it out. Various emotive and cognitive components, as well as the adoption of an incorrect model, allowed a predicted disaster to occur: hyper security and pathological risk propensity; egocentricity and organizational narcissism; the illusion of control and a confirmation bias; conformism to the flock effect. What is surprising is that the same formula that brought disaster in the case of LTCM – also known as the Black–Scholes case – remained popular until it finally contributed to the great crisis of 2008!

The LTCM disaster highlights a whole range of problems that were later responsible for the 2008 crisis. Some of them are related to the organizational and social *dyscrasia* that underpins risk evaluation and management in financial organizations. Two are particularly important. First of all, at an organizational level, risk managers are actually subordinate to traders. A company's purpose is to make deals, so if we are talking of risks, it tends to undervalue them and to take them. When a deal is presented, social pressure inside the company tries to communicate the positive aspects and opportunities, and to minimize the risks. So risk managers are seen as disturbances, something that often leads them to adopt attitudes that are not critical but conventional. And secondly, there is a cultural subservience to the rating agencies (which continues today). Their forecasts are considered oracles and represent a conscious or unconscious anchorage for a company's internal assessments. It is a shame that, as numerous cases show, they often make dreadful errors of judgement, and there is a serious problem of a conflict of interest between companies to be rated and rating agencies. How can we think that an agency rating can be objective if the company is paying and might not renew the contract the following year, if the agency often provides organizational consultancy inside the company itself, and if there is often an exchange of personnel between the agency and the company?

Many of the problems of social behaviour in the financial field could be neutralized, at least in part, by standards, rules and laws that induce the saver or finance operator to take care to avoid situations in which it is easy to make errors of judgement. The libertarian paternalism of Thaler and Sunstein (2008) tends to gently "NUDGE" the individual to protect his interests better and to prevent institutional mechanisms, like those of the rating agencies, from damaging the saver.[10] How can this be done? A few examples: we can help the individual to grasp the difference between real utility and perceived utility, by forcing him to consider, as in the case of some mortgage agreements in France, what he would have to pay if interest rates were to rise in future while the value of the property falls; we forbid mortgages with rates like those of hybrid American "2–28" and "3–27" mortgages (behind the subprime mortgages crisis), which trap borrowers with a very low initial rate, known as a "teaser", which then rises over the years; we do not allow conflicts of interest between rating agencies and companies, forbidding consultancy contracts with the same company being renewed more than once; we combat misleading advertising and make contract information cognitively and emotively "friendly"; starting at school, we systematically provide a financial education based on knowledge of behavioural and cognitive finance, introducing the techniques of "debiasing" and metacognitive control of our judgement and decision-making processes.[11]

In summary, what characterizes a behavioural approach to financial consumer policy and regulation should focus on the following general points (Petroni et al., 2015):

- Simplicity: the complexity of the banking and financial products is such that it renders them dull to the point that the choice made by

---

[10]   This is not the place to analyse the nudge theory critically. Many are the negative remarks to be made about the manipulative side of the theory, in particular to the default states (Viale, 2018). In any case, this theory also contains positive aspects when it supports the empowering of individual autonomy in decision making.

[11]   Financial education should not be based only on financial literacy. There are many data that show the low impact of financial literacy programmes in improving the financial skill of people. Only by adding risk literacy and behavioural finance training will the individual skill be really improved in financial decision making.

the consumer cannot often correctly represent the critical variables in play.

- Linguistic transparency: the use of a cryptic technical language and in particular of a formal language based on conditional probabilities and not on natural frequencies does not ease the understanding of risks.
- Salience: in the presentation of a product one should diversify the relative importance of the variables by increasing or decreasing their perceptual salience.
- Mapping: banking and financial products are not articulated in a way to promote the convergence between expected subjective utility and actual future reality. Namely, the mapping function between contingent choices and future well-being is missing. With the increased risk of traps and teasers.
- Disclosure: during disclosure, procedures should take into account and discount the psychological distorting effects on behaviour of the financial advisor (for example, moral licence to be less moral) and the person receiving the advice (burden of disclosure) (Sah et al., 2013).

To conclude, an emerging field in economics is that of behavioural finance. It is the result of the collection of many kinds of data coming from experimental, behavioural, cognitive economics and neuroeconomics. Financial behaviour is relatively easily studied in natural settings and artificial experiments. The results of these studies allow the control of hypotheses in cognitive economics and the generation of new insights in economic behaviour.

Observations of behaviour have moved social scientist inquiries from modelling decision-making based on an ideal agent to incorporating emotions and accounting for heuristics. This endeavour is further empowered by advances that allow access inside the human brain. These insights and findings can be formulated to inform financial policymaking towards achieving more stability, establishing sustainable security for the people and empowering the financial consumers.

# REFERENCES

Artinger, F., Pettersen, M., Gigerenzer, G. and Weibler, J. (2014). "Heuristics as adaptive decision strategies in management", *Journal of Organizational Behavior*, **36**(Suppl. 1), S33–S52.
Attia, C. and Hilton, D.J. (2011). *Decidere in Finanza*. Milan: Il Sole 24 Ore.

Balconi, M., Pozzali, A. and Viale, R. (2007). "The 'codification debate' revisited: a conceptual framework to analyze the role of tacit knowledge in economics", *Industrial and Corporate Change*, **16**(5).

Bazerman, M. (2009). *Quanto sei (a)morale?* Milan: Il Sole 24 Ore.

Berg, N. and Gigerenzer, G. (2010). "As-if behavioral economics: neoclassical economics in disguise?", *History of Economic Ideas*, **18**(1), 133–66.

Bingham, C.B. and Eisenhardt, K.M. (2011). "Rational heuristics: the simple rules that strategists learn from process experience", *Strategic Management Journal*, **32**(13), 1437–64.

Camerer, C., Loewenstein, G. and Prelec, D. (2005). "Neuroeconomics: how neuroscience can inform economics", *Journal of Economic Literature*, **XLIII**(1), 9–64.

Cleeremans, A. and Jimenez, L. (2002). "Implicit learning and consciousness: A graded, dynamic perspective". In R.M. French and A. Cleeremans (eds), *Implicit Learning and Consciousness: an Empirical, Philosophical and Computational Consensus in the Making* (pp. 1–40). Hove: Psychology Press.

Cooper, M.J., Dimitrov, O. and Rau, P.R. (2001). "A rose.com by any other name", *Journal of Finance*, **56**(6), 2371–88.

Damasio, A. (1994). *Descartes' Error.* New York: Avon.

Davidson, D. (1970). "Mental events". In L. Foster and J. Swanson (eds), *Experience and Theory.* Amherst, MA: University of Massachusetts Press.

Davidson, D. (1980). *Essays on Action and Events.* Oxford: Oxford University Press.

Davidson, D. (1984). *Inquiries into Truth and Interpretation.* Oxford: Oxford University Press.

Dennett, D. (1981). "Three kinds of intentional psychology". In R. Healey (ed.), *Reduction, Time and Reality.* Cambridge: Cambridge University Press.

Dennett, D. (1987). *The Intentional Stance.* Cambridge, MA: MIT Press.

Dosi, G., Marengo, L., Paraskevopoulou, E. and Valente, M. (2017). "A model of cognitive and operational memory of organizations in changing worlds", *Cambridge Journal of Economics*, **41**(3), 775–806.

Gal, D. and Rucker, D. (forthcoming). "The loss of loss aversion: will it loom larger than its gain?", *Journal of Consumer Psychology.*

Galbraith, J.K. (1954). *The Great Crash 1929* (Italian version Il grande crollo, Edizioni di Comunità, Milano, 1962). New York: Pelican.

Gigerenzer, G. (2007). *Gut Feelings: The Intelligence of the Unconscious.* New York: Viking Press.

Gigerenzer, G., Todd, P.M. and the ABC Research Group (1999). *Simple Heuristics that Make Us Smart.* New York: Oxford University Press.

Gigerenzer, G., Hertwig, R. and Pachur, T. (eds) (2011). *Heuristics.* Oxford: Oxford University Press.

Grice, H.P. (1989). *Studies in the Way of Words.* Cambridge, MA: Harvard University Press.

Hammond, K.R. (1996). *Human Judgement and Social Policy.* Oxford: Oxford University Press.

Hilton, D. (2001). "The psychology of financial decision-making: applications to trading, dealing, and investment analysis", *Journal of Behavioral Finance*, **II**(1), 37–53.

Kahneman, D. (2003). "Maps of bounded rationality: Psychology for behavioural economics", *American Economic Review*, **93**(5), 1449–75.

Kahneman, D. (2011). *Thinking, Fast and Slow*. New York: Farrar, Straus and Giroux.

Kahneman, D. and Tversky, A. (1979a). "Intuitive prediction: biases and corrective procedures", *Management Science*, **12**, 313–27.

Kahneman, D. and Tversky, A. (1979b). "Prospect theory: an analysis of decision under risk", *Econometrica*, **47**, 263–91.

Kruglanski, A.W. and Gigerenzer, G. (2011). "Intuitive and deliberative judgements are based on common principles", *Psychological Review*, **118**, 97–109.

Libet, B. (1985). "Unconscious cerebral initiative and the role of conscious will in voluntary action", *Behavior and Brain Sciences*, **8**, 529–66.

Loock, M, and Hinnen, G. (2015). "Heuristics and organizations: a review and a research agenda", *Journal of Business Research*, **68**, 2027–36.

March, J. and Simon, H. (1958). *Organizations*. New York: Wiley.

Oliver, D. and Ross, J. (2005). "Decision making in high velocity environments: the importance of guiding principles", *Organization Studies*, **26**(6), 889–913.

Osman, M. (2004). "An evaluation of dual-process theories of reasoning", *Psychonomic Bulletin & Review*, **11**(6), 988–1010.

Petroni, D., Giuliani, F. and Viale, R. (2015). "Bank nudging: opportunities and challenges for nudge strategies applied to the credit system". In G. Bracchi, U. Filotto and D. Masciandaro (eds), *European Banking 3.0*. Rome: Edibank.

Rizzolatti, G. and Vozza, L. (2008). *Nella Mente degli Altri*. Bologna: Zanichelli.

Rizzolatti, G., Fogassi, L. and Gallese, V. (2001). "Neurophysiological mechanisms underlying the understanding and imitation in action", *Nature Reviews Neuroscience*, **2**, 661–70.

Sah, S., Cain, D.M. and Loewenstein, G. (2013). "Confessing one's sins but still committing them: transparency and the failure of disclosure". In A. Oliver (ed.), *Behavioural Public Policy*. Cambridge: Cambridge University Press.

Sheffrin, H. (2005). *Behavioral Corporate Finance*. McGraw-Hill Education.

Slovic, P., Finucane, M., Peters, E. and MacGregor, D.G. (2001). "The affect heuristic". In T. Gilovich, D. Griffin and D. Kahneman (eds), *Heuristics and Biases: The Psychology of Intuitive Thought*. New York: Cambridge University Press.

Tetlock, P. (2005). *Expert Political Judgement*. Princeton, NJ: Princeton University Press.

Tetlock, P.E. and Gardner, D. (2015). *Superforecasting: The Art and Science of Prediction*. New York: Crown.

Thaler, R. (1999). "The end of behavioral finance", *Financial Analysts Journal*, **55**(6), 12–17.

Thaler, R. and Sunstein, C.R. (2008). *Nudge: Improving Decisions about Health, Wealth, and Happiness*. New Haven, CT: Yale University Press.

Tversky, A. and Kahneman, D. (1974). "Judgement under uncertainty: heuristics and biases", *Science*, **185**, 1124–31.

Viale, R. (2012). *Methodological Cognitivism: Mind, Rationality, and Society*. Heidelberg: Springer.

Viale, R. (2018). *Oltre il Nudge*. Bologna: Il Mulino.

Viale, R. (under review). "Architecture of the mind and libertarian paternalism: is the reversibility of System 1 nudges likely to happen?" *Frontiers in Cognition*.

## 2. Behavioral policymaking with bounded rationality

**Shabnam Mousavi**

Il meglio è nemico del bene[1]

For many decades in the modern era, economists reigned as superior consultants, analysts and recommendation providers for policymakers. Meanwhile, psychologists were by and large running psychological operations (PsyOps) in the government, where knowledge about the human psyche was used to channel or produce information that facilitated military or other governmental pursuits.[2] These psychologists had little or no influence on the formation of countrywide policies, which were shaped in part by cost–benefit analyses assessed and conducted by economists tasked with optimizing efficiency subject to legal constraints. Policymaking in general and regulations in particular were customarily presented to the public as a result of unavoidable trade-offs between efficiency and fairness (Shefrin and Statman, 2009; Mousavi and Shefrin, 2010), commonly phrased by politicians as "necessary compromises". The scene has changed considerably since the dawn of behavioral policymaking about a decade ago. The background academic work, as usual, started much earlier.

### WHY WOULD ECONOMISTS BOTHER WITH PSYCHOLOGY?

In the 1950s, just as economics was making strides in integrating two branches of decision theory developed during World War II, operation research (OR) and game theory (Mousavi and Gigerenzer, 2017), one political economist by training actively doubted the usefulness of

---

[1]  Italian adage: The best is the enemy of good.
[2]  See for example https://media.defense.gov/2017/Apr/07/2001728209/-1/-1/0/B_0018_ GOLDSTEIN_FINDLEY_PSYCHLOGICAL_OPERATIONS.PDF.

introducing more and more stylized facts into economics modeling as a fruitful strategy for understanding human behavior. Instead, he urged empirical-based theory building and went on to be the first professor of computer science and psychology to receive a Nobel Prize in economics. In his 1957 book, *Models of Man*, Herbert Alexander Simon wrote for the first time of *the principle of bounded rationality* (p. 200). Later, in 1972, he developed the basis for *theories of bounded rationality* in a chapter of the same name contributed to McGuire and Radner's edited volume *Decision and Organization*. In his Nobel Prize lecture (Simon, 1978) he keenly observed: "There are no direct observations that individuals or firms do *actually* equate marginal costs and revenues (emphasis added)." I personally find it useful to think of behavioral finance and behavioral economics as fields that have developed largely by efforts to unravel what individuals and firms "actually" do.

## Mathematics and Logic Are the Best

The rest of this chapter will have a heavy behavioral thrust, but before turning to that focus, I want to pause and briefly discuss a counter argument to the merit of a behavioral approach that stems directly from the dominant paradigm in which we economists have been trained ever since Paul Samuelson's revamp of economics education.[3] The argument is that the mere fact that a conduct (actually) exists or even persists does not imply its efficiency. Notwithstanding the fact that human conduct is most often delivered in uncertain and complex situations, the best forms of conduct are seen as being constructed on a logical and mathematical basis. And the reason for this is that the truism of mathematics and logic affords the type of clarity and coherence that is required for conceiving the well-thought-out steps toward the best conduct. Thus, to the economics theorist, no valid concerns can stem from differences that arise between stylized axioms of action and the governing principles *actually* observed in the world. The core premise here is that if mathematics and logic reveal a best conduct, it is indeed the best that can be acted upon. Many optimal and efficient solution concepts have been neatly generated by mathematicians in this fashion and have together built the body of knowledge referred to as decision theory – almost all of

---

[3]    Incidentally, he is the very first American economist to win the Nobel Prize in Economics, 1970. Samuelson's 1948 textbook quickly took over as the prominent text for teaching principles of economics and has captured the scene ever since. On the cover of the first edition *The Economist*'s praise reads: "It is difficult to exaggerate the world-wide impact of Mr. Samuelson's *Economics*."

which can be traced back to physics-based equilibrium analysis or to mathematics-based game theory. Notice that a direct and immediate corollary of the core premise above, that is, that the best conduct is based on mathematics or logic, is that any action deviating from the optimal/ best one can be improved upon at least in a Pareto-efficient fashion.[4] Named after the Italian polymath Vilfredo Federico Damaso Pareto (1848–1923), this involves a reallocation of resources by which no one is worse off but some are better off. Within this framework, economists dedicated to economics – defined as the science of resource allocation in the most efficient manner to achieve everyday, lifetime, political and social goals – have long engaged in coherent mathematical exercises that have generated many socio-economic policies.

**What is *Actually* Missing?**

Simon's plethora of arguments aimed specifically at the political influence of economists by scrutinizing the prescriptions of *armchair economics*, as appears, for example in his interview with *Challenge* (1986, p. 23):[5]

> *Challenge*:   Have economics put the wrong stress on optimization theory in consumer preference and resource allocation?
>
> Simon:   The stress is wrong and so is the methodology for testing their theories. Virtually no economics students get training in methods of observation that would lead the researcher to find out how the consumer *actually* makes choices, or go inside a business firm to see how decisions are *actually* made there. Marketing people in business schools are learning something about that, but it's not part of training of the Ph.D. economist. In business schools there is a surge of interest in decision-*making*, not in decision *theory*. As a matter of fact, in the Cathedral itself—the University of Chicago Business School—there is a very lively group working on decision-making.

Simon, in his many writings, pointed out that even though people do not follow the prescriptions for best conduct that are generated from mathematical and logical exercises, they fare amazingly well. We return to this "problem-solving orientation" of the bounded rationality approach later on. Notably, people's conduct cannot necessarily be

---

[4]  Pareto efficiency is not the only form of efficiency studied by economists. In fact, defining efficiency in other manners has been a frequent technical tool for modeling. This, however, does not imply complete clarity or consensus on the matter in the field. For a nice example of related work, see James Dow and Gary Gorton's 1995 NBER working paper, where they question and examine the very link between stock market efficiency and economic efficiency.

[5]  Source: http://digitalcollections.library.cmu.edu/awweb/awarchive?type=file&item=34 037.

*Note:*   The ant's path on the beach looks complex. The ant is following a very simple rule at every step, which it keeps repeating: change direction when there is an obstacle.

*Source:*   https://blog.seannewmanmaroni.com/simons-ant-2c7693335ff9.

*Figure 2.1    Simon's ant*

optimized if – as is the case in many real-world situations – an optimal form does not exist. Simon then proposed changing the scientific investigation method from simplifying complex problems of choice so as to fit in a mathematical structure to viewing actions as products of interactions between the agent and a likely complex environment. His famous example when discussing the psychology of thinking provides a new angle on the complex route that an ant takes on a beach to reach its nest, depicted in Figure 2.1.

Simon (1996) maintained that the ant is not executing a complex operation emerging from a high level of intelligence; rather, it is simply changing course whenever faced with an obstacle, which, on the irregular surface of the beach, happens to leave behind a mathematically complex path. By the same token, if humans are behaving in a complex environment, their behavior might appear complex, when in fact they are *actually* following simple rules, over and over again. These simple rules are known as heuristics. Another of Simon's (1990) related metaphors for understanding human decision-making is that of a pair of scissors, with cognitive capabilities as one blade, and the task environment as the other blade – emphasizing that these two indispensable elements for understanding and modeling action cannot be meaningfully attended to in isolation.

### From Modeling Reasonable Behavior to Sensible Modeling of Behavior

Psychology and other social sciences such as sociology and anthropology help economists move beyond decades of effort to build models of "reasonable behavior" (see, for a starter, the introduction to von Neumann and Morgenstern's original axiomatization, 1944) to developing sensible models of behavior, including reasoning processes themselves. In doing so, a central question arises: "How do humans *reason* when the conditions for rationality postulated by the model of neoclassical economics are not met?" This was asked perceptively by Simon (1989) and tackled over several decades by a good number of scientists, who have written elaborate answers to this question from the angle of their specialty. Of particular interest to our current discussion is Jonathan Bendor of Stanford's (2010) book *Bounded Rationality and Politics*, wherein he collated his three decades of reflections and collaborations on the relationship between bounded rationality and politics – policymaking being a domain where rationality requirements are more often, if not constantly, missing.

## BOUNDED RATIONALITY IN POLITICAL SCIENCE

Bendor wrote his book on bounded rationality (BR) in politics as "a tribute to Aaron Wildavsky, Marty Landau, and Herbert Simon". In addition to chapters recounting his co-advisor Wildavsky's and his main advisor and thesis chair Landau's work, three chapters of the book (3, 4 and 5) constitute "the intellectual core of the book. They study a concept central to the BR program, that of *heuristics*." Bendor starts his discussion of heuristics with "the most famous" satisficing, and describes Simon's orientation as a problem-solving approach that entails investigating the simple ways in which cognitively limited agents are able to deliver on many complex tasks, from playing chess to running organizations. This orientation also includes Lindblom's idea of seriality or sequential attention to reasons in what he called "muddling through" and Wildavsky's incrementalist view. Both muddling through and incrementalism accept the real treatment of information by boundedly rational agents to be fundamentally different from the comprehensive weighing and adding of the rational agent. Bendor then mentions another orientation of bounded rationality focused on discovering and improving cognitive limitations, which he calls heuristics-and-biases, named directly after the psychological study program that Kahneman, Tversky, and later on Slovic initiated in the 1970s. The list under this orientation continues with Kahan's cultural cognition concept and with the nudging agenda of Thaler and Sunstein. Other work in this orientation is also listed in the second column of Table 2.1. Bendor juxtaposes the heuristics-and-biases psychology with the fast-and-frugal heuristics research program pioneered by Gigerenzer, which he lists under the first

*Table 2.1   Two orientations of bounded rationality in political science*

| Problem-solving approach | Heuristics and biases |
| --- | --- |
| People manage to do reasonably well<br>Simon (1955, 1956, 1957) | People make mistakes even in simple tasks<br>Tversky and Kahneman (1974)<br>Kahneman et al. (1982) |
| Muddling through<br>Lindblom (1959) (seriality);<br>Braybrook and Lindblom (1963) | Cultural cognition + Debiasing<br>Kahan (2006)<br>Brest (2013) |
| Politics of the budgetary process<br>Wildavsky (1964) (incrementalism) | Nudge<br>Thaler and Sunstein (2008) |
| Risk savvy<br>Gigerenzer (2014) | Behavioral foundations of public policy<br>Shafir (2013) |
| Boost vs. Nudge<br>Grüne-Yanoff and Hertwig (2016)<br>Hertwig and Ryall (2016) | Nudging works. Now, do more with it!<br>Sunstein (2016) |
| Behavioral paternalism<br>Rizzo and Whitman (2009)<br>Whitman and Rizzo (2015) | Neuroliberalism<br>Whitehead et al. (2017) |

*Source:*   Drawn from Bendor (2010), with additions.

orientation of problem-solving approaches. Other work and scholars belonging to these two orientations can be found in Table 2.1. Bendor's categorization of policymaking-related academic work based on two different orientations of bounded rationality can be used as a tool for gaining clarity on the topic and ongoing discussions.

In the preface to his book, Bendor clarifies why this work is not a critique of the rational choice theory but instead a competitor. His interest is in finding operational alternatives, which he maintains do not exist. Also, he emphasizes the value of contributions and insights stemming from rational choice theory and the coherence it has afforded political economy. His position is one maintained by many economists who study bounded rationality. When rigorous treatments of the idea are attempted, they are always operationalized as deviations from the rational framework. In the next section, I will provide my personal take on the landscape of scientific work in the area and entertain the possibility of recasting bounded rationality in a self-sustained primary framework. This line of thought has accompanied me since I transitioned from engineering to economics almost two decades ago.

## CONTEMPLATING THE ELEMENTS OF BOUNDED RATIONALITY[6]

Examining the similarities and differences between full and bounded rationality reveals that bounded rationality should not be viewed as a deviation from full rationality. It simply does not make sense to assume that the same axiomatic framework serves to model both types of rationality. I believe that the main reason for building models of bounded rationality as departures from full rationality is that modelers of both types of rationality share the same notion of uncertainty about knowledge. In a framework where the (usually single) correct answer exists prior to the quest, rationality is goal-oriented. In that sense bounded rationality can be seen as a creature with two disparate legs: goal-orientation and cognitive limitations (see Figure 2.2). Incomplete but consistent models of bounded rationality are made by treating the second leg *as if* it belonged on the same ground. However, although the first leg of goal-orientation indeed has its place in the same paradigm as that for full rationality, the second leg of cognitive limitations is left in the air because it does not fit into that paradigm. I suggest that the problem be explored more deeply than by simply trying to modify yet another axiom. The problem might not be that we have chosen the wrong axiom(s) to modify, but rather that we are using an altogether inappropriate axiomatic framework. That is,

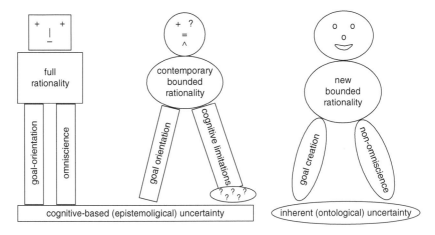

*Figure 2.2    Bounded rationality can be recast in a new paradigm*

[6]   I am grateful to Nicolaus Tideman for many helpful discussions that shaped major parts of this section.

instead of trying to distend the second leg to conform, we need to discover its origin and then find a corresponding first leg that stabilizes the creature.

It is popularly presumed that limitations of cognition are responsible for bounding rationality. The case-wise superior descriptive power of current models of bounded rationality derives from their incorporation of these limitations. In taking this direction, however, such models implicitly assume that (at least operationally) all departures from rationality can be traced to cognitive limitations: this assumption is the step that this second leg is expected to take, to follow the first leg of goal-orientation. But it cannot land where it does not belong; it is consistently incomplete!

Goal-orientation, which has been endorsed for convenience by bounded rationality modelers and hence has not been a matter of debate, is the source of futile modeling. While agreeing that the idea of bounded rationality is valuable and should be absorbed into economic studies, I believe that the correct way to do so is to replace the first leg, goal-orientation, with an alternative that better fits in the paradigm in which the second leg belongs. Notice that bounded rationality and full rationality share the leg of goal-orientation that I propose to replace with a new one. Notice also that the second leg of bounded rationality does not belong in the current paradigm and so cannot be adequately modeled by its practices and tools.

Admittedly, models of bounded rationality have extended our ability to better understand choice behavior and thus deserve acknowledgment.[7] Despite bounded rationality gaining immense attention for many years amongst thinkers with a wide variety of academic orientations, it still suffers from a lack of unified formal structure. A very challenging puzzle has thereby remained unexplored: how do we form a proper axiomatization of "somewhat rational" individuals? I maintain that the original idea of bounded rationality contains a rich capacity for valuation (as the general basis for any choice) but that the effort to fit bounded rationality into the standard economic paradigm emasculates this capacity. In my view, imposing the goal-orientation of full rationality on bounded rationality leads to structures that are doomed to fail. A shift from the currently predominant paradigm is therefore called for.

I assert that we will be able to fruitfully capture the bounded nature of rationality when it is implemented in a paradigm that allows us to replace the cognitive-based uncertainty that is embedded in full rationality

---

[7] A search (in April 2018) for books on bounded rationality on my computer returned several titles, of which I name a few: Rubenstein's (1998) *Modeling Bounded Rationality*, Gigerenzer and Selten's (2001) edited volume, *Bounded Rationality: The Adaptive Toolbox*, Salehnejad's (2006) *Rationality, Bounded Rationality and Microfoundations*, Spiegler's (2011) *Bounded Rationality and Industrial Organization*. There is even a novel by Pamela McCorduck (2012) with the title *Bounded Rationality*.

with a pragmatic notion of inherent uncertainty, where goals are created through intentional but not necessarily teleological quests. If we succeed in constructing a new paradigm for analyzing bounded rationality as a primary framework (rather than as a deviation from full rationality), it is my conjecture that a clean formalization of bounded rationality will then be possible. I suggest replacing goal-orientation with goal-creating intentionality, treating uncertainty as inherent, and delivering the complete second leg of non-omniscience formally. Thus, both legs of a new and creative (bounded) rationality will be grounded in an alternative paradigm that has the potential to be formalized as an operational framework. These new sturdy legs will equip the creature to deal comfortably with demonstrated inconsistencies in many processes of decision making. That would supplement the primary idea of bounded rationality and would eventually redirect research efforts onto an altogether new path.

I propose a first step toward building the new paradigm. It starts with a familiar distinction between risk and uncertainty and an extension of the old modes of information processing, namely deduction and induction, to include heuristics. This taxonomy is inspired by Frank Knight's (1921: *Risk, Uncertainty and Profit*) conception of uncertainty that what is important to problem-solving in the social sciences is not statistical probability, but instead those problems that do not lend themselves to the elegant and familiar actuarial configuration of risk. A first attempt to connect the concepts of Knightian risk versus uncertainty and heuristics was worked out in Mousavi and Gigerenzer (2014), reproduced here in Table 2.2. The idea is that formalizing action as the central problem of decision theory (recall the most famous work of Savage, 1954: *The Foundations of Statistics*) can incorporate behavioral science findings by adding heuristics to its information processes. This idea is organized by viewing action as a final outcome of a process that starts with a problematic situation of facing an unknown and continues by processing information that generates a sufficient amount of knowledge to induce action or otherwise endorse inaction – what I call *actionable* knowledge – and does not need to remove all unknowns or acquire/analyze all information: it can be a heuristic process.

I suspect that while undertaking to elaborate on the elements of this tabulated relationship between three paths from unknowns to knowledge generation, we will stumble upon insights that help in operationalizing a primary framework for bounded rationality.

*Table 2.2    Knowledge generated from information processes in risky vs uncertain situations*

| Nature of unknown | Knightian probability | Process of information | Associated methods | Generated knowledge |
|---|---|---|---|---|
| Risk | A priori (Design) | Deductive | Use probability theory to model the underlying structure | Objective odds; deterministic knowledge (as in lotteries) |
| Risk | Statistical (Frequencies in the long run) | Inductive | Sampling; Bayesian analysis; statistical inference; optimization | Stylized odds; stochastic knowledge (as in machine learning) |
| Uncertainty | Estimate | Intuitive | Heuristics; conduct based on opinion; not fully reasoned; exploratory data analysis | Intuited estimates; partial yet actionable knowledge (as in entrepreneurship) |

*Source:*    Mousavi and Gigerenzer (2014).

## SUMMARY AND CONCLUSION

In 2010, as Bendor was writing on bounded rationality as a competitor to rational choice theory (RC), he emphasized:

> Much better to be *strong and wrong* (Schotter 2006), to have produced *a beautiful theory [murdered] by a gang of brutal facts* (La Rochefoucauld 1678) than one that makes no interesting claims at all. RC theorizing has also given our discipline [political science] a badly needed measure of intellectual coherence.

Interestingly, the very advantage of one strong-but-maybe-wrong attitude, which guarantees coherence in the abstract domain of inquiries, is exactly what behavioral policymaking methodology has questioned and distanced itself from by promoting an experimental government (see Halpern, 2015; Mousavi, 2018). In my view, this distinction is at the bottom of methodological differences between the two orientations of bounded rationality applied to political sciences (see Table 2.1). As governmental advisors – even unknowingly – style policies in accordance with one or the other methodological orientation, it remains to be revealed empirically and gradually whether resulting outcomes are always different, sometimes overlapping, or insensitive to their orientations with respect to bounded rationality. The relationship to heuristics is, however, a clear one.

Boundedly rational policymakers use heuristics to make large-scale decisions with severe and long-term consequences. Behavioral policymaking refers to a framework that views both policymakers and policytakers as boundedly rational agents. A better understanding of heuristic decision-making processes used by these agents thus has the capacity for providing behavioral insights that in turn help improve the design and implementation of policies. This chapter provided an overview of select literature on bounded rationality in politics that reveals a close connection to the study of heuristics in psychology. Psychologists who have studied heuristics have done so either in association with cognitive biases that limit the ability to account for information fully, or alternatively as simple but effective strategies in the absence of or without considering complete information. I argued that building models of decision-making that are both reasonable and sensible necessitates extending our scientific inquiry tools to include heuristic processes on a par with mathematical and logical tools, namely deduction and induction, and provided an image of the resulting elements of a corresponding conception of bounded rationality conception that can be operationalized. Such efforts will contribute directly to the call by Harvard Kennedy School of Government visionary Zeckhauser (2014):

> Macroeconomics surely will have a different bent ten years from now, when its leading practitioners have digested the lessons of the unforeseen financial meltdown and its lingering aftermath. Technological advances is a watchword on the lips of most political and business leaders, but our mastery of our expanding capabilities remains rudimentary, as does our understanding of the entrepreneurs who are impelling us forward.

Such an endeavor is indeed materializing in junctures that bring together practitioners and entrepreneurs with academics and policymakers, such as at BEFAIRLY.

## REFERENCES

Bendor, J. (2010). *Bounded Rationality and Politics*. Oakland, CA: University of California Press.

Braybrook, D. and Lindblom, C. (1963). *A Strategy of Decision*. New York, NY: Free Press.

Brest, P. (2013). Quis custodiet ipsos custodes? Debiasing the policy makers themselves. In E. Shafir (ed.), *The Behavioral Foundations of Public Policy*. Princeton, NJ: Princeton University Press, pp. 481–93.

Dow, J. and Gorton, G. (1995). Stock market efficiency and economic efficiency:

Is there a connection? NBER Working Paper No. 5233, available at http://www. nber.org/papers/w5233.

Gigerenzer, G. (2014). *Risk Savvy: How to Make Good Decisions.* New York, NY: Viking.

Gigerenzer, G. and Selten, R. (2001). *Bounded Rationality: The Adaptive Toolbox.* Cambridge, MA: MIT Press.

Grüne-Yanoff, T. and Hertwig, R. (2016). Nudge versus boost: How coherent are policy and theory? *Minds and Machines* **26**, 149–83.

Halpern, D. (2015). *Inside the Nudge Unit.* London: Ebury Press.

Hertwig, R. and Ryall, M.D. (2016). *Nudge vs. Boost: Agency Dynamics Under 'Libertarian Paternalism'.* Available at http://ssrn.com/abstract=2711166.

Kahan, D.M. (2006). Cultural cognition and public policy. *Yale Faculty Scholarship Series.* Paper 103. Available at http://digitalcommons.law.yale.edu/fss_papers/103.

Kahneman, D., Slovic, P. and Tversky, A. (eds) (1982). *Judgment Under Uncertainty: Heuristics and Biases.* London: Cambridge University Press.

Knight, F.H. (1921). *Risk, Uncertainty and Profit,* Dover 2006 unabridged republication of the edition published by Houghton Mifflin Company, Boston and New York.

La Rochefoucauld, Duc de (1678). *Maxims.* New York, NY: Penguin Classics.

Lindblom, C. (1959). The science of "muddling through". *Public Administration Review* **19**, 79–88.

McCorduck, P. (2012). *Bounded Rationality: A Novel.* Santa Fe: Sunstone Press.

McGuire, C.B. and Radner, R. (eds) (1972). *Decision and Organization: A Volume in Honor of Jacob Marschak.* Volume 12 of Studies in Mathematical and Managerial Economics. Amsterdam: North-Holland Publishing Co.

Mousavi, S. (2018). What do heuristics have to do with policymaking? *Journal of Behavioral Economics for Public Policy* **2**(1), 69–74.

Mousavi, S. and Gigerenzer, G. (2014). Risk, uncertainty, and heuristics. *Journal of Business Research* **67**(8), 1671–78.

Mousavi, S. and Gigerenzer, G. (2017). Heuristics are tools for uncertainty. *Journal of Homo Oeconomicus* **34**, 361–79.

Mousavi, S. and Shefrin, H. (2010). Prediction tools: financial market regulation, politics, and psychology. *Journal of Risk Management in Financial Institutions* **3**(4), 318–33.

Rizzo, M.J. and Whitman, D.G. (2009). The knowledge problem of new paternalism. *Brigham Young University Law Review* **2009**(4), 905–68.

Rubenstein, A. (1998). *Modeling Bounded Rationality.* Cambridge, MA: MIT Press.

Salehnejad, R. (2006). *Rationality, Bounded Rationality and Microfoundations: Foundations of Theoretical Economics.* Basingstoke: Palgrave Macmillan.

Samuelson, P.A. (1948). *Economics: An Introductory Analysis.* New York, NY: McGraw-Hill.

Savage, L.J. (1954). *The Foundations of Statistics.* New York, NY: John Wiley and Sons. Reprinted in 1972 by Dover Publications.

Schotter, A. (2006). Strong and wrong: the use of rational choice theory in experimental economics. *Journal of Theoretical Politics* **18**(4), 498–511.

Shafir, E. (ed.) (2013). *The Behavioral Foundations of Public Policy.* Princeton, NJ: Princeton University Press.

Shefrin, H. and Statman, M. (2009). Striking regulatory irons while hot. *Journal of Investment Management* **7**(4), 29–42.

Simon, H.A. (1955). A behavioral model of rational choice. *The Quarterly Journal of Economics* **69**(1), 99–118.

Simon, H.A. (1956). Rational choice and the structure of the environment. *Psychological Review* **63**(2), 129–38.

Simon, H.A. (1957). *Models of Man: Social and Rational: Mathematical Essays on Rational Human Behavior in a Social Setting*. New York, NY: John Wiley.

Simon, H. (1972). Theories of bounded rationality. In C.B. McGuire and R. Radner (eds), *Decision and Organization*. Amsterdam: North-Holland, pp. 161–76.

Simon, H.A. (1978). Prize lecture: rational decision-making in business organizations. Available at: http://www.nobelprize.org/nobel_prizes/economic-sciences/laureates/1978/simon-lecture.html.

Simon, H.A. (1989). The scientist as problem solver. In D. Klahr and K. Kotovsky (eds), *Complex Information Processing: The Impact of Herbert A. Simon [21st Carnegie-Mellon symposium on cognition]*. Hillsdale, NJ: Erlbaum, pp. 373–98.

Simon, H.A. (1990). Invariants of human behaviour. *Annual Review of Psychology* **41**, 1–19.

Simon, H.A. (1996). *The Science of the Artificial*. Cambridge, MA: MIT Press.

Spiegler, R. (2011). *Bounded Rationality and Industrial Organization*. Oxford: Oxford University Press.

Sunstein, C.R. (2016). Nudging works: now do more with it. *Bloomberg Businessweek*, Accessed on 10 April 2018 at https://www.bloomberg.com/view/articles/2016-09-20/nudging-works-now-do-more-with-it.

Thaler, R.H. and Sunstein, C.R. (2008). *Nudge: Improving Decisions About Health, Wealth, and Happiness*. New Haven, CT: Yale University Press.

Tversky, A. and Kahneman, D. (1974). Judgment under uncertainty: Heuristics and biases. *Science* **185**(4157), 1124–31.

Von Neumann, J. and Morgenstern, O. (1944). *Theory of Games and Economic Behavior*. Princeton, NJ: Princeton University Press.

Whitehead, M., Jones, R., Lilley, R., Pykett, J. and Howell, R. (2017). *Neuroliberalism: Behavioural Government in the Twenty-First Century*. New York, NY: Routledge.

Whitman, D.G. and Rizzo, M.J. (2015). The problematic welfare standards of behavioral paternalism. *Review of Philosophy and Psychology* **6**(3), 409–25.

Wildavsky, A. (1964). *The Politics of the Budgetary Process*. Boston, MA: Little, Brown.

Zeckhauser, R. (2014). New frontiers beyond risk and uncertainty: Ignorance, group decision, and unanticipated themes. In M.J. Machina and W.K. Viscusi (eds), *Economics of Risk and Uncertainty*. North-Holland: Elsevier.

# 3. A taxonomy of behavioural policies
## Barbara Alemanni

## INTRODUCTION

Conventional economic theory has been the traditional base for public policymaking for many years; however, over the last decade a new behavioural movement has inspired interventions in several countries. Supporters of this new stream of thought advocate for its further diffusion, claiming that it is an ecological way to policymaking. A fruitful debate among academics, practitioners and policymakers is underway beyond the traditional scientific and political forums also testified by an article titled 'Economics behaving badly' written in 2010 by Loewenstein and Ubel (2010) for the *New York Times*. In that article, the two authors drew two main conclusions. First, mentioning the spreading of behaviourally inspired policies, they state:

> ..the field has its limits. As policymakers use it to devise programs, it's becoming clear that behavioral economics is being asked to solve problems it wasn't meant to address. Indeed, it seems in some cases that behavioral economics is being used as a political expedient, allowing policymakers to avoid painful but more effective solutions rooted in traditional economics.

The question on how far behavioural economics can go in policymaking is a crucial issue, discussed in other chapters of the present book, but it risks remaining too vague and theoretical if no agreement is reached upon the meaning of behaviourally-inspired policies. That leads to Loewenstein and Ubel's second conclusion. According to them:

> Behavioral economics should complement, not substitute for, more substantive economic interventions. If traditional economics suggests that we should have a larger price difference between sugar-free and sugared drinks, behavioral economics could suggest whether consumers would respond better to a subsidy on unsweetened drinks or a tax on sugary drinks.

For many, including the author of this chapter, what Loewenstein and Ubel have just described is a behavioural based policy.

In practice, policymakers have so far agreed on an array of policies often labelled as 'behavioural policies', encompassing randomized controlled trials (RCT), financial incentives, comparison web portals, and nudges, among others. The behavioural suffix in policy application is used to describe quite heterogeneous and diverse interventions. It is often unclear to which aspect of a policy formulation the term 'behavioural' refers, where practitioners, policymakers and researchers often use or assume quite different definitions of the term 'behavioural'.

## DEFINING BEHAVIOURALLY INSPIRED POLICIES

To shed some light on this, we must start by making a distinction between the two main ingredients of so-called 'behavioural' public policies, namely methods and insights.

The first source of potential misunderstanding in behavioural aspects of policy formulation relates to the fact that practitioners and policymakers tend to define a policy instrument under the behavioural umbrella merely because it entails the use of RCTs as a method of generating evidence (Galizzi, 2017).

The focus on the use of RCTs as a fundamental defining criterion for 'behavioural' policies calls for some conceptual clarifications. The use of RCTs has to do with the methods employed to gather evidence for policy purposes, not with the content and insights of such evidence. Outside the context of policymaking the use of RCTs is far from novel and RCTs are certainly not a distinguishing feature only of behavioural policy, behavioural science or behavioural economics. In addition, RCT is a vague and misleading term to use for experiments for policy formulation purposes as it does not convey key information on the exact nature and typology of the experiment. There is not one single type of experiment for policy formulation purposes; rather, a broad spectrum of different types of experiments spanning from the lab to the field could prove useful.

What is relatively novel in the policy formulation arena is that there is currently, probably for the first time ever, a diffused and open-minded interest by decision-makers and practitioners in rolling out rigorous tests of envisaged policy interventions prior to their full-scale implementation. In financial systems, such an experimental approach to regulation is well testified by the sandboxes that several financial markets supervisors are using with start-up companies in the FinTech world.

Nevertheless, it is worthwhile mentioning that when using RCTs in fields such as medicine or pharmacology, subjects are always asked to provide informed consent before participating in RCTs. This is not the case in the majority of so-called RCTs used for policymaking

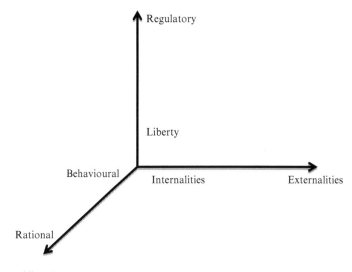

*Source:*   Oliver (2015).

*Figure 3.1    Oliver's classification of public policies*

purposes. This leads to obvious but profound ethical and political implications.

A second source of potential misunderstanding in the 'behavioural' aspects of policy formulation is concerned with the nature and insights, rather than the methods, of the behavioural policies. When formulating policies, researchers and decision-makers are ultimately interested in knowing which type of policies would work effectively to change behaviour. To that extent, Oliver (2015) classifies policies along three dimensions, as presented in Figure 3.1. A first feature of policies is their regulatory power. Policies fare in a continuum ranging from the preservation of the liberty of choice (full antiregulatory policies) to full regulation. A second dimension deals with its application, which can be informed by behavioural economics rather than the standard, conventional model of rational choice. Finally, policies can address internalities or externalities.

A similar, though somewhat different, categorization is put forward by Loewenstein and Chater (2017) and presented in Table 3.1.

Public policies fit into a matrix where rows represent the reasons for intervening. Policy interventions can be justified on traditional economic grounds, such as externalities or market failures; on behavioural grounds, typically internalities; and on both. The columns of the matrix deal with the types of intervention. Traditional economic interventions are taxes and

*Table 3.1    Loewenstein and Chater's (2017) classification of public policies*

| Rationale for intervention | Type of intervention | | |
| --- | --- | --- | --- |
| | Traditional economics (e.g. taxes) | Hybrid policies (e.g. carefully 'framed' taxes) | Behavioural |
| Traditional economic (e.g. externalities) | A (pure rational approach) | B | C |
| Hybrids (e.g. companies optimally responding to consumer biases) | D | E | F |
| Behavioural economics (e.g. internalities) | G | H | I (pure behavioural approach) |

*Source:*    Loewenstein and Chater (2017).

subsidies among others and behavioural interventions are well exemplified by nudges. The intermediate column deals with hybrid policies, where conventional interventions benefit from the insight of behavioural clues.

Both classifications insist on a dynamic graduation of interventions ranging from a full conventional approach – cluster A in Loewenstein and Chater's scheme and fully regulatory, standard informed and addressing externalities in Oliver's approach – to a full behavioural one – cluster I for Loewenstein and Chater and antiregulatory, behavioural informed and addressing internalities according to Oliver. Within the extremes, there lies a full collection of intermediate to hybrid policies (B, E, H), which have been neglected so far (Loewenstein and Chater, 2017, p. 29).

## A MORE PRAGMATIC CLASSIFICATION OF PUBLIC POLICY

Rather than resolving the fundamental issue of whether the assumptions of conventional or behavioural economics are correct at a general level, economists and social scientists are increasingly embracing a pragmatic approach (Galizzi, 2014; Bhargava and Loewenstein, 2015; Chetty, 2015; Laibson and List, 2015). In essence, and consistently with Oliver and

Loewenstein and Chater's classification, this approach considers behavioural economics as a natural progression of conventional economics. Take, for example, tax and subsidies-based policies. These are policies based on regulation and often address 'externalities'. Traditionally, they have been firmly grounded on conventional economics, however as Loewenstein and Ubel suggest, there is an immense potential to combine these traditional but effective public economics tools with new insights from behavioural science. For instance, how can we design specific schemes around well-known human biases so that we can 'supercharge' taxes and subsidies with behavioural insights to enhance their long-term effectiveness? This seems one of the most exciting and promising areas where more experimental evidence is currently needed in behavioural public policy and where 'what works' units such as the British and American ones are focusing their attention.[1]

From this perspective, behavioural insights (BIs) represent an input to the policy process, and can be fully integrated with and inform other traditional forms of intervention (that is, regulations, incentives, information requirements). In this sense, BIs may support a broader range of policy instruments. Being an input to the policy process, BIs, contrary to nudges, to which we will turn our attention later, do not warrant a specific type of output, and indeed sometimes suggest that no intervention, or a conventional one, is the best solution.

At the UK Financial Conduct Authority (FCA) this pragmatic approach has been broadly implemented and several interventions are consistent with this blurring distinction between conventional and behavioural spheres.

In financial markets, an interesting example of behavioural regulation is what Oliver (2015) defines 'budge policies'. Classic budges are regulations against harmful, behavioural economics informed supply side activities. Budge policies will fit into cluster D, E and F in Loewenstein and Chater's (2017) matrix. Here, we refer to policy responses to financial offers such as payday loans, teaser rates and other practices designed to extract payments from imperfectly rational individuals. The effectiveness of regulatory changes requires a hybrid of behavioural and conventional economic analysis.

Budge policies might have to deal with what Heidhues et al. (2016) define 'exploitative' as opposed to value-increasing innovations. Regulators need to investigate when firms – quite often in the financial industry – show incentives to invest in innovative products or services aimed at increasing the hidden prices they collect from naïve/irrational consumers. Reliably

---

[1] https://www.gov.uk/government/news/dr-david-halpern-reappointed-as-what-works-national-adviser.

identifying whether an innovation is value-increasing or exploitative, or whether a product is socially wasteful, might be extremely difficult, and it is important to develop general methods with which regulators can make these determinations and subsequent actions.

A general method to approach hybrid policies is presented in Barr et al. (2009). Specifically, they adopt a framework that considers in more depth firms' incentives to respond to behaviourally motivated regulation. The outcomes are seen as equilibrium interactions between individuals with specific psychologies and firms that respond to those psychologies within specific market contexts. Regulation must then address failures in this equilibrium.

This perspective produces two dimensions to consider. First, the psychological biases of individuals can either help or hurt the firms they interact with; hence firms' and policymakers' interests are sometimes misaligned and sometimes not. This distinction in market responses to individual psychology is central to the framework. In some cases, the market is either neutral or wants to overcome consumer fallibility. In other cases, the market would like to exploit or exaggerate consumer fallibility. Take the example of consumers failing to understand the effect of compounding of interest. Such a bias could lead to under-saving or over-borrowing. Society would prefer that the individual did not have such a bias in both contexts. Rules which take away the negative effect of this bias on under-saving might turn out to be more effective than those trying to tackle over-borrowing, since in the first case both regulators and firms share the same type of incentive, while in the second, incentives are opposite. Firms are keen on helping individuals to reduce the bias to under-save, so that funds intended for investment and fee generation would not diminish, but, at least over the short term, financial institutions would not worry if the same individuals over-borrow. Note the parallelism in these examples: firm incentives to alleviate or exploit a bias are not an intrinsic feature of the bias itself. Instead, they are a function of how the bias plays itself out in the particular market structure. The market response to individual failure can profoundly affect the effectiveness of the regulation.

A second implication of this equilibrium model of firms interacting with individuals with specific psychologies is that the mode of regulation chosen should take account of this interaction. Regulators hold two different levers of change: rules and scoring. When forcing disclosure of the Annual Percentage Rate (APR), for example, the regulator effectively changes the 'rules' of the game: what a firm must say. A stronger form of rule change is product regulation: changing what a firm must do. Behavioural rule changes, such as creating a favoured starting position or default, fall between these two types. When changing liability or providing tax incentives, by contrast, the regulator changes the way the game is 'scored'.

In this stylized model, the regulator can either change the rules of the game or change the scoring of the game. Setting a default is an example of changing the rules of the game, as is disclosure regulation. Specifically, the rules of the game are changed when there's an attempt to change the nature of firm–individual interactions, as when the regulation attempts to affect what can be said, offered or done. Changing the scoring of the game, by contrast, changes the payoffs a firm will receive for particular outcomes. This may be done without a particular rule about how the outcome is to be achieved. Typically, changing the rules of the game without changing the scoring maintains the firms' original incentives to help or hurt consumer bias. By contrast, changing the scoring of the game can alter those incentives.

## DEALING WITH INTERNALITIES: NUDGES VS. BOOSTS

A chapter apart must be opened when we deal with the so-called nudge policies. Moving from the original definition provided by Thaler and Sunstein in 2008, a nudge is: 'any aspect of the choice architecture that alters people's behavior in a predictable way without forbidding any options or significantly changing their economic incentives' (p. 8). Consequently, a nudge preserves liberty and is therefore antiregulatory, its applications are informed by behavioural economics and it addresses internalities.

Nudges are policy formulation tools that are most genuinely and firmly grounded on insights from the behavioural sciences. For this reason, 'nudging' interventions should be regarded as a policy type that comfortably sits under the umbrella of behavioural, rather than conventional, economics. Nudges are best employed to deal with 'internalities' (Galizzi, 2014; Bhargava and Loewenstein, 2015). Internalities are the failure of decision-makers to take full account of the costs or benefits of their choices to other (usually future) selves. Herrnstein et al. (1993) coined the term and defined it as: 'a within-person externality . . . which occurs when a person underweighs or ignores a consequence of his or her own behavior for him- or herself' (Herrnstein et al., 1993, p. 150). Internalities' costs originate from our own errors and failures in judgement and decision-making, rather than from market failures.

Internalities are perhaps a more fundamental source of flaws and failures than externalities, as they pre-exist in markets and economic institutions. They also represent a bigger challenge as they cannot be removed by conventional policy formulation instruments such as taxes and subsidies. In principle, the internal failures and biases in human decision-making are likely to survive even when externalities are addressed by direct market interventions.

The application of nudges to policy formulation is relatively recent, but it has been very influential in several new policies' decisions. However, by and large, self-proclaimed nudgers are often not, strictly speaking, nudging. This matters because it draws a veil over the intellectual clarity of nudge-based policy. The impression is that the term 'nudge', which is used to represent a collection of diverse policy proposals, appears conceptually vague and possibly not fully coherent. Therefore at least a few different types of nudges should be individually analysed.

Fisher and Lotz (2014) propose a taxonomy of nudges based on several distinctions: intentional vs. unintentional behaviour, utility vs. probability components of expected utility, and monetary vs. non-monetary costs. They distinguish between nudges that address people's intentional behaviour as utility maximizers and nudges that address unintentional (automatic) behaviour. Based upon these dimensions they figure out four types of nudges.

The choice of a utility maximizer can be influenced by changing either utilities derived from different possible outcomes of a choice option or by changing the subjective probability of this outcome occurring. When outcomes are manipulated it counts as a nudge if there is an alteration of non-monetary utility derived from an outcome.

Type 1 and type 2 nudges in Fisher and Lotz's classification are consistent with this framework. Type 1 – *discomfort nudges* – are interventions that impact expected utility by changing the non-monetary (psychological or social) utility of outcomes. Strictly speaking, the differences between Type 1 nudges and traditional economic incentives can be seen in the fact that the nudge manipulates the non-monetary utility of a choice consequence, rather than its monetary utility, and does so only 'marginally'. Type 2 – *probability nudges* – are policies that impact expected utility by changing the subjective probability that certain outcomes are realized.

These two types, however, do not cover all policies that Thaler and Sunstein designate as nudges. Consequently, Fisher and Lotz propose additional nudge typologies. Type 3 – *indifference nudges* – are measures that exploit gaps in the utility function or individuals' indifference when choosing between alternatives and that induce people to form specific and predictable ad hoc preferences. Type 4 nudges – *automatism nudges* – are those which use the absence of intentionality to control unintended behaviour. In this respect, Types 2 and 4 share the common goal of attempting to prevent unintended consequences. The difference between the two types lies in the fact that with Type 2 there is a (partially) conscious processing of information that contributes to a utility calculation, whereas with Type 4 the processing of information occurs on an unconscious level and directly affects behaviour.

This classification has been challenged by Sampson (2014), who proposes to approach nudges from a decision analysis perspective: simply imagining the structure of an individual's decision process and considering the different points at which an individual could be influenced. Based on the Thaler–Sunstein definition, a nudge can affect any part of a person's decision process. Based on this, there are three points of influence: (1) before an individual's preferences are defined; (2) after the definition of preferences but before the observation of the choice set; and (3) once the choice set has been recognized. Once preferences are defined and the choice set has been recognized there are two means of influencing choice: utility or probability.

Such classifications need to be further investigated; however, they represent interesting attempts as they both try to disentangle different psychological mechanisms underlying decision-making processes that are affected by nudging policies and consequently their different political and ethical consequences.

In terms of law and public policy, Sunstein (2016) puts forward a different distinction between non-educative and educative nudges. The former include default rules and strategic decisions about how items are ordered and are aimed at exploiting system 1 – intuitive – cognitive operations in the human mind (Kahneman, 2011). On the other hand, educative nudges include disclosure requirements, reminders and warnings, which are specifically designed to increase people's own powers of agency – perhaps by augmenting their knowledge and their capacities, perhaps by making relevant facts salient. Educational nudges address system 2 – deliberative – processes.

According to Sunstein, some types of educational nudges might be described as 'boosts' as long as they represent an attempt to improve people's capacity to make choices for themselves, for example by improving statistical literacy. However, advocates of boosting policies partially disagree with Sunstein's classification (Grüne-Yanoff and Hertwig, 2017) and assert that boosts belong to a separate and somehow alternative category to nudges.

The theoretical foundations of boosting are different from those inspiring nudging. Grüne-Yanoff and Hertwig (2016) claim that the necessary assumptions of nudging and boosting are implied by theoretical commitment to the heuristics-and-biases (for example, Kahneman, 2003; 2011; Kahneman et al., 1982) vs. the simple heuristics and ecological rationality (for example, Gigerenzer et al., 2011) research programmes, respectively.

Although undoubtedly influential, the heuristics-and-biases programme is not the only view about human decision-makers and their competence, nor have its conclusions remained unquestioned. Among alternative research programmes stands the simple heuristics (or fast and frugal heuristics) approach. The starting premise of this programme has been that individuals and organizations cannot help but rely on simple heuristics in conditions of uncertainty, lack of knowledge, and time pressure. Rather than conceptualizing heuristics as inherently error-prone, however, the programme has provided evidence that less information, computation and time – conditions embodied by heuristics – can help improve inferential and predictive accuracy.

Here the cognitive system relies on an 'adaptive toolbox' of simple strategies, and successful performances are the result of so-called ecological rationality, being the ability to select and match the mind's tools to the current social or non-social environment (Gigerenzer et al., 1999; 2011; Hertwig et al., 2013). Of course, heuristics may still fail (for example, when applied in the wrong environment), but this approach emphasizes that, relative to resource-intensive and general-purpose normative strategies, heuristics can be surprisingly efficient and robust (Gigerenzer et al., 2011).

Boost policies are deeply rooted in the simple heuristics research stream and they share the goal of empowering people by expanding (boosting) their competences and thus helping them to reach their objectives. Boosts are interventions that target competences rather than immediate behaviour. These competences can be context-transcending – for instance, statistical literacy – or relatively context-specific, such as making fast and good decisions in a professional context. At least three classes of boost policies can be distinguished. Policies can:

1. change the environment in which decisions are made;
2. extend the repertoire of decision-making strategies, skills and knowledge;
3. do both.

Grüne-Yanoff and Hertwig (2017) distinguish two kinds of boosts. Some are *short-term*, and while they foster a competence, the improvement in performance is limited to a specific context. Others are *long-term* boosts: 'Ideally, these permanently change the cognitive and behavioural repertoire by adding a new competence or enhancing an existing one, creating a "capital stock" (Sunstein, 2016, p. 32) that can be engaged at will and across situations' (Grüne-Yanoff and Hertwig, 2017, p. 977).

In such a context, educative nudges and short-term boosts largely overlap. Both represent local fixes to a given problem and require – in contrast to classic nudges, such as defaults – a modicum of motivation and cognitive skill.

A possible classification of long-term boosts follows the framework of the behaviour change wheel (Michie et al., 2011). Within such a framework long-term boost interventions would be classified under 'education', 'training', 'environmental restructuring', 'modelling' and 'enablement'.

One dimension on which boosts can be classified is according to the competence to be boosted.

Risk literacy boosts establish or foster the competence to understand statistical information in domains such as health, weather and finances. This competence can be achieved through several representation methods: graphical, as in Lusardi et al. (2014), experienced-based (Kaufmann et al., 2013), free of framing biases (Gigerenzer et al., 2007) and so on and so forth.

Boosts targeting risk literacy work as long as people have access to actuarial information about risks. Often, however, people need to make decisions under uncertainty, with no explicit risk information available. In this case, they need other mental tools. Uncertainty management boosts establish or foster procedural rules for making good decisions, predictions and assessments under uncertain conditions with the help of other strategies such as fast and frugal decision trees or simple heuristics (for example Drexler et al., 2014; Hertwig and Herzog, 2009).

Additionally, boosts can be motivational and can foster the competence to adjust one's motivation, cognitive control and self-control autonomously (Shefrin and Thaler, 1981). Here policy interventions could capitalize on the strategic use of automatic processes (Gollwitzer, 1999) or on the implementation of reward-bundling exercises (Ainslie, 1992; 2012).

Boosts and nudges are, of course, not perfect substitutes. Yet there are domains in which either nudges or boosts could be used, including food choices, financial decisions and self-control problems. In each of these classes, individuals' competences can be boosted, nudged, or both. Conceptual clarity is the key to understanding the toolbox available to public policymakers and appreciating each tool's pros and cons. Although two tools may aim to bring about the same behavioural effect, they can tread different causal pathways. Nudging and boosting represent different causal pathways to behaviour change. Making this distinction explicit contributes to the normative debate on behavioural policies, and it offers policymakers a choice.

## CONCLUDING REMARKS

Traditional public policymaking provides a powerful framework for policy analysis, but it relies on a model of human behaviour that the new science of behavioural economics increasingly calls into question. Not only can public financial policy incorporate many lessons of behavioural economics but they can also serve as a solid foundation from which to apply insights from psychology to questions of economic policy. A new approach to policy should be a unified analytical approach that encompasses both traditional policy levers, such as taxes and subsidies, and more psychologically informed instruments. The net result of this innovative approach is a fully behavioural public finance, an integration of psychology and the economics of the public sector that is explicit, systematic, rigorous and realistic.

## REFERENCES

Ainslie, G. (1992), *Picoeconomics: The Strategic Interaction of Successive Motivational States Within the Person*, Cambridge: Cambridge University Press.

Ainslie, G. (2012), 'Pure hyperbolic discount curves predict "eyes open" self-control', *Theory and Decision*, **73** (1), 3–34.

Barr, M.S., S. Mullainathan and E. Shafir (2009), 'The case for behaviorally informed regulation', in D. Moss and J. Cisternino (eds), *New Perspectives on Regulation*, Cambridge, MA: The Tobin Project, pp. 25–61.

Bhargava, S. and G. Loewenstein (2015), 'Behavioral economics and public policy 102: beyond nudging', *American Economic Review: Papers and Proceedings*, **105** (1), 396–401.

Chetty, R. (2015), 'Behavioral economics and public policy: a pragmatic perspective', *American Economic Review*, **105** (5), 1–33.

Drexler, A., G. Fischer and A. Schoar (2014), 'Keeping it simple: financial literacy and rules of thumb', *American Economic Journal: Applied Economics*, **6** (2), 1–31.

Fisher, M. and S. Lotz (2014), 'Is soft paternalism ethically legitimate? The relevance of psychological processes for the assessment of nudge-based policies', CGS Working Paper, **5** (2).

Galizzi, M. (2014), 'What is really behavioral in behavioral health policy? And does it work?', *Applied Economic Perspectives and Policy*, **36** (1), 25–60.

Galizzi, M. (2017), 'Behavioral aspects of policy formulation: experiments, behavioral insights, nudges', in M. Howlett, I. Mukherjee and S. Fraser (eds), *Handbook of Policy Formulation*, Cheltenham, UK and Northampton, MA, USA: Edward Elgar Publishing.

Gigerenzer, G., W. Gaissmaier, E. Kurz-Milcke, L.M. Schwartz and S. Woloshin (2007), 'Helping doctors and patients to make sense of health statistics', *Psychological Science in the Public Interest*, **8** (2), 53–96.

Gigerenzer, G., R. Hertwig and T. Pachur (eds) (2011), *Heuristics: The Foundations of Adaptive Behaviour*, Oxford: Oxford University Press.

Gigerenzer, G., P.M. Todd and ABC Research Group (1999), *Simple Heuristics that Make Us Smart*, New York, NY: Oxford University Press.

Gollwitzer, P.M. (1999), 'Implementation intentions: strong effects of simple plans', *American Psychologist*, **54** (7), 493–503.

Grüne-Yanoff, T. and R. Hertwig (2016), 'Nudge versus boost: how coherent are policy and theory?', *Minds and Machine*, **26** (1–2), 149–83.

Grüne-Yanoff, T. and R. Hertwig (2017), 'Nudging and boosting: steering or empowering good decisions', *Perspectives on Psychological Science*, **12** (6), 973–86.

Heidhues, P., B. Koszegi and T. Murooka (2016), 'Exploitative innovation', *American Economic Journal: Microeconomics*, **8** (1), 1–23.

Herrnstein, R.J., G.F. Loewenstein, D. Prelec and W. Vaughan (1993), 'Utility maximization and melioration: internalities in individual choices', *Journal of Behavioural Decision Making*, **6** (3), 149–85.

Hertwig, R. and S.M. Herzog (2009), 'Fast and frugal heuristics: tools of social rationality', *Social Cognition*, **27** (5), 661–98.

Hertwig, R., U. Hoffrage and ABC Research Group (2013), *Simple Heuristics in a Social World*, New York, NY: Oxford University Press.

Kahneman, D. (2003), 'A perspective on judgment and choice: mapping bounded rationality', *American Psychologist*, **58** (9), 697–720.

Kahneman, D. (2011), *Thinking, Fast and Slow*, New York, NY: Farrar, Straus & Giroux.

Kahneman, D., P. Slovic and A. Tversky (eds) (1982), *Judgement under Uncertainty: Heuristics and Biases*, New York, NY: Cambridge University Press.

Kaufmann, C., M. Weber and E. Haisley (2013), 'The role of experience sampling and graphical displays on one's investment risk appetite', *Management Science*, **59** (2), 323–40.

Laibson, D. and J.A. List (2015), 'Principles of (behavioural) economics', *American Economic Review: Papers and Proceedings*, **105** (5), 385–90.

Loewenstein, G. and N. Chater (2017), 'Putting nudges in perspective', *Behavioural Public Policy*, **1** (1), 26–53.

Loewenstein, G. and P. Ubel (2010), 'Economists behaving badly', *New York Times*, 14 July.

Lusardi, A., A.S. Samek, A. Kapteyn, L. Glinert, A. Hung and A. Heinberg (2014), 'Visual tools and narratives: new ways to improve financial literacy', NBER Working Paper No. 20229.

Michie, S., M.M. van Stralen and R. West (2011), 'The behavioural change wheel: a new method for characterising and designing behavior change interventions', *Implementation Science*, **6** (1), 42.

Oliver, A. (2015), 'Nudging, shoving, and budging: behavioural economic-informed policy', *Public Administration*, **93** (3), 700–714.

Sampson, C. (2014), 'A taxonomy of behavioural interventions', *The academic health economists' blog*, accessed at www.aheblog.com.

Shefrin, H. and R. Thaler (1981), 'An economic theory of self control', *Journal of Public Policy*, **89** (2), 392–406.

Sunstein, C. (2016), *The Ethics of Influence: The Government in the Age of Behavioural Sciences*, Cambridge: Cambridge University Press.

Thaler, R. and C. Sunstein (2008), *Nudge: Improving Decisions About Health, Wealth, and Happiness*, New Haven, CT: Yale University Press.

# 4.   Do regulators know better?

## Umberto Filotto

## 1.   INTRODUCTION

Those that visit the beautiful city of Naples and happen to walk in the narrow and central street of Via Egiziaca a Pizzofalcone, will pass by and certainly stop in front of the imposing Palace Serra di Cassano. What most tourists probably ignore is that until 1999 the front doorway of the Palace, which is facing the Naples Royal Palace, was closed and that it had been so for two hundred years. In 1799 the owner of the Palace, the Duke Serra di Cassano, ordered the main entrance to be shut in sign of mourning and protest against the king for the beheading of his youngest son Gennaro, deputy commander of the National Guard of the Neapolitan Republic which, thanks to the determinant backing of Horatio Nelson and of the Royal British Navy, was defeated by the conservative troops of the "Santa Fede" (Holy Faith), thus reinstating the cruel and die hard former king Ferdinando I of Borbone. Before being executed Gennaro Serra looked at the cheering crowd of Piazza del Mercato and sadly said "I always fought for their wellbeing and now I see them celebrate my death".

The reason why I think the story of the Neapolitan Republic[1] deserves to be remembered here is that the typical Enlightenment approach of emancipating people top down without taking into consideration their opinions (which are probably wrong), didn't, in this and many other occasions, prove successful. Experience tells us that believing that some benevolent paternalistic entity is entitled to decide what is good and what is wrong for others not only is a bit arrogant but it might also have undesirable consequences.

Luckily enough, at least in this part of the world, this kind of controversy has less dramatic outcomes nowadays; still, the rejection of State paternalism, no matter how benevolent it might be, is however definitely vivid. Just think about the harsh debate on the "nanny approach" of

---

[1]   On the story of the Neapolitan Republic see Benedetto Croce (1912), *La Rivoluzione Napoletana del 1799: Biografie, Racconti, Ricerche*; see also the novel based on the biography of Eleonora Fonseca Pimentel by Enzo Striano (1986), *Il Resto di Niente*.

Michael Bloomberg when his administration introduced a ban on extra-large soft drink cans and servings (Gostin, 2013; De Maria, 2013). Besides the fact that funnily enough (but I am sure neuroscientists – or maybe lobbyists? – are ready to explain to us that this is perfectly natural) people tend to overreact when you touch on food, while they tend to be a lot quieter when you send them to fight in a war to be, very likely, killed, it is striking, at least for me, that sound, rational and humanitarian policies designed by qualified, well-meaning and objective regulators can be rejected, sometimes with violence, precisely by those who should benefit from those provisions. But why and how do people fiercely resist being led to the good?

Reflecting on this might very easily throw us into confusion. On one side, being researchers, who prize competence and excellence, we are inclined to believe that knowledge and experience and a positive and rational approach is in any circumstance (be it research or government) preferable to chaos and thus those who are better educated and cleverer should lead the crowd. On the other side, after Darwin, we are aware that there is no absolute best and that only a trial-and-error process can lead to progress, a word which has to be taken only in a time dimension as, we know, evolutionism is absolutely anti-teleological. In the latter perspective rejecting any kind of "intelligent design" (and designers) can certainly generate several mistakes but, in the long run, might not necessarily determine negative or worse outcomes.

The antinomy between guidance and self-determination will certainly be one of the *fils rouges* of the research agenda of the Behavioral Financial Regulations and Policy initiative (from now on BEFAIRLY). Actually, if we accept as a postulate that we need a regulation of financial markets, as we have clear evidence that they do not naturally reach a state of equilibrium, there are a few things that have to be dealt with when we draft the agenda of our behavioral regulation research initiative.

## 2.   WHAT WE NEED BEFORE WE START

The first one, clearly, is acquiring an adequate understanding of the financial ecosystem. In the last decades major progress in the comprehension of how markets, institutions and decision makers interact in the financial environment has been made. For sure we do not have a complete and reliable vision of reality and while this happens in most scientific domains (otherwise there would be nothing to research for), the fact that in our case the comprehension gap is definitely very wide could be highly frustrating even though it is not unusual. Think, for example, about quantum mechanics or neurology: very little is known, but this does not restrain physicists in investigating the subatomic level nor neurologists and neurosurgeons in treating patients. Compared to the latter domains, however, in economics we have a significant advantage: we can fill in the knowledge gap with models and because same or similar models are used in the regulations, not only are they a viable proxy to reality but they also tend to shape it. But the issue remains: do we have an adequate understanding of the financial environment and of the "natural" mechanisms which determine the outcomes to be able to design effective interventions?

The ambition to shape reality leads us to the second rule that should be respected when designing regulations: what is the desirable and viable shape? To answer this question what is needed is a clear and shared vision of the world, that is, a common *Weltanschauung* which should be the background and the source of inspiration for the decisions of policymakers and regulators. Do we have it? Maybe I am not able to perceive it, but I really cannot see such a common vision; I also have the impression that while after the Great Crisis of the 1930s such a common *Weltanschauung* was developed (no matter if right or wrong), one of the consequences of this crisis has been the definitive dissolution of any common vision of what financial markets should finally look like.

Despite the fragility of its foundations, as the volatility and the inclination of financial markets to instability is evident and strong, regulation is nevertheless not an option but an obligation; as a matter of fact even stubborn deregulators do not go so far in their ideology as to deny the necessity of rules for financial markets and institutions.

## 3.  SOME CONCERNS

So regulation was, and, in its overall structure, still is definitely prescriptive; this consideration applies not only if we refer to the banking legislation of the 1930s, but is ultimately true even if we look at the Basel Accords and to all the supposedly "lighter" prudential regulation. Then, if mandatory and authoritative regulation is admissible, the introduction of a behavioral, thus "softer", approach should ease possible objections to the current model of disciplining, without creating new criticism.

While logical in principle this consideration has to be tested against a few possible counterarguments:

- the first one is, by now, a classical one: while some disagree (Gigerenzer, 2014), in common understanding, also of policymakers, the main tool for behavioral regulation is nudging (Thaler and Sunstein, 2008), but are we sure that the gentle push is "better" (that is, not only more effective but overall more acceptable) than mandatory rules?

- the second one is: if we accept the fact that regulators have the right, and the duty, to regulate are we sure they are competent enough?
- and the final one: what happens, who is responsible and what are the consequences if things go wrong?

There is already a vast body of literature on the first topic. Sunstein's (2016) *The Ethics of Influence* is the natural reference for those that compare nudge with other ways to drive behaviors. Sunstein's conclusions are, not surprisingly, that, yes, nudge is overall better where applicable (there are of course situations in which mandatory rules and bans are necessary and others which do not require regulations).

One would wonder why the issue is on the table; at the end of the day having the option to opt out instead of being compelled to comply with a mandatory rule is definitely better. But criticism is just as obvious: on one side, just because it is "lighter", nudging could be, and is, used in a wider number of situations, also those in which a mandatory rule would be rejected as being too authoritarian. Just think about the can size dispute; nobody would have ever accepted criminal law to be applied to this issue so that manufacturers or consumers could be put in jail or fined because they sold or drank too many soft drinks. This means that the perimeter of regulation tends to widen and to cover issues that are usually considered outside the scope of public rule. In parallel with this, nudging is normally delegated to regulatory bodies that are composed of very clever, well-meaning and excellently schooled people but that often do not have a clear democratic mandate (we will come back to this). On the other side because nudging is based on the use of a decision-making mechanism it is not explicit and, to some possibly significant extent, manipulative (Selinger and Whyte, 2011).

The "nudgers" obviously fight back: while they admit that nudging does not always apply and recognize its limitations and the necessity to use it appropriately (that is, promoting welfare, not violating people's dignity and so on), they claim that in a vast number of circumstances it is an efficient, cheap (or cheaper), and respectful way of regulating and protecting citizens (see Halpern, 2015; Halpern and Sanders, 2016). However, what is more convincing is that Sunstein produces evidence that not only nudges work, but that most people like them. If rules are an intrusion into people's self-determination and liberty, who could object to measures whose introduction is strongly demanded by those who are subject to the discipline? Chapter 6 of *The Ethics of Influence* is entirely dedicated to this topic and contains several examples of very popular nudges; being Italian I have necessarily to refer also to a 2016 paper (Reisch and Sunstein, 2016) because its results show that, contrary to the stereotype of Italians being intrinsically anarchists and impossible to govern, my fellow countrymen and women do indeed love to be nudged.

That said, criticism of pro-nudgers is abundant and robustly motivated (Gigerenzer, 2015): the most profound, wise and long-term oriented objection is that even if they like it, nudging is not necessarily healthy for people. Actually the accusations of nannification and of inducing people to discharge their responsibilities are based on solid grounds and it is likely that nudging could deprive people of real incentives to learn and to fully master their lives. Also, objecting to nudging compared to mandatory rules at constant perimeter is certainly possible if you consider the aforementioned long-term effects and/or if you fear a possible subtle manipulation of individuals. However, what is even more critical is that because nudging is gentler and allows people to make different choices without any sanction, the scope of regulation tends to be much wider, with regulators feeling less constraint in interfering in behaviors that would be normally considered private, the can size case giving clear evidence. What actually happens is that, because the box contains soft tools there is a sense that they can be used more broadly, like if, given their different and apparently less intrusive quality, nudging mechanisms could be used in larger quantities.

Of course the intentions are generally good (as they were for Gennaro Serra di Cassano), but are they also fair? Something is indeed unpleasant and is the self-definition of nudgers as "choice architects". Yes, of course, we are aware that also in a world without nudge units at work, there will always be somebody, in the state, in the private sector and in our private life, trying to drive us to make certain choices. But the idea that a comprehensive and coordinated set of mechanisms is put in place to influence our choices in order to shape, widely, our society and economic system is rather scary (Campbell, 2017). There are indeed several arguments that can be used to object to the approach. One, which is not commonly used, is that trying to determine people's choices in detail diminishes the amount of randomness and of unexpected decisions that, while apparently wrong, might end up as being the most appropriate given the circumstances. This is a pure Darwinian consideration and it might also look to some extent irresponsible as it does not consider the effects of giving up protecting individuals from their own stupidity; however, it is known to be true that in several, probably most, cases innovation, like evolution, was not generated by any intelligent designer worried about making the right (that is, already proven successful) thing, but by somebody making "wrong" choices. From the discovery of penicillin to x-rays, from rubber vulcanization to Viagra, the story of science is rich in "unintended" (and certainly unplanned) innovations.

But the idea of Big Brother deciding for everybody also raises criticism for other more obvious reasons. One which will be discussed more thoroughly later concerns the mandate of these "choice architects". Because we do not question that in a democracy the legitimacy to take decisions on others' lives must be limited and has to stem from a very clear and unambiguous consensus, the question is whether "choice architects", that usually operate in independent authorities and bodies not directly elected, are entitled to such a wide power of determination. Other arguments used to question putting wide powers in the hands of one single architect are true classics. First, the "harm principle" by J.S. Mill (1859): how can the "architect" know what is good for you as he/she has less information on what you like than you do? Everybody who went through the renovation of a house knows, having gone through lengthy discussions with interior designers, how well grounded this argument could be. But also F. von Hayek (1945) contributes to this discussion in a very convincing way: because information is dispersed, and the sum of total knowledge is much higher than what could be available to one single agent, decisions cannot be taken properly in a concentrated way. These arguments have been, and still are, the spearhead of conservative advocates against state intrusion. While being certainly relevant, the information argument is, however, not definitive either in one sense or in the other. Because our perspective is behavioral we are well aware that information is certainly important but, alas, insufficient to guarantee that people would make good choices: no matter how much information decision makers have, and how good it is, they are biased and make mistakes. This could be a good argument to justify the necessity for a superior and illuminated guidance; because decision makers are biased, they need somebody wiser than them (that is, than us) to guide appropriate choices; but because we also care for freedom of choice we do not want to be submitted to coercive rules and prefer to be guided gently to our Shangri-la.

With this we move on to the second of our concerns on the appropriateness and preferability of a "nudge based" regulatory agenda; that of the competence, in a broad sense, of regulators. The issue is twofold: on one side we refer to competence in its strict meaning of the possession of knowledge and skills that enable individuals to perform appropriately in a given situation. On the other side, we will also consider the several cognitive limitations that steer final decisions and that explain why the mere fact of being better educated and more experienced does not necessarily correspond to better choices. Discussing the first dimension should be, and actually is, easier. In most countries regulatory authorities and bodies are usually able to attract the most brilliant and better motivated graduates together with distinguished scholars; this should make the issue of mere competence a non-issue. But this is also a pitfall; because they have to defend competence against ignorance, simply because they "know better", officials tend to fall into what we might call the "Serra trap", that is, imposing on others solutions that are indeed deemed for the good but that might be not only too abstract but also not appropriate for those who should benefit from them. And, as it was for Serra, ideology can be a dangerous enemy; many of those well-intentioned officials chose to be public servants instead of accepting better paid private employment because they had an ideal that they wanted to achieve. So they do have a *Weltanschauung* and such a strong and demanding one that they very often forget to consider a reality that dares not match with their vision. Also, it is not only the noble intention of changing the world that motivates those officials; in some, not too rare cases, it is also preferring a lower paid, but safer job, to the challenges and risks of private employment. This means that some of them have a natural inclination to be conservative and risk avoiding.

The combination of intellectual arrogance and risk aversion might offset the advantages of higher competence; ultimately what is relevant is not how good you are but how good are your decisions and, unfortunately, this is not guaranteed by a better education.

But this is not the only problem: actually, how can we be sure that our sapient archimandrites do not suffer from the same limitations that we have (Schnellenbach and Schubert, 2014)? Of course they have first class education, outstanding IQs, experience and vision but unless they are relatives of Doctor Spock, and have been raised on planet Vulcan, they are, like us, prey to those same unpleasant emotions and have that strange amygdala (Tasic, 2011). . .

Yes, it is certainly true that the conditions in which we make our personal financial decisions compared to those in which financial rules and incentives are designed by someone who is not directly affected by the results are completely different; the latter should be less vulnerable to emotions and cognitive biases. Less vulnerable, yes, but unfortunately not totally immune; some biases (framing, hyperbolic discounting, herding and so on) are personal characteristics, systematic states of mind not significantly influenced by the fact that what is at stake is directly related to you. Actually there is no evidence showing that being aware that you theoretically suffer from cognitive limitations, simply like everybody else, immunizes you against the risk of making the same mistakes others make.

However, the impression one gets going through the literature on nudging and its implementations is that its advocates implicitly reject the hypothesis of being very close kin to those that they wish to regulate and protect, as if they had received the gift of the real truth (Lodge and Wegrich, 2016). There is a high risk of intellectual arrogance in this perspective which, by the way, contradicts one of the foundations of the behavioral approach, that is, that we all are human beings with inevitable natural limitations. Another aspect which should be considered is that when "choice architects" are wrong, the consequences of their mistakes, instead of being individual, will be generalized and publicly enforced. This has severe consequences for public welfare as people will be induced, against their natural inclination, to make sub-optimal choices they would not have made if they were left alone. And while this is, even more, true when we consider bans and mandatory rules, the usual considerations apply: being softer, nudges tend to be used in more circumstances and on a larger scale and, as they are less explicit, using them leaves regulators with freer hands and fewer responsibilities. This leads us to the final step of this discussion, which is the issue of accountability: if a well-intentioned but inexperienced or unlucky regulator nudges me in the wrong direction, who is responsible for the consequences?

Before we get to this point, however, we have once again to remind ourselves that the alternative in our case is not regulation versus no regulation, as we know that an unregulated financial market would certainly be unstable and politically unacceptable. Once this is accepted we end up with the same recursive question: why should mandatory rules (which would be written by those same imperfect regulators) be preferable to nudging? The latter at least gives individuals the possibility to opt out, thus to "self-correct" the mistakes made by regulators. If, for example, unnecessary or misleading health screenings were made mandatory, the possible negative effects would apply in 100 percent of cases, while if they were only nudged, savvy or even lazy individuals would avoid negative consequences.

Like before when we were considering the perimeter of the two regulatory approaches, *ceteris paribus*, this observation is correct; but as previously discussed, softer rules tend to have wider scope and application, and, because they are not explicitly coercive, they escape the same severe criteria of effectiveness and appropriateness that apply to mandatory regulations. For the same reasons "nudgers", being perceived as liberal and tolerant regulators, keeping themselves at arm's length, could be exempt from the responsibility criteria that apply to their authoritarian paternalistic equivalents who would be more exposed to legal responsibilities or to the risk of being laid off.

But if they are "choice architects", if they influence others' behavior, choices and ultimately lives, shouldn't their responsibilities at least be the same? So what happens if something goes wrong, if the wise, but pervasive design is simply mistaken?

The topic of the accountability of regulators is a very delicate one (Scott, 2000). There is a very fragile, and once again human, equilibrium between making regulators accountable and the risk of having them avoid responsibilities or drifting to a very formalistic approach. Of course regulators, like everybody else, must take the risk of being wrong, the alternative being making no decisions; this would, however, be unacceptable as their task is precisely that of making choices. But if the choices are wrong, or better, too wrong, if they were made carelessly, against evidence or the general will, in the regulator's own interest or to follow an abstract ideology or a twisted *Weltanschauung*, why should they be immune to any consequence?

To avoid this logical stalemate the approach we will take is essentially political in the sense that those that are given the power to steer other people's choices may, and must, do so and because of this they can possibly be wrong. However, this power and franchise should be strictly limited by an explicit and verifiable mandate.

And if mandates are not given by the grace of God, they normally result from a democratic process in which people (or organizations) explicitly delegate somebody else to act in order to pursue what they (the delegators) considered the common good at the cost of giving up part of their intrinsic rights and of their liberty. Because the aforementioned cost is so crucial, the issue of the limits of the mandate and of its recipient is essential. In political science literature this debate is immense but we have to concentrate on what is relevant for our discussion, the two main questions being: do "nudgers" have an explicit mandate from those they want to save from their own stupidity? And if so, which kind of domain does this mandate cover and what are its boundaries?

Answering the question about the mandate of regulators (see, for example, Tison, 2003–2004; Cafaggi, 2006) and to what extent elected representatives can delegate to technocrats some of the powers they have received from voters would open another Pandora's box: there are fierce discussions on this topic among political scientists and in administrative law academia. But, sticking to our specific field of interest, that is, the mandate of "nudgers", are we reasonably confident that they are entitled to exert the influence they have in shaping people's choices? Serious doubts are legitimate: despite the fact that we do not have empirical evidence supporting this conclusion, while maybe for some Obama voters being nudged was a hidden desire, it is very difficult to believe that Conservatives wanted Dr Halpern to shape their lives. The issue of the questionability of the subtle, soft, though manipulative, approach of nudging emerges once again. As we are still discussing whether unelected regulators are really entitled to impose rules on the basis of powers which are delegated to them, we have even stronger doubts regarding individuals or organizations, which in some cases, being private think tanks, have no public statute and control, that develop measures that steer people's lives. It is clear that ultimately the responsibility rests with the politician, hopefully elected, who adopts the proposed measure, but isn't there an issue of ethics in conducting inexplicit experiments that guide decision making and aim to shape society? Admitting the expression might be too strong, isn't this a kind of social eugenics, certainly deemed for the good, but not authorized by its potential beneficiaries? And if there is no clear mandate, nor authorization, nor clear and statutory limits, who can be held accountable for mistakes deriving from induced improper conducts? Gerd Gigerenzer's studies on the ill-effects of excessive disease screenings are true classics: what I want to point out here is that those that are responsible for inducing these behaviors will not, and cannot (after all there is no obligation to comply) be held responsible for that, which also might have as a consequence making the redressing of malfunctioning mechanisms more difficult and slow.

## 4.  CONCLUSIONS

Behavioral regulation is on the agenda of politicians and authorities of most countries. Mandatory approaches and coercive legislation have financial, but also political, costs that are becoming more and more difficult to afford; also the effectiveness and the applicability of these kinds of rules in some domains is in question. This puts alternative solutions like the ones that are within the scope of the BEFAIRLY initiative at the center of the academic and policy debate. But because they are popular, and fashionable, and blessed by a huge recent success, these approaches might be misinterpreted and misapplied.

To avoid this possible outcome a serious and critical debate has to develop; not all measures are equivalent, not all of them are effective and appropriate in any situation. A critical attitude from those who are certainly convinced of the necessity of adopting a behavioral perspective is appropriate and advisable to try to avoid mistakes.

In this chapter I wanted to give my contribution on issues which I consider essential for structuring the next steps of our initiative such as the necessity to develop a common and shared vision of objectives, once an adequate comprehension of the actual economic framework is reached, to discuss the suitability of soft compared to hard approaches to regulation, to consider the competence and accountability of regulators.

Naturally no definitive conclusion was reached, but for these topics, as for most of the topics which are on our research agenda, we are just starting a difficult but exciting journey.

# REFERENCES

Cafaggi, Fabrizio (2006), 'La responsabilità dei regolatori privati: un itinerario di ricerca tra mercati finanziari e servizi professionali', *Mercato Concorrenza e Regole*, (1), 9–60.

Campbell, David (2017), 'Cleverer than command', *Social and Legal Studies*, **26** (1), 111–26.

Croce, Benedetto (1912), *La Rivoluzione Napoletana del 1799: Biografie, Racconti, Ricerche*, Bari: Laterza, reprinted by Bibliopolis, Naples, 1999.

De Maria, Anthony M. (2013), 'The nanny state and "coercive paternalism"', *Journal of the American College of Cardiology*, **61** (20), 2108–109.

Gigerenzer, Gerd (2014), *Risk Savvy: How to Make Good Decisions*, New York, NY: Viking.

Gigerenzer, Gerd (2015), 'On the supposed evidence for libertarian paternalism', *Review of Philosophy and Psychology*, **6** (3), 361–83.

Gostin, Lawrence O. (2013), 'Bloomberg's health legacy: urban innovator or meddling nanny?', *The Hastings Center Report*, **43** (5), 19–25, Georgetown University Law Center.

Halpern, David (2015), *Inside the Nudge Unit*, New York, NY: Random House.

Halpern, David and Michael Sanders (2016), 'Nudging by government: progress, impact and lessons learnt', *Behavioral Science and Policy*, **2** (2), 54–65.

Lodge, Martin and Kai Wegrich (2016), 'The rationality paradox of nudge: rational tools of government in a world of bounded rationality', *Law and Policy*, **38** (3), 250–67.

Mill, John Stuart (1859), *On Liberty*, London: John W. Parker and Son, reprinted and translated as *Saggio sulla Libertà*, Milan: Il Saggiatore, 2009.

Reisch, Lucia A. and Cass R. Sunstein (2016), 'Do Europeans like nudges?', *Judgment and Decision Making*, **11** (4), 310–25.

Schnellenbach, Jan and Christian Schubert (2014), 'Behavioral political economy: a survey', CESifo Working Paper No. 4988, pp. 1–54.

Scott, Colin (2000), 'Accountability in the regulatory state', *Journal of Law and Society*, **27** (1), 38–60.

Selinger, Evan and Kyle Whyte (2011), 'Is there a right way to nudge? The practice and ethics of choice architecture', *Sociology Compass*, **5** (10), 923–35.

Striano, Enzo (1986), *Il Resto di Niente*, Milan: Rizzoli, reprinted 2004.

Sunstein, Cass R. (2016), *The Ethics of Influence*, New York, NY: Cambridge University Press.

Tasic, Slavisa (2011), 'Are regulators rational?', *Journal des Economistes et des Etudes Humaines*, **17** (1), 1–19.

Thaler, Richard H. and Cass R. Sunstein (2008), *Nudge*, New Haven, CT: Yale University Press.

Tison, Michel (2003–2004), 'Challenging the prudential supervisor: liability vs regulatory immunity', University of Gent, Working Paper 2003-04, presented at the SUERF Conference 2003 in Tallin, Estonia.

Von Hayek, Friedrich (1945), 'The use of knowledge in society', *American Economic Review*, **35** (4), 519–53.

# 5. Behavioral finance and the effects of non-conventional monetary policies

**Benoit Mojon, Adrian Penalver and Adriana Lojschova**

## 1. INTRODUCTION

The financial crisis has put central banks at center stage of macroeconomic and financial stabilization policies. They have extended and diversified their set of tools to intervene in financial markets and influence economic activity and inflation. Where before 2007 their main tool was the level of short-term interest rates, they had to design and implement alternative instruments after these rates reached their "physical" minima, near zero, the so-called "zero or effective lower bound on interest rates".

Two main "unconventional tools" have emerged: forward guidance and large-scale asset purchases. Forward guidance boils down to a commitment on future decisions on interest rates. The US Federal Reserve for instance announced in August 2011 that it would not raise interest rates before 2013 Q2 at the earliest. The European Central Bank (ECB) announced in July 2013 that it would not raise short-term interest rates for an extended period of time, and then after its asset purchase program began, rates would not increase "well past" the end of its net purchases.

In addition, large-scale asset purchases consist of issuing money to push up bond prices in order to lower interest rates at longer maturities. Just to fix ideas, the Federal Reserve, the ECB and the Bank of Japan have purchased bonds up to 25, 25 and 60 percent of GDP, respectively, and held them on their books. Prior to the crisis, these portfolios were an order of magnitude smaller.

The emergence of these new instruments raises important analytical challenges that are close to the research agenda initiated by Herbert Simon. Indeed, both forward guidance and large asset purchases will influence markets and economic activity if and only if a majority of economic agents understand their purpose and act upon them. In this chapter, we show that bounded rationality that can either limit (in the case of forward guidance) or amplify (in the case of large asset purchases) the effectiveness of central banks' policies.

In section 2 we report empirical evidence that the ability of the Federal Reserve to influence expectations through its forward guidance has been diverse and incomplete. As shown in Andrade et al. (2018), only a minority among professional forecasters took the Federal Reserve 2011–12 forward guidance as a means to stimulate economic activity. A majority instead took this commitment of not increasing interest rates for at least two years as a bad omen on the economic outlook. To the extent that this majority would act upon such reassessment, for instance revising their investment plans down, the intent of the Fed can turn out to be counter-productive in slowing down the economy instead of stimulating it.

In section 3 we show instead that a large asset purchase program can be more effective thanks to a form of bounded rationality. Akiyama et al. (2017) reproduced large asset purchase programs, also known as quantitative easing or QE, in laboratory experiments with students. It seems that the announcement that the central bank will buy assets and either eventually sell them or keep them up to maturity pushes prices of these assets persistently above their fundamental value.

These two studies illustrate that we cannot, when evaluating the effectiveness of central bank policies, overly rely on standard macroeconomic models in which agents form rational expectations. While we still need further research to understand properly the formation of inflation expectations in the real world, it seems necessary to keep an open mind and base our assessments on multiple models with various hypotheses of the effects of monetary policies on output and inflation.

## 2.   CENTRAL BANK COMMUNICATION AND THE FORMATION OF EXPECTATIONS

Since 2008, forward guidance has become a key element of monetary policy. The Federal Reserve, the Bank of Japan, the ECB and the Bank of England have all provided forward guidance about future policy rates in various forms, some qualitative, others quantitative, and in some cases conditional on specific economic developments, including the evolution of real variables such as the unemployment rate.

However, there is ample evidence that it took time for markets to understand what central banks meant by forward guidance. As shown in Figure 5.1, forward interest rates remained much higher than effective short-term interest rate until very late in the crisis. From the Lehman crisis in 2008 until August 2011, investors were convinced that short-term interest rates

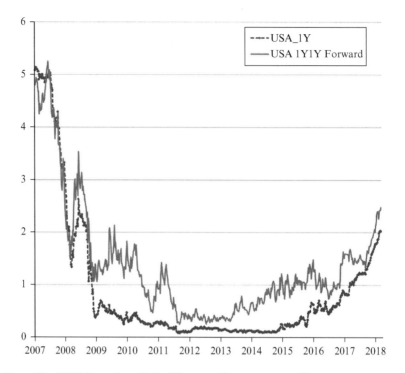

*Note:*   The 1Y1Y forward rate is the 1Y rate markets expect a year from now.

*Source:*   Authors' calculation using Bloomberg data.

*Figure 5.1    US 1 year and 1Y1Y forward interest rates*

would rise again within two years. With hindsight, we know that the Fed started to increase interest rates only in late 2015.[1]

Yet we see a much better understanding of markets from August 2011 until the end of 2012. This is when the Federal Reserve communication on future interest rate was very precise in terms of date, using what is now called fixed date forward guidance. The Federal Reserve communicated a horizon until when it would not raise interest rates. And we see from Figure 5.1, this is when forward rates were the closest to what short-term interest rate were eventually.

---

[1]   Financial markets are often prone to myopia. In this respect, the great financial crisis can be seen as an even more striking combination of myopia and herd behavior. As we describe in the Appendix, in 2007 the expected default probability of the banks reached a minimum.

However, we argue that even during this specific episode, when forward guidance was very effective in bringing down expected interest rates, it is far from clear that this policy stimulated the economy.

How forward guidance statements are interpreted depends fundamentally on what those listening think central banks can do. Those who believe that central banks can commit to future policy rates today will behave differently from those who believe that central banks cannot commit. A first set of evidence on such a different interpretation can be shown from the survey of professional forecasters. In particular, we can compare the level of disagreement across forecasters on future interest rates and on future economic activity. Andrade et al. (2018) show that while the period of fixed date forward guidance is one of exceptional consensus on future interest rates, there is very persistent disagreement on future inflation and future growth of consumption.

This indicates that communicating your intention on future interest rates need not facilitate the coordination of expectations on a faster growth of the economy. Actually, if the proportion of people who believe that the central bank can commit is too small, then forward guidance becomes counter-productive.

To understand why, notice that central banks' announcements that future rates are expected to remain low for some time could signal either a weak macroeconomic outlook – which is bad news – or a more accommodative policy stance – which is good news. Andrade et al. (2018) present a model in which agents are unsure about the nature of forward guidance announcements, that is, whether they are *Odyssean* (a signal of a commitment to future accommodation) or *Delphic* (a signal that the economy will be forced to remain at the zero lower bound (ZLB) by weak future fundamentals.[2] In their benchmark model, policies are constrained by the ZLB during a liquidity trap of exogenously determined length. As a result, a pure Delphic or an Odyssean policy implies similar policy rates until the end of the liquidity trap. Only after the liquidity trap ends do the policies diverge. Under an Odyssean policy, rates will stay low but under a Delphic policy rates will rise as economic fundamentals improve.

Before the end of the trap, signaling with policy rates may be impossible. On the one hand, credibility is hampered by the fact that a Delphic type can easily send the same signal without suffering a cost to its reputation

---

[2] This terminology was introduced by Campbell et al. (2012). See also Ellingsen and Soderstrom (2001) for a seminal contribution in which monetary policy decisions are either related to new information about the economy or to changes in the preferences of the central banker.

of raising interest rates at the end of the trap – a cost the Odyssean central banker would have to pay. For example, Barthelemy and Mengus (2016) show that signaling Odyssean forward guidance can only take place before the liquidity trap begins. Signaling instruments other than rates may be available such as communication, transparency on central banks' beliefs (for example through the release of forecasts) or unconventional monetary policy instruments.[3]

One way to limit the fraction of those who believe the central bank is making a Delphic statement would be to be much clearer about the nature of the commitment. As argued by Woodford (2012), the announcement of a clear commitment by the central banker can be a way to make *ex post* deviations from the central bank's commitment costly ("to cause embarrassment", to borrow Woodford's words) and thereby convince those who believe it is Delphic to change their views on the type of policy. Yet, such announcements can be also made by Delphic central bankers. And again, the latter will not bear the cost of reneging whilst it pockets the *ex ante* gains related to increasing the proportion of optimists. In the end, communication on commitment is plagued by cheap talk problems: to the extent that it costs nothing for the Delphic central banker to pretend to be an Odyssean central banker, such communication provides no information on types of policy. This cheap talk aspect of forward guidance announcements is developed in Bassetto (2015).

Another way to increase the belief that the central bank is Odyssean could be to communicate on fundamentals and to try to coordinate agents' beliefs on shorter liquidity traps than the horizon of the zero interest rate policy. This can be achieved by releasing forecasts of macro-economic variables, as frequently done by central banks, or by committing to temporarily overshoot the inflation target (the Fed, the Bank of England and more recently the Bank of Japan have made such announcements).

Finally, quantitative easing policies and the purchase of long maturity bonds at very low rates, or supplying liquidity at long horizons at zero interest rates amount to "putting your money where your mouth is". This can provide a strong signal about the central bank's willingness not to raise policy rates in the future. Indeed, such policies can imply a cost to the central bank in case it deviates from its commitment because an increase in interest rate leads to capital losses to the central bank (see Bhattarai et al., 2014 for an investigation of this mechanism). Yet such a signaling

---

[3]   These include quantitative easing or loan policies such as the targeted long-term refinancing operation (TLTRO) implemented by the ECB. Some evidence of the signaling effect of the Asset Purchasing Program has been documented by Coenen et al. (2017).

device hinges on the central bank's aversion to capital losses and the extent to which it cannot be rescued by the fiscal authority in case of negative equity.

## 3. A QUANTITATIVE EASING EXPERIMENT

Another unconventional monetary policy instrument available to central banks when their policy interest rates hit the effective lower bound is quantitative easing (QE). QE in its most basic form is the purchase of government bonds in exchange for central bank reserves with the intention to retain them for a significant length of time.[4] In an era in which interest is paid on reserves, this amounts to the exchange of one interest-bearing liability of the state for another. In textbook models with frictionless and complete markets and fully rational and infinitely living agents and no arbitrage, such a transaction can have no temporary or permanent effects on any macroeconomic variables (Eggertsson and Woodford, 2003). In particular, short-term and long-term interest rates will be unchanged and there will be no effect on output and inflation.[5]

There is, however, strong evidence that QE programs have moved bond prices and yields, although the scale and duration of such effects is still debated (Joyce et al., 2011; Krishnamurthy and Vissing-Jorgensen, 2011). The literature has focused on two departures from the textbook model to explain these effects. One theory is that central bank money and government bonds are not perfect substitutes (Tobin, 1958) perhaps because markets are segmented due to investors' "preferred habitat" (Vayanos and Vila, 2009) or because investors do not like holding the interest rate risk associated with long-term bonds. If long-term government bonds and central bank reserves are not perfect substitutes, a fall in the volume of long-term bonds in private hands can raise the price and drop the yield relative to short-term rates. The alternative explanation is that QE is a means by which central banks can give credibility to forward guidance commitments to deviate from established monetary policy behavior, such as a Taylor rule (Eggertsson and Woodford, 2003). QE reinforces the signal that the short-term rate will remain low for longer than a time-consistent policy

---

[4]   The scale of the purchases and the holding period distinguish QE from standard open market operations. QE programs have also bought non-government bonds but this is outside the scope of this discussion.
[5]   Older irrelevance propositions for open market operations were described in Wallace (1981) and Sargent and Smith (1987).

rule would suggest. Lowering the expected path of short-term rates drags down long-term rates through the expectations hypothesis of the term structure.

In this section, we present experimental evidence documented in Akiyama et al. (2017) that QE can still work even if bonds and central bank cash are perfect substitutes. The subjects participating in this experiment are put in the situation of large commercial banks that hold a portfolio of bonds and central bank reserves. In a benchmark case, they trade bonds for reserves in a call market over 11 rounds without any involvement by the central bank. Two variants of QE are considered: one in which the central bank buys specified amounts on known dates and holds the purchases to the end of the experiment, and a second in which the central bank buys and then sells all of its accumulated portfolio on known dates.

Under fully rational expectations, neither of these QE operations should change the price. Although it might be thought that prices will rise because the central bank will buy in the future and therefore that prices should rise in advance, each trader has an incentive to try to price just under the existing marginal trader to sell all their bonds at any price above the fundamentals. If each trader follows the same strategy, any price above the fundamental price will be undercut until it disappears.

Figure 5.2 shows that on average the market price in the benchmark case was very close to the fundamental value. However, prices rose well

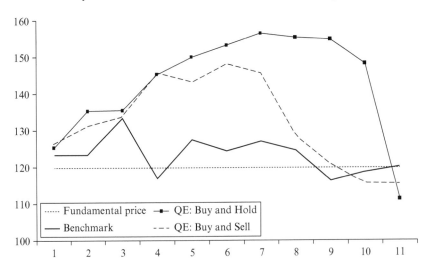

*Source:* Akiyama et al. (2017).

*Figure 5.2    Average price paths for each treatment group across 11 periods*

above the fundamental value under QE with buy and hold, only converging on the fundamental price by period 11. By contrast, when the central bank bought and then sold, prices rose above fundamentals but then fell below as the central bank sold. Since the only difference between these experiments is the nature of the central bank's actions, we ascribe the different price paths observed to differences in beliefs about the impact of the central bank's operations.

Overall, these experiments suggest that shifts in beliefs could be part of the explanation for the effect of QE on bond prices (although it doesn't exclude the other channels either). Accepting this possibility does not affect any aspects of the transmission mechanism from bond yields to economic activity and ultimately inflation. Where it does matter is whether QE has effects after net purchases have stopped. According to either of the prevailing theories, it is the stock of purchases that matters, so a buy and hold strategy sustains a constant accommodative stance. The policy is sustainable fundamentally. In these experiments, prices only remain high after purchases have stopped because of the persistence in beliefs about prices, a phenomenon that in real markets could be revised or overturned by alternative shocks. The accommodative stance after purchases have stopped is thus sustained only by coordination of beliefs, which is a less stable equilibrium.

## 4. CONCLUSION

Policy making in models with fully rational agents is often straightforward. What will or won't work and how are commonly understood by everyone concerned. Policy making in practice is as much art as science because there is not complete clarity. Not everyone is fully rational, not everyone is paying full attention to policy making, and people hear different things from the same words just to take a few departures from the world of simple models. Policy making in the real world has to take into account how people actually behave. This can impose constraints in some cases and open up opportunities in others.

In this chapter we have explored two examples of how beliefs can alter the effectiveness of unconventional monetary policy. In the first example, we explained that whether people believe that central banks can commit to future policy matters a lot, and if too many people think it cannot and that forward guidance on low interest rates in fact sends a negative signal about the outlook, then forward guidance can become counter-productive. In the second example, we showed that quantitative easing can still work even if bonds and cash are close substitutes and quantitative easing does not send any signal about future interest rates. If people believe that central bank purchases of bonds will raise bond prices, then they will go up.

These models are obviously not the only way that central banks view how these instruments work. Central banks use multiple models from multiple perspectives, including those with fully rational, forward-looking, infinitely living representative agents. Behavioral models have a role to play in the suite of models central banks use to provide a perspective that is otherwise hidden from view.

## REFERENCES

Acharya, V. and P. Schnabl (2009), "How Banks Played the Leverage 'Game'", NYU Stern White Paper. Executive summary of chapter 2, V.V. Acharya and M. Richardson (eds), *Restoring Financial Stability: How to Repair a Failed System*, Hoboken, NJ: John Wiley and Sons.

Akiyama, E., Y. Funaki, N. Hanaki, R. Ishikawa and A. Penalver (2017), "A Quantitative Easing Experiment", Banque de France Working Paper No. 651, November.

Altunbas, Y., L. Gambacorta and D. Marques-Ibanez (2010), "Bank Risk and Monetary Policy", *Journal of Financial Stability* **6** (3): 121–9.

Andrade, P., G. Gaballo, E. Mengus and B. Mojon (2018), "Forward Guidance and Heterogeneous Beliefs", CEPR Discussion Papers No. 12650.

Barthelemy, J. and E. Mengus (2016), "The Signaling Effect of Raising Inflation", mimeo, HEC Paris and Sciences Po.

Bassetto, M. (2015), "Forward Guidance: Communication, Commitment, or Both?", 2015 Meeting Papers 216, Society for Economic Dynamics.

Bernanke, B. (2010), "Monetary Policy and the Housing Bubble", Speech given at the Annual Meeting of the American Economic Association, Atlanta, Georgia, 3 January.

Bhattarai, S., G.B. Eggertsson and B. Gafarov (2014), "Time Consistency and the Duration of Government Debt: A Signalling Theory of Quantitative Easing", mimeo.

Blundell-Wignall, A. and P. Atkinson (2008), "The Sub-prime Crisis: Causal Distortions and Regulatory Reform", paper presented at the Reserve Bank of Australia conference on "Lessons from the Financial Turmoil of 2007", Sydney, Australia, 14–15 July.

Campbell, J.R., C.L. Evans, J.D. Fisher and A. Justiniano (2012), "Macroeconomic Effects of Federal Reserve Forward Guidance", *Brookings Papers on Economic Activity* **44**: 1–80.

Coenen, G., M. Ehrmann, G. Gaballo, P. Hoffmann, A. Nakov, S. Nardelli, E. Persson and G. Strasser (2017), "Communication of monetary policy in unconventional times", ECB Working Paper Series No. 2080, June.

Dubecq, S., B. Mojon and X. Ragot (2015), "Risk Shifting with Fuzzy Capital Constraints", *International Journal of Central Banking* **11** (1): 71–101.

Eggertsson, G.B. and M. Woodford (2003), "The Zero Bound on Interest Rates and Optimal Monetary Policy", *Brookings Papers on Economic Activity* **34** (1): 139–235.

Ellingsen, T. and U. Soderstrom (2001), "Monetary Policy and Market Interest Rates", *American Economic Review* **91** (5): 1594–607.

Financial Stability Forum (2008), "Report of the Financial Stability Forum on Enhancing Market and Institutional Resilience", April.

Gilchrist, S. and B. Mojon (2014), "Credit Risk in the Euro Area", Banque de France Working Paper No. 482 and NBER Working Paper No. 20041.

Joyce, M., M. Tong and R. Woods (2011), "The United Kingdom's Quantitative Easing Policy: Design, Operation and Impact", *Bank of England Quarterly Bulletin* **51** (3): 200–212.

Krishnamurthy, A. and A. Vissing-Jorgensen (2011), "The Effects of Quantitative Easing on Interest Rates: Channels and Implications for Policy", *Brookings Papers on Economic Activity* **43** (2): 215–87.

Rochet, J-C. (2008), "The Future of Banking Regulation", Toulouse School of Economics Notes No. 2.

Sargent, T.J. and B.D. Smith (1987), "Irrelevance of Open Market Operations in Some Economies with Government Currency Being Dominated in Rate of Return", *American Economic Review* **77** (1): 78–92.

Tobin, J. (1958), "Liquidity Preference as Behavior Towards Risk", *Review of Economic Studies* **25** (2): 65–86.

Vayanos, D. and J-L. Vila (2009), "A Preferred-Habitat Model of the Term Structure of Interest Rates", NBER Working Papers 15487, National Bureau of Economic Research.

Wallace, N. (1981), "A Modigliani-Miller Theorem for Open-Market Operations", *American Economic Review* **71** (3): 267–74.

Woodford, M. (2012), "Methods of Policy Accommodation at the Interest-Rate Lower Bound", in *The Changing Policy Landscape*, Federal Reserve Bank of Kansas City.

## APPENDIX: FURTHER EVIDENCE ON MYOPIA IN FINANCIAL MARKETS

The financial crisis that unfolded in 2007 and 2008 was the direct result of vulnerabilities and imbalances which had been growing steadily and then combined in ways that few foresaw. Few, if any, anticipated how severe the unwinding of these imbalances would be for the functioning of the financial system.

Three major stylized facts from the period preceding the sub-prime crisis stand out.[6] First, there is broad consensus that US financial intermediaries *increased their risk exposure* during the decade leading up to the crisis. This took the form of an expansion of balance sheets and increased leverage on the part of US investment banks. For instance, the Security and Exchange Commission (SEC) reports that between 2003 and 2007, the mean leverage

---

[6] For details, see Dubecq et al. (2015).

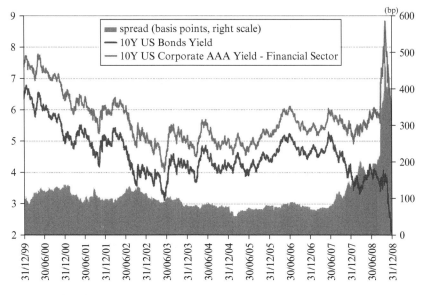

*Source:*  Bloomberg.

*Figure 5A.1    Spread between ten-year US treasury bonds and ten-year
bonds of US AAA financial companies*

ratio of the five major investment banks[7] (defined as the ratio of overall debt to bank equity) jumped from 22 to 30.

Among these five investment banks, only one survived the crisis as a stand-alone institution. This expansion in the size of banks' balance sheets was accompanied by an increase in "off-balance-sheet leverage", as documented in Acharya and Schnabl (2009). This leverage in turn allowed financial intermediaries to generate higher profits without additional capital, in spite of increased potential future losses: in *ex ante* terms, the unit of risk borne by each dollar of the US banking system's equity increased markedly. We also note that the increase in banks' assets was concentrated among assets that require very low capital funding. These products, considered to be quite safe by regulatory standards, were, however, at the root of significant losses for banks after the beginning of the financial crisis.

Second, the *perceived* riskiness of the US financial intermediaries did not increase as measured by the market risk premiums on their debt. If anything, the spread between the yields on bonds issued by US financial

---

[7]   Lehman Brothers, Bear Stearns, Merrill Lynch, Goldman Sachs and Morgan Stanley.

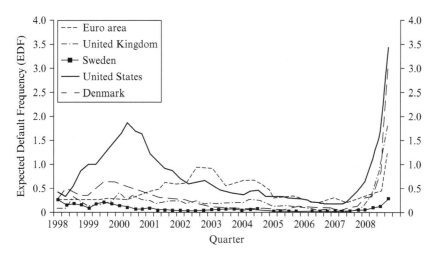

*Note:* Over a one-year horizon (averages by country and groups of countries).

*Source:* Moody's KMV and Altunbas et al. (2010).

*Figure 5A.2  Expected default frequency of banks*

companies and US government bonds declined somewhat between 2002 and 2007 (Figure 5A.1).

The change in banks' expected default frequencies (EDFs) is another indicator of the ease with which banks accessed market funding between 2002 and 2007. Banks' EDFs decreased worldwide between 2002 and 2007 (see Figure 5A.2), suggesting that market investors either assigned lower probabilities to defaults in the banking sector or required lower risk premiums to invest in banks' debt instruments. The same observation that credit risk for banks was perceived to be negligible can be made by comparing credit default swap (CDS) contracts on US banks intermediaries and on issuers in other economic sectors.[8]

Third, the *effective level of banks' capital was difficult to assess* during the period. Several factors help explain why capital requirements and capital norms were weak during this period. The most critical factor was that Basel II authorized banks to use internal risk models. Blundell-Wignall and Atkinson (2008) and Rochet (2008) highlight the difficulty for outsiders to obtain extensive information on the level of risk borne by financial intermediaries, although it is clear *ex post* that it was

---

[8]  This is also particularly striking when comparing banks and non-financial corporate credit spreads in the euro area between 2000 and 2007 (Gilchrist and Mojon, 2014).

exploited to reduce their capital base. Such complexity must have led financial intermediaries to minimize risk per unit of risk in line with the vested interest of the industry. Finally, accounting rules concerning the consolidation of off-balance-sheet entities were singled out by the Financial Stability Forum (2008) for creating "a belief that risk did not lie with arrangers and led market participants to underestimate firms' risk exposures."[9]

It's fairly clear that no model with full information and rational expectations can explain the first two facts. The smaller the equity buffer relative to the stock of risky assets, the greater the risks borne by bank creditors and the higher the risk premiums they should have paid. The absence of proper market discipline is probably explained by the third fact, although here too one might expect that accounting opacity would cause premiums to rise.

---

[9]   This issue is actually on the agenda of the G20, and similar concerns about off-balance-sheet vehicles have been brought up by academics (see Acharya and Schnabl, 2009), official regulators, and central bankers (see, for instance, the speech by Ben Bernanke in 2010).

# 6. The psychology of financial choices: from classical and behavioral finance to neurofinance

## Massimo Egidi and Giacomo Sillari

October. This is one of the peculiarly dangerous months to speculate in stocks. The others are July, January, September, April, November, May, March, June, December, August and February.
Mark Twain, *Pudd'nhead Wilson*

## 1. BEATING THE MARKET

"Beating the market", that is, earning more in the stock market than the traders' average, which is equivalent to the stocks' riskiness, is the hope of fund managers and individual traders operating in financial markets. It is not an easy goal to achieve since constructing a portfolio that performs better than average requires understanding which stocks are overvalued and which are undervalued, as well as making predictions on their future trends. With what degree of confidence could one possibly evaluate stocks, given a market that has, by nature, a high level of uncertainty? This is a crucial problem not only for traders, but also and above all for business managers who, needing to evaluate assets and liabilities in their own budgets, would have to predict stock price trends in relevant markets without making excessive errors. If a business wants to finance a new investment through issuing stock, it would, in fact, have to formulate expectations on many elements, among which are future earnings on these emissions, keeping in mind that stock pricing will at least partially depend on the expectations of buyers and sellers regarding the company's future activities. Expectations thus play a dominant role in the formulation of financial portfolios and, more generally, in financial planning.

But, how does one decide if a stock is over or undervalued? Here, we must distinguish between two different frames of reference: the world of financial operators and the world of academics. While prescriptions from the two worlds coincide from time to time, there is a notable divergence in most cases. We will first concern ourselves with the academic tradition.

From this perspective, the fundamental value of a stock is defined by the net current value of future earnings that the stock guarantees, appropriately discounted. The problem, in the case of stocks, is that future earnings are far from certain, since those who issue stock do not assume any responsibility vis-à-vis stockholders, other than sharing profits through dividends. Consequently, future earnings depend on a large number of variables connected to the business, the operating sector, and general economic developments.

An investor, to establish a portfolio's strategy, needs to possess relevant and, for the most part, certain information prior to performing a complex calculation. This aspect of the problem, derived from the very complexity of economic models, presented itself from the beginning of the development of business theory and economic equilibrium. Once the general theory of equilibrium was developed, many academic economists rightly asked how managers and economic operators could be attributed with the capacity for making such difficult calculations. To obtain optimal results, an investor would need to be able to use complex models and conduct difficult calculations. Today, one may be tempted to trust portfolio management to a collection of artificial intelligence programs in the hope that these calculations would be solved automatically, and, in fact, the web is rife with bots and algorithms for trading. However, in the 1950s, when the problem came to light, this was not even remotely possible.

A highly successful answer to the problem of complex calculations came from the interpretation of equilibrium adjustment as adaptation processes. The idea, developed by Harrod, and then by Alchian and Friedman, is that, whatever the operative and predictive capacity of operators and the calculations they pose, the market rewards those who obtain the best economic results, and therefore selection occurs through the expulsion of those who do not perform well. Alchian (1950) sustains that the Darwinian elimination of less capable operators leads to the emergence of more successful behavior. Friedman (1953) is also of this opinion, and further attributes the positive role of re-equilibrating the market to speculators. If, in the short term, stock prices deviate from equilibrium, the traders who simultaneously buy undervalued stock and sell analogous overvalued stock would rebalance the system, conducting what is defined as arbitrage.

Since the crux of the problem consists of calculating whether a stock is under or overvalued, and since this type of calculation is very uncertain and extremely complex, Friedman (1953) added an important element: he argued that investors and speculators act "as if" they are trying to rationally maximize expected returns with full knowledge of necessary data for succeeding in their attempt. The idea of "as if" contains a methodologically relevant core, which forms a central problem of social sciences: the relationship between intentional and non-intentional action. However, the idea itself, united by the two stated corollaries, favored a division between (normative) economic theory and psychology, with its connected technical experimentation, a division that persisted at least until the 1970s. Thus, the mantra derived from Friedman's idea was that the analysis of individual behavior could be completely irrelevant, since they could be safely considered, in aggregate, as if they were rational.[1]

The high level of uncertainty characterizing the calculation of a stock's intrinsic value made it such that the world of finance and trading confronted this problem with different methods and with different degrees of success.[2] There are two common methods. "Fundamentalists" rely on the analysis of fundamental economic variables determining value – an analyst wanting to estimate future earnings operates based on an estimate of expected growth rate, expected dividend payments, the level of risk, and the future interest rate on the market. On the other hand, "technical analysts" try to find short-term regularity in terms of price developments, generally maintaining that the temporal sequence of prices can be used to identify trends and patterns that allow for predictions (at least in the near future) to beat the market.

Even though much debate occurs between supporters of the two methods, they actually share common ground – if it is possible to identify persistent mispricing, that is, the deviation of a stock's value from its fundamental value, without committing systematic errors, it should be possible to predict (within a set confidence interval) the value that a stock will assume when it returns to its fundamental value. The implication of this assumption is that the historical trend of stock prices would have to show autocorrelation (the variation in prices between today and tomorrow must be correlated with their variation between yesterday and today). Therefore, the central point for understanding if profits greater

---

[1]  It should, however, be noted that this concern was well presented in the scientific community, so much so that a large part of the "calculation" was correctly reduced to a simple rule. The neoclassical school (in all its versions, and with particular analytical depth in the Austrian variation by Von Mises and Von Hayek) always correctly avoided attributing the capacity of conducting overly complex calculations to individuals, that is, the market is an institution that conducts the necessary tasks of simplifying information and making calculations, permitting the individual to make rational choices based on extremely simple calculations.

[2]  According to Malkiel (1973), Warren Buffet is an example of a famous financier who made his fortune (so to speak) through basic analysis; on the other hand, it should be recognized that John Maynard Keynes did not believe in the efficacy of this type of analysis due to uncertainty surrounding the factors determining business earning potential in the long term, although he did make millions of pounds sterling for his personal estate and increased the market value of King's College in Cambridge tenfold.

than the market average can be obtained on a stock is based on whether or not the historical trend of that stock is random.

The conclusion that follows is extremely obvious. If a method or algorithm capable of calculating mispricing without systematic errors exists, and if it were applied in non-instantaneous arbitrage, the historical trend of this stock would *not* be a random process, and vice versa. However, if a reliable method for calculating mispricing were possible, this method would either be available to a monopolist who would keep it a secret, and this would be immediately observable through this person's exponential enrichment, or this miraculous algorithm would be available to all, thus returning the market to the equilibrium as soon as the mispricing occurs.

There are only two sequiturs to this reasoning. One could presume that a miraculous algorithm permitting the rational use of all relevant information exists (or that the markets behave in aggregate "as if" it does) and is available to all – this is the assumption of Eugene Fama's efficient market hypothesis (EMH), which further assumes that all adjustments have instantaneous effects. Otherwise, one could presume that a general and always valid algorithm does not exist, but that it is possible to identify autocorrelation patterns in the short term. This is the assumption of behavioral finance.

## 2.   EFFICIENT MARKETS

In the efficient market hypothesis Fama proposed, traders are fully informed and perfectly rational. Fully informed means that they understand all the relevant publicly available information. Perfectly rational means that the decisions they make:

1.  result from coherent choices (according to the utility theory's model, about which we will further elaborate); and
2.  are based on rational expectations.

Until the 1960s, rational behavior in the sense of point (1) was considered compatible with a variety of different types of expectations. The adaptive expectation was the most widespread, as demonstrated in the debate surrounding the Phillips curve, but it was also applied to other types of expectations, such as the extrapolative ones. When it came to economic equilibrium, it implied that subjects could form expectations incoherent with economic developments, committing systematic prediction errors. Muth assumed, instead, that economic agents could not make systematic errors and, therefore, expressed "rational" expectations, that is, those that, on average, came to pass.

According to the rational expectations theory, it is not possible for all economic and financial operators to commit systematic predictive errors, and therefore their expectations about a stock must (on average) coincide with the stock's value. In this manner, the approach assumes coherence in the behaviors of economic operators and the characteristics of their decision-making models. This vision obviously does not take into account the difficulties involved in calculating a stock's fundamental value, assuming, in fact, that operators know all the relevant information, including the economic system's characteristics.[3]

Applying the rational expectations theory, it follows that mispricing would be corrected instantaneously by arbitrage, and therefore, if there are price distortions, they can only come from external information, which by definition is unpredictable and random. But then, even stock price oscillations must be random. For Fama's theory, empirical validation of the hypothesis that stock prices evolve randomly is thus crucial.[4]

If *future* price developments, based on information that will be available in the future, cannot be predicted, then the theoretical conclusion's practical inference is that markets cannot be beaten[5] and that an unsophisticated

---

[3]    The theory was born in the Graduate School of Industrial Administration (GSIA) at Carnegie Mellon at the end of the 1950s and early 1960s, from the working group in which John Muth, Herbert Simon, Charles C. Holt and Franco Modigliani were members. John Muth developed the concept of rational expectations while Herbert A. Simon created the basis for his theory of bounded rationality, which underlined the individual's limited ability to make calculations.

[4]    Empirical evidence supporting the efficient market hypothesis started building beginning in the 1960s, when the Center for Research in Stock Prices (CRSP) in Chicago made long-term stock price data of various markets available. These empirical tests (see Fama, 1970) allowed the distinguishing of the efficient market hypothesis' various degrees of strength. A *weak* version posits that investors cannot profit based on information contained in these prices and past returns on investment. A *semi-strong* version posits that investors cannot profit based on any publicly available information. A *strong* version posits that it is not possible to profit through information that has not yet become part of the public domain. In the 1960s and 1970s, Fama and others gathered a notable quantity of empirical evidence on the fact that stock trends evolved randomly, the fact that reactions to new fundamental information are fast and precise, and the fact that prices do not react to information unrelated to the fundamentals, supporting at least the weak and semi-strong versions of the hypothesis. Starting in the 1980s, however, as will be evident in the remainder of this section and the one following, the environment changed and strong theoretical and empirical arguments against the hypothesis of efficient financial markets began to firm.

[5]    If the prices of a stock perfectly reflect all the information connected to that stock and therefore its precise fundamental value, then a way to beat the market would not exist. We assume that stock XYZ is worth €50 and that a trader, based on publicly available information, knows for sure that it will be worth €60 in the future. This trader, naturally, will buy as much of stock XYZ as he can at €50 so he may resell it at €60, resulting in the stock's price almost instantaneously rising to €60, wiping away any possibility of earnings. Therefore,

investor would be able theoretically to obtain a return on investment equal (on average) to those obtained by more capable professionals, on the condition that the stock portfolio is sufficiently diversified. Burton Malkiel (1973) vivaciously illustrates this property with the famous quote: "a blindfolded monkey throwing darts at a newspaper's financial pages could select a portfolio that would do just as well as one carefully selected by experts."

The conclusion that it is not possible to beat an efficient market is subject, obviously, to a qualification. It is in fact quite possible to achieve returns higher than the market average when one also assumes the risk of inferior returns. If the returns on my portfolio exceed the market average, a possible explanation could be, contrary to the market's efficiency, the mispricing of stock in my possession; on the other hand, there is a different possible explanation in keeping with the efficient market hypothesis: my portfolio is more risky than the market average.

The efficient market hypothesis, from the moment of its introduction, suffered from the observation that stock prices are not autocorrelated. However, starting in the 1980s, numerous empirical findings putting its solidity very much in doubt began to accumulate. We will consider some of the more important ones.

One of the first studies making the efficient market hypothesis a subject of debate was done by Shiller (1981). If one of the hypothesis' crucial assumptions is the rationality of stock values, or rather the correspondence between stock prices and their fundamental values, and if the fundamental value of a stock is composed of the sum of its future dividends discounted based on the year already under way, then, according to Shiller, the fundamental values intrinsic to the stocks' past can be exactly reconstructed *ex post*. In other words, we can calculate the fundamental value of a stock in a given year in the past by considering the dividends paid out in successive years, appropriately discounted, and thus identifying the fundamental value of this stock in the year under examination (that is, the value that an agent, given rational expectations, would attribute to a stock given the stock's real dividend payout). Applying Shiller's conclusion to the Standard & Poor's index from 1871 to 1979[6] for the United States shows, as can be seen in the graph in Figure 6.1, that stocks have an illegitimately higher volatility than their fundamental values. Stock trends, in sum, far

---

under the efficient market hypothesis, it is not possible to obtain results superior to the market average.

  [6]  The graph, updated upon the awarding of the Nobel Prize Shiller shared with Fama in 2013, continues to show excessive volatility in stock prices relative to their fundamental values.

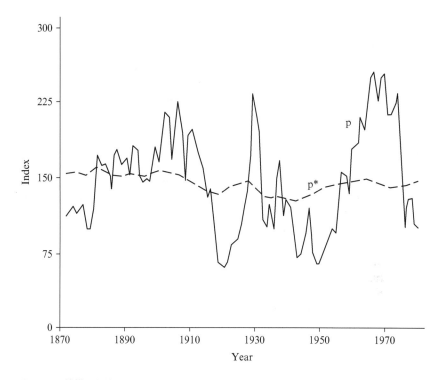

*Source:* Shiller (1981).

*Figure 6.1 Comparison between S&P index values between 1871 to 1979 (the line indicated with the letter* p*) and the fundamental values calculated* ex post *of the companies making up the index (the dotted line indicated with the letter* p*)*

from being efficient, show much more volatility than the fundamental values Shiller reconstructed or, in other terms, show constant mispricing that is far from instantaneously corrected by the market.

A second fundamental empirical study that undermined the efficient market hypothesis was conducted by Mehra and Prescott (1985), on the so-called equity premium puzzle. In their paper, the two authors considered historical values over the course of 100 years for two categories of emissions: stocks on the one hand and the practically risk-free bonds issued by the US Federal Reserve on the other. As is obvious, returns on stock are higher than those on bonds. According to the Merton–Lucas model, this difference can be rationalized, but the empirical data gathered by Mehra and Prescott do not allow the deviation to be justified without attributing impossible levels of risk aversion to agents.[7] In other words, the returns offered by the stock market are greater than those that would be expected for any other market model. This is puzzling because, if the effective premium is this cheap, what rational trader would buy bonds? For the efficient market hypothesis, then, the returns on bonds would have to increase, closing the gap between stock and bond returns.

A third empirical study by De Bondt and Thaler (1985) considered trader overreaction to positive or negative news regarding stocks.[8] The empirical investigation considered US stock and divided them over an observation period of five years. A portfolio containing the 35 best-performing stocks was categorized as "winners" and one containing the 35 worst-performing stocks was categorized as "losers". In an efficient market that does not allow the future to be predicted based on the past; both portfolios should offer the same returns. Systematically, however, the "winners" portfolio underperformed compared to the "losers", suggesting that traders react excessively to information.[9] A possible response to the argument that this result represents empirical refutation of the efficient market hypothesis rests on the fact that the returns of a portfolio can be higher than those of the market as a whole, based on the portfolio's riskiness. In this sense, the more extreme winners and losers of De Bondt and Thaler's paper would have performances superior and inferior to that of the market because it is more or less risky than the market average, respectively. However, for the CAPM – the Capital Asset Pricing Method, that is the most common model for measuring a portfolio's risk level – the "losers" portfolio's risk was *less* than that of the "winners", that is, the opposite of what supporters of the efficient market hypothesis would predict.

---

[7] It should be noted that the level of risk aversion necessary to justify the relevant premium (around 7 percent) would be that of an agent who prefers a certain return of €51 300 over a possible return of either €50 000 or €100 000, with each having a 50 percent probability.

[8] This study is particularly relevant since it assumes an excessive psychological reaction that causes a systematic deviation from the rational ideal to emerge. The efficient market hypothesis can support the presence of non-rational agents to the extent that deviations in their rationality are not correlated and thus allows the "as if rational" hypothesis. If, however, the deviations in their rationality are systematic, as was the case with De Bondt and Thaler, then the efficient market hypothesis would face serious difficulty.

[9] Here, "excessive" signifies a manner incoherent with Bayes' Rule, that is, the good news (for the "winners") weighing in an excessive manner relative to the bad news (for the "losers").

## 3.   THE LIMITS OF EFFICIENCY

As we have explained up to this point, the efficient market hypothesis is subject to assumptions about the rationality of agents and their expectations. Countering this hypothesis, in the same years the articles cited above were published, a theoretical argument also emerged. The idea, originally attributed to Aumann (1976) and applied to the financial context by Milgrom and Stokey (1982) in the so-called "no-trade theorem" is, informally, that if two traders share a common vision of the markets (including their rationality), then they must have identical opinions on the prices of individual stock, including when the two traders have asymmetric information on the stocks in question. Thus, the agents' intentions to buy or sell these stocks reveal their private information, rendering it officially public. Therefore, the decisions the two traders reach must be the same, rendering purely speculative buying and selling impossible since, at any given instance, both traders would want to buy (or sell). Thus, theoretically, the securities exchanges would have extremely low or completely absent trade volumes, an evident departure from reality. Also for this reason, Grossman and Stiglitz (1980) introduced to the economic literature the concept of "noise traders", traders that receive signals categorized by background noise, and who are, therefore, unable to receive clear information on demand and supply in the market but nonetheless decide to trade.

The noise trader, therefore, does not follow rational expectations, and their presence in the markets thus becomes one of the reasons why arbitrage could fail in the task of bringing the price of a stock to its fundamental value. The presence of these "irrational" operators, in fact, could impede the instantaneous return to equilibrium prices and therefore render arbitrage operations risky, when they should in fact be *risk-free*. Suppose that the price of stock A is less than a twin stock B due to irrational pessimism of noise traders against stock A. An arbitrage opportunity would present itself in the purchase of stock A and the sale of stock B until the price of A and B realign. However, if irrational noise traders depress the prices of A, an arbitrager taking advantage of the opportunity would have to recognize the possibility that noise traders would *continue* to act irrationally, presenting the risk of loss if pessimism over stock A persists or depresses the prices even further. This does not mean that arbitrage is impossible, only that an arbitrager's operating timeframe would set a limit on the opportunity for arbitrage.[10]

---

[10]   The so-called "limits of arbitrage" are not limited to the presence of noise traders but encompass other aspects that tend to assign a positive risk to arbitrage trades that should theoretically be risk-free. Among these other aspects lies the fact that arbitrage is often

The market efficiency can therefore be put in doubt by the presence of limitedly rational traders in the same market. Behavioral economics, studying systematic deviations in economic rationality, presents a decisive critique of the efficient market hypothesis. Models with heterogeneous agents, limitedly rational, thus become essential for understanding what happens in the world of financial transactions.[11] Before, however, analyzing behavioral critiques and their consequences for financial market operators, we will briefly digress.

At the end of the 1960s, Benoit Mandelbrot, the father of fractal geometry, used empirical challenges to the efficient market hypothesis to subvert the infrastructure of classical finance in an even more radical way than the challenges posed by behavioral finance, leading to the proposal of a fundamental rethinking.

### 3.1   Fractal Markets

The consequence of stock prices being a random walk is, as already stated, that returns on a diversified portfolio, on average, should be equal to market returns. This means that, given a sufficiently high number of well diversified portfolios, their returns would be distributed in a Bell (Gaussian) curve, according to the so-called *normal* distribution. Mandelbrot (1997) observed, however, that if the distribution of returns were effectively normal, markets would manifest degrees of volatility far lower than what is observed. This means that big variations, say plus or minus over 4.5 percent, would occur with a much lower frequency than in actual fact. The 22 percent crash in 1987 on Wall Street, for instance, would occur at a probability of 1 in $10^{50}$, a number so low as to have no empirical significance. According to Mandelbrot, the assumption of independence for stock prices is not plausible: a stock that increases for three consecutive days has a lower probability of increasing for a fourth time than a stock that remained at the same value for the entire period, but, according to Mandelbrot, this type of market "memory" could actually persist for years.

If a random walk can be represented by a Gaussian curve, what type of representation should be used when stock prices, as Mandelbrot suggests, are *not* a random walk? According to the Polish mathematician, stock

observed in the trade of two "twin" stocks, with one being over or undervalued with respect to the other; however, almost never can these two stocks be considered perfect substitutes for one another. The additional aspect is the friction resulting from transactional costs which, when price realignment does not occur quickly, could introduce relevant risk.

[11]   For example, the broad survey conducted by Cars Hommes (2006).

price developments on the markets manifest a degree of autosimilarity. A graph that represents the Dow Jones weekly closings for a year is similar to one representing the daily closings for a month, or the hourly closings for a week, or the values captured every five minutes for a day, and so on. Magnifying (or shrinking) any part of the graph, we find a shape with details very similar to the larger whole. This *homothetic* property belongs to fractals, and if market movements can be interpreted as fractals,[12] then the Gaussian curve cannot be adequately representative for calculating the probable returns of a portfolio.

A curve adequate for representing the strong "turbulence" due to excessive market volatility is a curve known to economists. Vilfredo Pareto, at the beginning of the 20th century, represented the distribution of wealth in a society using an *exponential* curve. In society, an infinitesimal fraction of the population is enormously rich, a small number of people are very rich, while an overwhelming majority of the population is moderately rich or poor. Similarly, market trends show an infinitesimal fraction of extreme variations, a small number of very big variations, and an overwhelming majority showing small or non-existent variations. This type of volatility is better represented by an exponential rather than a Gaussian curve.

The consequences for the world of finance are various. The efficient market hypothesis fails because homothetic properties presuppose some level of correlation or market "memory". Likewise, ideas surrounding the risk of financial operations implicit in the randomness of market fluctuations and the normal distribution of returns also fail. In particular, the risk of financial operations, in Mandelbrot's model, is significantly higher than those of traditional models, and thus requires more careful and attentive offsetting activities.

## 4. THE REUNION BETWEEN ECONOMICS AND PSYCHOLOGY

After a long period of intellectual prevalence, the efficient market hypothesis and the rational expectations hypothesis faced a series of difficult analytical challenges and experimental anomalies between the 1970s and

---

[12] If a line is a mathematical object with a *single* dimension, a random walk, simplified, represents a mathematical walk with two dimensions since it at least covers the entire two dimensional plane. Fractals are mathematical objects with "incomplete" dimensions, and Mandelbrot (1962) calculated the fractal dimension of the S&P between 1950 and 1988 to be 1.28.

the century's end, which led to its weakening role and the emergence of the behavioral approach. As Malkiel (2003) wrote:

> Many financial economists and statisticians began to believe that stock prices are at least partially predictable. A new breed of economists emphasized psychological and behavioral elements of stock-price determination, and they came to believe that future stock prices are somewhat predictable on the basis of past stock price patterns as well as certain "fundamental" valuation metrics.

The behavioral approach to economic and financial decisions emerged both from the experimental studies that cast doubt on the concept of market processes as a random walk and from alternatives to the utility theory applied to behavioral anomalies related to choice. This is not the place for a detailed analysis of the characteristics of expected utility theory[13] (EUT), so we will limit ourselves to restating that, when subjected to experimental scrutiny, the theory's theoretical assumptions revealed relevant anomalies. The theory is essentially based on four axioms that characterize the way a logically coherent individual makes choices.[14] In 1950, Allais showed the systematic violation of the independence axiom, according to which the choice between two risky alternatives does not change if an equivalent addition is made to both. This induced many attempts to create alternative theoretical paths, resulting from the modification of certain EUT assumptions. However, the attempts to obtain a new decision-making theory through the modification or attenuation of the EUT's properties did not allow for a solution with complete experimental validation.

At the end of the 1970s, Kahneman and Tversky experimentally showed the systematic violation of the most important axiom: continuity. When choosing between alternatives, individuals are predisposed to risk if the choice is presented in terms of loss, and adverse to risk if it is presented in terms of gain. In other words, the same problem generated diverse choices depending on how it was presented. It is not difficult to understand why this "framing effect" was of particular relevance to the analysis of decisions in the financial field.

---

[13] Fundamentally, expected utility theory (EUT) assumes that individuals have a well-defined preference system and that they act to maximize utility under conditions of uncertainty that are subjective (Savage) or objective (Von Neumann–Morgenstern). Subjects imagine the outcomes of all uncertain alternatives that could come to pass and act as if they were calculating the average value of all the possible outcomes, based on their utility. They maintain their preferences in a coherent manner, although they could be manipulated.

[14] The four axioms of the expected utility theory that define a rational decision maker are completeness, transitivity, independence and continuity.

These anomalies explain how the behavior of individuals faced with choices involving risk are guided by cognitive and emotional factors that superimpose themselves over and overrule logic and coherence when making decisions. As will be shown in section 5, neurofinance identified neurophysiological factors that correspond to some of these emotional and psychological mechanisms, thus systematically influencing financial decisions.

Kahneman and Tversky's approach diverged in a crucial way from previous attempts because they tried to incorporate cognitive and emotional biases into their new Prospect Theory, refusing to limit themselves to modifying EUT axioms and instead restructuring the entire problem around mental processes involved in decision making. Two relevant developments followed. On the one hand, systemic behavioral "anomalies" were classified and studied. Meanwhile, and more importantly, because real behavior showed systematic deviations from EUT predictions, explanations were needed, and this could only come through understanding the cognitive processes involved in choice.

With Kahneman and Tversky's results, the long-standing divorce between economics and psychology, made official in the 1950s by Milton Friedman, ended. Instead, analyzing cognitive biases related to choice became the most relevant avenue for providing alternative behavioral predictions. A particularly important context for experimental studies on decision making, given the richness of conditions offered to players, is the game of chess. Studies conducted on chess players by Simon and his colleagues in the 1970s showed that, while novices had to arduously calculate good moves, and therefore needed time and exerted notable effort, master chess players, based on their long experience, automatically and immediately recalled strategic options from memory, based on the distribution of chess pieces on the board at the time. "What was once accomplished by slow, conscious deductive reasoning is now arrived at by fast, unconscious perceptual processing. It is no mistake of language for the chess master to say he 'sees' the right move."[15]

A large part of conscious reasoning thus interacts with "automatic" processes recalled from long-term memory, which occurs without the individual's conscious control and requiring neither attention nor effort. The reasoning process is founded, in a certain sense, on moving sand, because we do not consciously control elements that our memory brings to our attention. "Because people have little or no introspective access to these processes, or volitional control over them, and these processes were

---

[15]   Chase and Simon (1973).

evolved to solve problems of evolutionary importance rather than respect logical dicta, the behavior these processes generate need not follow normative axioms of inference and choice."[16]

It follows that our logical deliberative capacity, which would have to precede our choices, does not always appropriately regulate behavior. Simon maintained that an individual's ability to make rational calculations and complex decisions is limited by memory and by the necessity to accumulate vast experiential data. This is the theory of bounded rationality.

Progressive accumulation of experiential data allows the extrapolation of rules of play, simple strategies that allow a player to quickly solve situations without having to conduct complex mental calculations. These rules are called heuristics. Through the use of heuristics, expert players can drastically limit their analysis of available alternatives, greatly simplifying the analysis while implicitly introducing the possibility of errors.

Heuristics are not only used by chess players but in every decision-making and problem-solving activity. Based on the bounded rationality theory, starting at the end of the 1970s, Amos Tversky and Danny Kahneman launched a research project[17] documenting systematic judgment and decision-making errors of humans *tout court*. The project, titled *Heuristics and Biases*, is based on the idea that some heuristics could be generating systematic errors when, instead of providing an approximately correct solution for the problem at hand, they provide misleading solutions. In the next subsection, we will more closely examine some of these heuristics or behavioral systems, analyzing their impact, particularly on financial decisions.

### 4.1   Representativeness

A heuristic often used whenever we need to make a probabilistic judgment is representativeness. Instead of making a judgment based on the probability of a certain event, we judge the degree to which this event is similar to a prototype, and namely how it is representative of a certain class. In fact, judging the similarity of an event to a reference point is often simpler than judging its probability. However, utilizing representativeness could be misleading, since stereotypes used for making judgments based on representativeness often do not coincide with actual probabilistic frequencies. To take an example from Bazerman and Moore (2013), even if a woman

---

[16]   Camerer et al. (2005).
[17]   For an exhaustive, updated, and engaging synthesis of the project, its results, and future prospects, see Kahneman (2011).

is defined as "a shy poetry lover", it remains more probable that she is a student of business administration than of medieval Chinese literature, given the numbers of students in the two disciplines.

Representativeness is in play in the case of analysts excessively reacting to new information as well, as identified in the study by De Bondt and Thaler (1985), cited in section 2. An analyst observing a series of extremely positive quarters, in fact, could become convinced that the series is representative of the "real" distribution of quarterly earnings. In other words, the analyst could believe that the company's management is particularly able and the business particularly good and therefore, that the probability of the positive trend continuing in a similar fashion in the future is high, but only because the positive series is representative of management ability. Representativeness makes it difficult to predict a mediocre result under these circumstances because, according to the analyst, if a company were to produce mediocre results, it would have had to do so in the past as well, contrary to empirical data. A similar reasoning would apply to "bad" companies that underperform in the market.

This type of reasoning is precisely what causes excessive reactions to the types of information De Bondt and Thaler identified. In fact, the results of a company do not exclusively depend on managerial ability or the intrinsic goodness of a company, its product, and so on. A relevant factor, in this case, especially given the series of exceptionally positive quarters, is that the company experienced a significant dose of good luck. More relevant is the randomness factor (which obviously can never be zero) and the fact that future results tend to be less extreme, bringing the company's performance back to the market average. De Bondt and Thaler (1985) apply this intuition to the stock market, and the better earnings of the "losers" portfolio with respect to the "winners" exactly reflect the regression toward average values that the heuristic of representativeness tends to systematically distort.

Distinguishing managerial ability from merely stochastic elements and therefore taking into account the natural regression toward average values is perhaps a crucial responsibility of financial analysts who do not want to become victims of distortions due to representativeness.

## 4.2  Availability

The second heuristic often used for obviating the complexity of probabilistic judgments is availability. In this case, instead of the (difficult) measurement of the probability of a certain event, we resort to the more (immediate) measurement of the ease with which an event is available in our minds. This aspect of availability is salience: if an event recently occurred, perhaps repeatedly, then it would be easily available for recall and thus judged as a high probability event. An application of this idea to the financial crisis is found in Gennaioli et al. (2012). The authors constructed a model in which, when the economic trend is positive, low probability is assigned to negative shocks (and therefore operators have an excessive tendency to approve, for example, sub-prime loans). On the other hand, right after a critical phase (when the availability of bad economic news is high), the probability of negative economic events is overestimated, causing the credit market to stall.

Distortions due to the availability heuristic can also affect probability judgments about stock trends. For example, instead of evaluating the probability that a certain stock increases in price, one uses the availability of this stock in memory, making a stock widely covered in the media seem better than those that receive less coverage in financial news channels. Gadarowski (2002) analyzes the relationship between stock profits and media coverage, noting that stocks with high media coverage, which are therefore extremely available to the mind, tend to underperform in the two following years.

Conversely, however, Gerd Gigerenzer studied a phenomenon close to availability – the recognition heuristic – showing that, in certain cases, this heuristic could compensate for a lack of information. Gigerenzer et al. (1999) tested the recognition heuristic on a selection of stocks. After showing a list of stocks to hundreds of passersby in Chicago and asking them to identify those they have heard of, they compiled a list containing 10 percent of the most recognized stock. The portfolio comprised of these stocks, after a year, was compared with a randomly selected portfolio, a portfolio containing the 10 least recognized stocks, a portfolio of blue chip stock, and a portfolio containing the entire Dow Jones index. In almost all instances, the portfolio containing the most recognized stock outperformed the other four.

### 4.3  Overconfidence

The majority of people think they drive better than average. The majority of students in a course think they will get a higher than average grade. Ostensibly, the majority of individual investors on the market believe that they can obtain better than average returns. Often, in short, we think we have more control over our circumstances when in reality we do not. Furthermore, one remains systematically victim of a certain overconfidence. We think we are right or successful much more than we really are. For example, in an experiment by Lichtenstein and Fischhoff (1977), participants were given a report on 12 stocks in the US market and asked to predict their future trend. Even though the correct predictions only made up 47 percent of the total, the subjects remained convinced that they had, on average, a 65 percent probability of making the right prediction. Terrence Odean (1998b) raised the practical implications of this overconfidence for private investors. Analyzing 10 000 anonymous deposit accounts in the United States, Odean concluded that the majority of investors who sold stocks to buy others were victims of excessive optimism and security. In fact, investors obtained, on average, 3 percent inferior returns on their stock relative to what they would have earned if they kept the originals. In general, Barber and Odean (2000) noted that, on average, increased exchanges within a portfolio corresponded to lower profits. It is interesting that Barber and Odean (2001) found men more active in stock trading and, in fact, their portfolios performed less well than those managed by women on average. Overconfidence, represented as a systematic psychological tendency, could at least in part explain the discrepancy between the results of Milgrom and Stokey (1982)'s no-trade theorem, cited in the third section, and market realities.

The illusion of possessing a particular aptitude for financial transactions in the end results in costly losses, especially for private investors. Barber et al. (2009) showed that the Taiwanese market is at least in part characterized by a gigantic transfer of wealth from individual investors to financial institutions, equal to 2.2 percent of GDP.

## 4.4 Framing

When considering preference construction by agents, we continue to see systematic errors relevant to financial choices. The utility theory upon which classical microeconomics was built assigns a certain value (utility) to determinants of wealth or well-being. A million euros in wealth has a precise utility $x$, variable from person to person, but independent of whatever other reference point. A brief moment of introspection is sufficient to make evident the descriptive inadequacy of this theory. Imagine two investors whose portfolios yesterday were worth 500 000 euros and 5 million euros respectively; today, both portfolios are now worth a million. According to classical theory, the two investors would assign identical utility to both portfolios, since they are worth the same. However, is this really plausible? Clearly, one would imagine a discrepancy in value attribution given that the first portfolio's value resulted from a net gain while the second resulted from a loss. To incorporate this aspect in the function attributing value to wealth, we cannot only evaluate simple *states* of wealth, as per traditional theory, but must take into account the *prospects* of gain or loss relative to a reference point, which is often arbitrary. We would consider an item bought with a credit card *overpriced* if there is a surcharge over the price in cash, which is our reference point. However, if the displayed price includes the credit card surcharge, then the cash price would appear *discounted*. A return of 10 percent for a particular investment fund could be framed as a gain of 9 percent compared to the 1 percent interest on sovereign bonds or a loss of 15 percent compared to a different fund that had 15 percent returns. A stock bought a year ago for €15 that is now €20, but which was worth €40 last month, could be framed as either a €5 gain over the purchase price or a €20 loss with respect to last month's value.

Framing a prospect as a gain instead of a loss has very relevant implications for our decisions. As explained at the beginning of this section, many experiments in fact demonstrated that people tend to be *risk averse* when it comes to gain and *risk prone* when it comes to losses. An implication of this is that a trader could assume more risk as his performance worsens. In other words, once performance becomes negative, placing the trader in the context of *loss*, a psychological tendency to assume excessive risk to return once again to the breakeven point activates. Naturally, this tendency further increases the probability that the losses the trader incurs become greater.

## 4.5 Loss Aversion

An additional, crucial aspect of prospect theory is loss aversion. We are averse to losses in the sense that the value attributed to a loss is greater than the value attributed to an equivalent gain. Any investor who monitors his or her portfolio daily knows well that a 2 percent loss brings far more distress than the satisfaction reaped from a 2 percent gain. In short, the value function for losses is steeper than the value function for gains. Empirical estimates put the relationship between losses and gains slightly in excess of 2, implying that a 1000 euro loss is equal to, in absolute terms, a gain of a little more than 2000 euros.

An important application of this psychological trait governing preferences is the equity premium puzzle identified by Mehra and Prescott (1985), discussed at the end of section 2. Mehra and Prescott documented how stock market profits, in the long term, are much higher than bond returns to a degree that cannot be reconciled using classic risk-return models. Benartzi and Thaler (1995), in a paper that represents a real cornerstone of behavioral finance, provides a plausible explanation for the puzzle in terms of loss aversion. The puzzle is solved if investors behave in a shortsighted manner regarding their investments. Agents averse to loss attribute a negative psychological value to a portfolio that increases by 2 percent today and decreases by 2 percent tomorrow, even though the portfolio's value at the beginning of today is identical to that of tomorrow. So, then, the more investors check their stock portfolios, the more opportunities there are to observe losses, and thus the smaller the psychological value assigned to these portfolios relative to ones containing less volatile bonds. How long would the time horizon have to be before investors express a preference for a stock portfolio over a bond portfolio? Through simulations, Benartzi and Thaler show that a time horizon greater than 13 months (with a loss aversion coefficient of 2.25) would be necessary for an investor to prefer a stock portfolio over one comprised of bonds. Patient investors (who consider longer time horizons) can effectively pocket a risk premium of 7 percent over more shortsighted investors.

An additional application of the loss aversion concept is the *disposition effect*, that is, the tendency to sell "winning" stocks too early and "losing" stocks too late, contrary to the proverb "cut your losses and let your profits run". The disposition effect is clearly documented by Odean (1998a) through the analysis of 10 000 anonymous bank accounts belonging to US traders. The disposition effect is explained to a certain degree by loss aversion. As long as a losing stock remains in the portfolio, the loss is "virtual" rather than real. Loss aversion thus translates in this case to an aversion to realizing virtual losses. Given a choice between selling a losing stock and a gaining stock, one tends to prefer the second option. Odean (1998a) shows how this tendency can be detrimental to portfolio returns for individual investors, in part because they are not fiscally optimized, but more importantly because the stocks they sell, in the following years, tend to outperform the ones they keep. The disposition effect is also utilized in the context of the real estate market to explain the reluctance to sell after a generalized fall in real estate prices (Genesove and Mayer, 2001).

## 5.   NEUROFINANCE

The psychological tendencies that influence our choices in the manner described in previous sections have corresponding physiological and neural aspects. Thanks to technological progress in the last ten years, we are able to observe many biological and neural correlates of our choices. This frees us from the limitation of observing and studying economic choices and their effects, instead allowing the study of underlying neural and biological mechanisms that guide our choices. Neuroeconomics utilizes a variety of investigative models (for example, psychophysiology, electroencephalograms, and functional magnetic resonance imaging, fMRI) to study neural and biological correlates of economic choices.

Many behavioral phenomena described in preceding sections are analyzed in neuroeconomics, allowing the identification of neural correlates. For example, patients with damaged amygdala no longer show loss aversion (De Martino et al., 2010). Additionally, fMRI studies show that decisions that reveal risk aversion in the context of gains and risk propensity in the context of losses (that is, typical behavior surrounding risk according to prospect theory) is accompanied by the activation of parts in the amygdala that are not activated when making atypical decisions, such as the propensity for risk in the context of gains, and risk aversion in the case of losses (De Martino et al., 2006).

These investigative techniques were applied to financial choices as well. Among the pioneers of neurofinance are Kuhnen and Knutson (2005), who studied risk propensity and aversion and noted that the two different attitudes toward risk translate into the activation of different areas of the brain, specifically the nucleus accumbens in the case of risk aversion and the insular cortex in the case of risk propensity. Bruguier et al. (2010) studied the surprising ability of uninformed traders, even novices, to infer information from the trading process – intuiting the presence of traders with insider information. They identified an important correlation between this ability and the human capacity to discern malicious or benevolent intent, which they called the theory of mind (ToM).

An interesting neurofinance study (Frydman et al., 2014) was done on neural correlates of the disposition effect described at the end of the previous section. The idea is that the disposition effect is really the result of psychological values obtained from the realization of concrete losses and virtual profits. The laboratory experiment was devised such that (exogenous) prices of stock that increased in the past would probably continue to increase and those of stock that decreased in the past would probably continue to decrease. Therefore, the optimal behavior, contrary to the disposition effect, would be to sell the losing stocks and keep the winning stocks. Participants in the experiment behaved in an all but rational manner, very similar to the results Odean (1998a) obtained, as cited in the previous section. The part of the brain that activates during a sale is the ventromedial prefrontal cortex (vmPFC), which activates upon the psychological impact of a stock's sale. The more the vmPFC area activates in a subject during a realized return, the more the subject manifests the disposition effect (Frydman et al., 2014).

Another relevant laboratory study for neural aspects of financial decisions considers the neural correlates of individual financial choices that, in aggregate, give rise to the phenomenon of speculative bubbles

(Smith et al., 2014). This study uses laboratory techniques to endogenously generate situations in which the stock prices that participants are exposed to become significantly higher than their fundamental value. The experiment is thus based on two goods: risky (represented by stock) and not risky (represented by liquidity). The risky good pays an uncertain dividend $E(d)$, while liquidity pays an interest $r$. Stocks that the participants possess at the end of the experiment are converted to liquidity at a rate $F$. The parameters $F$, $r$ and $d$ allow the assignment of a fundamental value to stocks traded in the experimental market. In the majority of sessions, bubbles are generated, with characteristics not dissimilar to speculative bubbles in the stock market (for example, an asymmetry between the bubble's relatively slow formation and the rapid and pronounced crash). From a behavioral point of view, the experiment identifies three general types of traders: (1) the "fundamentalists", who sell their stocks at the beginning of the experiment at the fundamental value and simply wait for the final conversion to liquidity; (2) the "momentum" traders, who start to buy at the beginning of the bubble and continue to buy even after it bursts; and (3) the "smart", who buy when the stock prices begin to rise and sell prior to the peak. The latter type realizes the highest returns, at the expense of the second group. This behavioral difference corresponds to differences in cerebral activity. Of the two most relevant findings, one is the correlation between the aggregate activity of the nucleus accumbens of all participants (in a certain sense, the neural activity of the "market") and the evolution of risky stock prices, so much so that the peak in aggregate activity of the nucleus accumbens corresponds to the peak of the speculative bubble. In a certain sense, the increase in activity in the nucleus accumbens implies risk propensity and the illusion that the increase in prices will continue uninterrupted. The traders that make less are those more susceptible to buying based on the activity of the nucleus accumbens, victims, one could say, of irrational exuberance. The second difference in relevant cerebral activity is the activation of the insular cortex (an area already identified as connected, among others, to uncertain financial situations), which is greater in "smart" traders. These participants, in some way, inferred that something could go wrong and concluded, therefore, that the increase in prices could not continue in the long term. It is interesting to note that the smart traders, when they start to sell risky stock, are not able to do so on the basis of statistical signals (given that the trend is singularly increasing) and have to do so on the basis of some type of subjective intuition, similar to what was identified by Bruguier et al. (2010), as cited above. Inversely to what was stated regarding the activation of the nucleus accumbens, in this case the greater the propensity of a trader to sell upon activation of the insular cortex, the greater that trader's returns.

As famously stated by Warren Buffett, "be fearful when others are greedy and greedy when others are fearful". Smith et al. (2014), discussed above, in a certain sense, offers a neural correlate: "activate your insular cortex when others activate their nucleus accumbens". Neurofinance, in sum, can help us identify the heterogeneous types of traders present on the market, explaining and potentially allowing predictions about the market's aggregate behavior.

# REFERENCES

Alchian, Armen A. (1950). "Uncertainty, evolution, and economic theory". *Journal of Political Economy*. **58**(3): 211–21.

Aumann, Robert J. (1976). "Agreeing to disagree". *The Annals of Statistics*. **4**(6): 1236–9.

Barber, Brad M. and Terrance Odean (2000). "Trading is hazardous to your wealth: The common stock investment performance of individual investors". *The Journal of Finance*. **55**(2): 773–806.

Barber, Brad M. and Terrance Odean (2001). "Boys will be boys: Gender, overconfidence, and common stock investment". *The Quarterly Journal of Economics*. **116**(1): 261–92.

Barber, Brad M., Yi-Tsung Lee, Yu-Jane Liu and Terrance Odean (2009). "Just how much do individual investors lose by trading?" *Review of Financial Studies*. **22**(2): 609–32.

Bazerman, Max and Don A. Moore (2013). *Judgment in Managerial Decision Making*. 8th edn. New York, NY: John Wiley & Sons.

Benartzi, Shlomo and Richard H. Thaler (1995). "Myopic loss aversion and the equity premium puzzle". *The Quarterly Journal of Economics*. **110**(1): 73–92.

Bruguier, Antoine J., Steven R. Quartz and Peter Bossaerts (2010). "Exploring the nature of "trader intuition". *The Journal of Finance*. **65**(5): 1703–23.

Camerer, Colin, George Loewenstein and Drazen Prelec (2005). "Neuroeconomics: How neuroscience can inform economics". *Journal of Economic Literature*. **43**(1): 9–64.

Chase, William G. and Herbert A. Simon (1973). "Perception in chess". *Cognitive Psychology*. **4**(1): 55–81.

De Bondt, Werner F.M. and Richard Thaler (1985). "Does the stock market over-react?" *The Journal of Finance*. **40**(3): 793–805.

De Martino, Benedetto, Colin F. Camerer and Ralph Adolphs (2010). "Amygdala damage eliminates monetary loss aversion". *Proceedings of the National Academy of Sciences*. **107**(8): 3788–92.

De Martino, Benedetto, Darshan Kumaran, Ben Seymour and Raymond J. Dolan (2006). "Frames, biases, and rational decision-making in the human brain". *Science*. **313**(5787): 684–7.

Fama, Eugene F. (1970). "Efficient capital markets: A review of theory and empirical work". *The Journal of Finance*. **25**(2): 383–417.

Friedman, Milton (1953). *Essays in Positive Economics*. Chicago, IL: University of Chicago Press.

Frydman, Cary, Nicholas Barberis, Colin Camerer, Peter Bossaerts and Antonio Rangel (2014). "Using neural data to test a theory of investor behavior: An application to realization utility". *The Journal of Finance*. **69**(2): 907–46.

Gadarowski, Christopher (2002). "Financial press coverage and expected stock returns". Available at SSRN: https://ssrn.com/abstract=267311.

Genesove, David and Christopher Mayer (2001). "Loss aversion and seller behavior: Evidence from the housing market". *The Quarterly Journal of Economics*. **116**(4): 1233–60.

Gennaioli, Nicola, Andrei Shleifer and Robert Vishny (2012). "Neglected risks, financial innovation, and financial fragility". *Journal of Financial Economics*. **104**(3): 452–68.

Gigerenzer, Gerd, Peter M. Todd and the ABC Research Group (1999). *Simple Heuristics that Make Us Smart*. New York, NY: Oxford University Press.

Grossman, Sanford J. and Joseph E. Stiglitz (1980). "On the impossibility of informationally efficient markets". *The American Economic Review*. **70**(3): 393–408.

Hommes, C.H. (2006). "Heterogeneous agent models in economics and finance". *Handbook of Computational Economics*. **2**: 1109–86.

Kahneman, Daniel (2011). *Thinking, Fast and Slow*. Macmillan.

Kuhnen, Camelia M. and Brian Knutson (2005). "The neural basis of financial risk taking". *Neuron*. **47**(5): 763–70.

Lichtenstein, Sarah and Baruch Fischhoff (1977). "Do those who know more also know more about how much they know?" *Organizational Behavior and Human Performance*. **20**(2): 159–83.

Malkiel, Burton G. (1973). *A Random Walk Down Wall Street*. New York, NY: W.W. Norton.

Malkiel, Burton G. (2003). "The efficient market hypothesis and its critics". *The Journal of Economic Perspectives*. **17**(1): 59–82.

Mandelbrot, Benoit (1962). "Paretian distributions and income maximization". *The Quarterly Journal of Economics*. **76**(1): 57–85.

Mandelbrot, Benoit (1997). "The variation of certain speculative prices". In *Fractals and Scaling in Finance*. New York: Springer. pp. 371–418.

Mehra, Rajnish and Edward C. Prescott (1985). "The equity premium: A puzzle". *Journal of Monetary Economics*. **15**(2): 145–61.

Milgrom, Paul and Nancy Stokey (1982). "Information, trade and common knowledge". *Journal of Economic Theory*. **26**(1): 17–27.

Odean, Terrance (1998a). "Are investors reluctant to realize their losses?" *The Journal of Finance*. **53**(5): 1775–98.

Odean, Terrance (1998b). "Volume, volatility, price, and profit when all traders are above average". *The Journal of Finance*. **53**(6): 1887–934.

Shiller, Robert J. (1981). "The use of volatility measures in assessing market efficiency". *The Journal of Finance*. **36**(2): 291–304.

Smith, A., T. Lohrenz, J. King, P.R. Montague and C.F. Camerer (2014). "Irrational exuberance and neural crash warning signals during endogenous experimental market bubbles". *Proceedings of the National Academy of Sciences*. **111**(29): 10503–508.

# 7. Behavioral re-evolution: how behavioral economics has evolved and is evolving

**Enrico Maria Cervellati**

[. . .] we now account for approximately 6% of all Nobel economics prizes ever
awarded.
Robert J. Shiller

## INTRODUCTION

George Stigler used to say: "There's nothing new in economics. Adam
Smith had said it all." Indeed this seems also to be the case in behavioral
economics (Ashraf et al., 2005). Thus, Smith is not only the first economist
in history, but also the first *behavioral* economist in history. A few mentions are enough to recognize the statement. Smith described what we
now call "overconfidence", in his *Wealth of Nations* as "the over-weening
conceit which the greater part of men have of their own abilities" (Smith,
1776 [1981], I, x, 1). In *The Theory of Moral Sentiments*, he claimed
that "Pain. . . is, in almost all cases, a more pungent sensation than the
opposite and correspondent pleasure" (Smith, 1759 [1981], III, ii, 176–7),
a perfect description of "loss aversion". Again, he wrote: "The pleasure
which we are to enjoy ten years hence, interests us so little in comparison
with that which we may enjoy today [. . .]" (Smith, 1759 [1981], IV, ii, 273),
anticipating the concepts of "present bias" and of "limited self-control".

Coming to the twentieth century, Herbert A. Simon claimed that
"The phrase 'behavioral economics' appears to be a pleonasm. What
'non-behavioral' economics can we contrast with it? The answer to this
question is found in the specific assumptions about human behavior that
are made in neoclassical economic theory" (Thaler, 2016). Simon has
surely anticipated behavioral economics, thus somebody may claim that
he was "biased" in his judgment. However, Vilfredo Pareto, also one of
the fathers of "traditional" economics, asserted that "The foundation
of political economy, and, in general of every social science, is evidently
psychology. A day may come when we shall be able to decide the laws of

social science from the principles of psychology" (Pareto, 1906 [2014]). Another "traditional" economist, John Maynard Keynes, considered the father of modern macroeconomics, may actually be regarded as the first behavioral financial economist (Thaler, 2016). His idea of "animal spirits" in financial markets anticipated the work of many modern behavioral economists such as Robert J. Shiller, Nobel Laureate in Economics in 2013.

## 1.   BEHAVIORAL ECONOMICS 1.0

Coming to the present day, psychologist Daniel Kahneman, Nobel Laureate in Economics in 2002, is by most considered the father of "modern" behavioral economics, for his joint work with the late Amos Tversky. Their research signaled the birth of modern behavioral economics, as well as of the application of the behavioral approach to other fields such as politics. Richard Thaler is considered the first "modern" behavioral economist since he has probably been the first one to fully understand the importance of the work of the two psychologists and to start applying it to economics. What is usually considered the first study in behavioral economics written by an economist is his 1980 paper "Toward a positive theory of consumer choice" (Thaler, 1980), followed by his joint work with Hersh Shefrin on the limits of self-control (Thaler and Shefrin, 1981).

Turning to finance, apart from Robert Shiller, the other two pioneers of modern behavioral finance are, in my view, Hersh Shefrin and Meir Statman. One of their fundamental contributions is the development of "Behavioral Portfolio Theory" (Shefrin and Statman, 2000), which differs in several respects from the traditional "Modern Portfolio Theory" by Harry Markowitz (Markowitz, 1952a). Interestingly, in 1952 Markowitz actually wrote two papers, reflecting two definitely different views of investors' behavior. The most famous one, "Portfolio selection" (Markowitz, 1952a), theorized the mean-variance approach. Markowitz himself clarified that mean-variance portfolio theory is a "production" theory (Das et al., 2011, p. 25) – that is, a theory that allows investors to produce efficient portfolios that combine expected returns and volatilities in an optimal way – but it does not say anything about what investors want to do with the money invested in these efficient portfolios. There is no reference to possible investors' goals such as funding their retirement, leaving a bequest to their children, and so on. Indeed, producing mean-variance efficient portfolios should be a way to achieve investors' objectives. Instead, behavioral portfolio theory combines efficient portfolios and investors' goals. In the second, less famous, paper (Markowitz, 1952b), Markowitz extended the "insurance-lottery framework" developed by Friedman and Savage (1948) in which people buy lottery tickets at the same time as buying insurance, thus displaying both risk-seeking and risk-averse attitudes. People buy lottery tickets – or lottery-like stocks – because they aspire to achieve a higher social status, while they buy insurance – or very safe assets – as protection against the possibility of losses that will force them to reduce their status. Prospect theory (Kahneman and Tversky, 1979) extends Markowitz (1952b), describing the behavior of people when they perceive themselves either in a domain of losses or in a domain of gains, with respect to a given reference point or an aspiration level. While in the domain of gains people display a risk-averse behavior, in the domain of losses the same people show a risk-seeking attitude. Thus, somehow, Markowitz may be considered a behavioral economist too. As a matter of fact, in a recent paper together with Sanjiv Das, Jonathan Scheid and Meir Statman (Das et al., 2010), Markowitz developed the "Mental Accounting Portfolio Theory", which combines the traditional mean-variance approach with behavioral portfolio theory, especially focusing on the role of investors' goals and mental accounting.

While Meir Statman continued to focus on investors' behavior, Hersh Shefrin laid the basis for the application of the behavioral approach to many branches of finance and related fields, namely: asset pricing (Shefrin, 2005; 2008a); corporate finance (Shefrin, 2007; 2018); management (Shefrin, 2008b); and risk management (Shefrin, 2016).

Of course, many others scholars contributed to applying the behavioral approach to finance and economics. Too many to mention. However, among others it is worth citing Colin Camerer, who pioneered the field of "behavioral game theory" (Camerer, 2003) as well as neuroeconomics (Glimcher et al., 2009). Neuroeconomics is contributing greatly to behavioral economics, reinforcing the findings of the behavioral literature. A future Nobel Prize in Economics could be awarded to a neuroeconomist.

## 2.   BEHAVIORAL ECONOMICS 2.0

While the 1980s saw the appearance of the first papers in behavioral economics and behavioral finance, raising a lively debate between traditional and behavioral economists, in the 1990s the behavioral approach grew substantially, leading to the 2002 Nobel Prize being awarded to Kahneman. At the end of the 1990s and the beginning of the 2000s, the seeds of what has been called "Behavioral Finance 2.0" or "Behavioral Finance in Action" (Benartzi, 2011) were planted, but they emerged in 2008 with the publication of *Nudge* (Thaler and Sunstein, 2008). While behavioral economics 1.0 presented a list of biases, but little guidance on what to do to avoid them, or at least to mitigate their negative effects, the *nudges* at the center of the "behavioral finance in action" approach led to proposals on what to do. Of course, this approach has been – and still is – controversial. Initially called "libertarian paternalism", it has attracted strong criticism from those who are against a paternalistic approach. I will not discuss these criticisms here – even though I consider them important – because I want to stress the shift from behavioral economics 1.0 to 2.0, that is, the passage from a somehow descriptive approach to a prescriptive one.

A notable example of the second generation of behavioral studies is what has been called the *Save More Tomorrow* (SMART) program, developed by Richard Thaler and Shlomo Benartzi (Thaler and Benartzi, 2004). The SMART approach is a *smart* example of how to use behavioral biases to benefit people. The case in point is investment choices for retirement. People, on average, tend to under-save for their retirement and to invest too little in shares. Even acknowledging the importance of these kinds of decision, they tend to procrastinate, overwhelmed by choice overload, or excessively focusing on the short run, partly due to self-control problems that lead people to attach too much importance to the present and too little to the future. In theory, the best solution would be to let people understand their mistakes so that they would rationally change their behavior in their best interest. However, the reality is different and much evidence shows that people hardly change their behavior, even once they are aware of the errors committed. The solution proposed by the SMART program is based on the automatic enrollment of employees in private pension plans, giving them the possibility to opt out. The possibility of opting out is the difference between paternalism and "libertarian" paternalism. Of course, knowing that people tend to procrastinate, and remain in the status quo, the designers of the program may anticipate that many people will not opt out, and will remain in the plan. The other key characteristic of the program is that the contribution rate will automatically increase whenever employees get a salary raise. Once the raise arrives, even if it is slightly lower due to the increase in the contribution rate, the employee will still be happy given the overall increase in salary. The impact of the SMART program has been quite impressive, and many other similar programs have been implemented, such as the "Borrow Less Tomorrow" program (Karlan and Zinman, 2012).

Nudges are nowadays so widespread that they have impacted many fields in economics and finance, but also in politics, leading to the creation of "nudge units" all over the world. As mentioned, Richard Thaler has contributed to applying the behavioral approach in many branches of economics and finance, but his idea of nudge has been explicitly mentioned and recognized by the Nobel committee in assigning him the prize. The probable reason is the tangible impact they had in so many fields of real life.

There are of course many more examples of behavioral economics 2.0 "in action", but this chapter is a personal (and thus biased) view of the evolution of behavioral economics and, most importantly, its focus is on the evolutionary process and not on its details. For more details on how behavioral economics evolved, see Thaler (2015).

## 3.   BEHAVIORAL ECONOMICS 3.0

In the early 2000s, behavioral scholars (Statman and Wood, 2004), but also practitioners (Pompian and Longo, 2005) started considering investors' personalities in behavioral studies. More recently, they structured what I now personally call "Behavioral Finance 3.0" or "Personalized Behavioral Finance" (Pompian, 2012; Pan and Statman, 2013). Pompian (2012) explicitly refers to the theory of personality temperaments proposed by Dr. David Keirsey (Keirsey and Bates, 1984; Keirsey, 1998). Keirsey built on previous theories of the twentieth century such as Jung's theory of psychological types (Jung, 1923), the theory of personality types developed by Myers and Briggs (Myers, 1980), and the Big-Five theory (McCrae and Costa, 1992), underlining the five main personality traits that characterize people. However, it is possible to claim that Keirsey's four personality temperaments find their roots in Hippocrates' traditional four temperaments, which date back more than 2000 years. Pompian (2012) moved from Keirsey's four temperaments to propose four corresponding Behavioral Investor Types (BITs). The author claims that specific cognitive biases can be associated to each BIT, because a specific BIT is more prone to some biases than others. Linking cognitive biases to personalities is thus important in several respects. For example, financial advisors may improve their relationship with clients once they understand their corresponding BIT. Investors themselves may improve their behavior and decisions once they recognize that they have a specific personality that predisposes them to peculiar biases. Considering individual personality has far more important implications, as I suggest in Cervellati (2017). For example, with regard to financial education, the level of financial literacy is quite low in several countries. In recent years, governments all over the world have implemented programs in financial education, trying to raise the literacy level, the results of which have not been very encouraging. There are many reasons for these poor results. I personally believe that there are at least two major issues that are not adequately considered in financial education programs. First, they typically do not incorporate behavioral economics findings, thus often the financial education programs follow traditional paths, resulting in their being too technical and often even boring. As a matter of fact, it seems that the most effective financial education programs with children – but the same holds with adults – are the ones that are based on games (Shefrin, 2013). In addition, traditional financial education programs often focus on issues that are not really central in people's life. The other major issue for which they eventually become ineffective is that they do not take into account individual differences in terms of personality that affect the way people perceive and understand things. The communication style has to be different with distinct people. In other words, "one size does not fit all". Nowadays, the challenge is to identify specific strategies suitable to distinct personality types.

## 4.   CONCLUSIONS

As Robert Shiller noted, considering other Nobel Laureates in Economics who have contributed to behavioral economics, such as Robert Fogel, George Akerlof, Daniel Kahneman, Elinor Ostrom, Richard Thaler, and himself, behavioral economists account for approximately six percent of all Nobel Economics prizes ever awarded. In this chapter I mentioned the evolution of behavioral economics in what I called the first, second and third generations of studies. There will probably be a fourth one, a fifth one or even more. Or maybe people will eventually stop talking about behavioral economics. This may happen not because of the diminishing importance of the behavioral approach, but exactly for the opposite reason, that is, because people, and economists among them, will finally recognize that economics is behavioral in nature. In the (hopefully near) future, we will eventually witness the "End of Behavioral Finance" – and, in general, of behavioral economics – as Richard Thaler advocated (Thaler, 1999). A future in which people, and economists, will stop adding the adjective *behavioral* before the word *economics*.

## REFERENCES

Ashraf, N., C.F. Camerer and G. Loewenstein (2005), "Adam Smith, behavioral economist", *Journal of Economic Perspectives*, **19** (3), Summer, 131–45.
Benartzi, S. (2011), "Behavioral finance in action", CFA working paper.
Camerer, C.F. (2003), *Behavioral Game Theory. Experiments in Strategic Interactions*, Russell Sage Foundation, Princeton, NJ: Princeton University Press.

Cervellati, E.M. (2017), "One size does not fit all. The importance of investors' personality in financial education", *Quaderni di Finanza Consob*, **84**, 77–87.

Das, S., H. Markowitz, J. Scheid and M. Statman (2010), "Portfolio optimization with mental accounts", *Journal of Financial and Quantitative Analysis*, **45** (2), 311–34.

Das, S., H. Markowitz, J. Scheid and M. Statman (2011), "Portfolios for investors who want to reach their goals while staying on the mean-variance efficient frontier", *The Journal of Wealth Management*, **14** (2), 25–31.

Friedman, M. and L.J. Savage (1948), "The utility analysis of choices involving risk", *Journal of Political Economy*, **56**, 279–304.

Glimcher, P.W., C.F. Camerer, E. Fehr and R.A. Poldrack (eds) (2009), *Neuroeconomics: Decision Making and the Brain*, Burlington, MA, USA, San Diego, CA, USA and London, UK: Elsevier.

Jung, C.G. (1923), *Psychological Types*, New York, NY: Harcourt Brace.

Kahneman, D. and A. Tversky (1979), "Prospect theory: An analysis of decision making under risk", *Econometrica*, **47**, 263–91.

Karlan, D. and J. Zinman (2012), "Borrow less tomorrow: Behavioral approaches to debt reduction", Working Paper, Financial Security Project at Boston College, MA, USA.

Keirsey, D. (1998), *Please Understand Me II: Temperament, Character, Intelligence*, Del Mar, CA: Prometheus Nemesis.

Keirsey, D. and M.M. Bates (1984), *Please Understand Me: Character and Temperament Types*, Del Mar, CA: Prometheus Nemesis.

Markowitz, H. (1952a), "Portfolio selection", *Journal of Finance*, **7**, 77–91.

Markowitz, H. (1952b), "The utility of wealth", *The Journal of Political Economy*, **60**, 151–8.

McCrae, R. and P. Costa (1992), "An introduction to the five-factor model and its applications", *Journal of Personality*, **60**, 175–215.

Myers, I.B. (1980), *Gifts Differing*, Palo Alto, CA: Consulting Psychologists Press.

Pan, C.H. and M. Statman (2013), "Investor personality in investor questionnaires", *The Journal of Investment Consulting*, **14** (1), 15–23.

Pareto, V. (1906), *Manual of Political Economy*, reprinted in A. Montesano, A. Zanni, L. Bruni, J. S. Chipman and M. McLure (eds) (2014), *Manual of Political Economy: A Critical and Variorum Translation Edition*, Oxford: Oxford University Press.

Pompian, M.M. (2012), *Behavioral Finance and Investor Types: Managing Behavior to Make Better Investment Decisions*, Hoboken, NJ: John Wiley & Sons.

Pompian, M.M. and J.M. Longo (2005), "The future of wealth management: Incorporating behavioral finance into your practice", **18** (3), 58–63.

Shefrin, H. (2005), *A Behavioral Approach to Asset Pricing*, Burlington, MA, USA, San Diego, CA, USA and London, UK: Elsevier.

Shefrin, H. (2007), *Behavioral Corporate Finance: Decisions that Create Value*, New York, NY: McGraw-Hill.

Shefrin, H. (2008a), *A Behavioral Approach to Asset Pricing*, 2nd edn, Burlington, MA, USA, San Diego, CA, USA and London, UK: Elsevier.

Shefrin, H. (2008b), *Ending the Management Illusion: How to Drive Business Results Using the Principles of Behavioral Finance*, New York, NY: McGraw-Hill.

Shefrin, H. (2013), "Born to spend? How nature and nurture impact spending and borrowing habits", Chase Blueprint.

Shefrin, H. (2016), *Behavioral Risk Management: Managing the Psychology That Drives Decisions and Influences Operational Risk*, London: Palgrave Macmillan.

Shefrin, H. (2018), *Behavioral Corporate Finance: Concept and Case for Teaching Behavioral Finance*, 2nd edn, New York, NY: McGraw-Hill.

Shefrin, H. and M. Statman (2000), "Behavioral portfolio theory", *Journal of Financial and Quantitative Analysis*, **35** (2), 127–51.

Smith, A. (1759), *The Theory of Moral Sentiments*, reprinted in D.D. Raphael and A.L. Macfie (eds) (1981), Indianapolis, IN: Liberty Fund.

Smith, A. (1776), *An Inquiry into the Nature and Causes of the Wealth of Nations*, Volumes I and II, reprinted in R.H. Campbell and A.S. Skinner (eds) (1981), Indianapolis, IN: Liberty Fund.

Statman, M. and V. Wood (2004), "Investor temperament", *Journal of Investment Consulting*, Summer, 1–12.

Thaler, R.H. (1980), "Toward a positive theory of consumer choice", *Journal of Economic Behavior and Organization*, **1**, 39–60.

Thaler, R.H. (1999), "The end of behavioral finance", *Financial Analysts Journal*, **55** (6), 12–17.

Thaler, R.H. (2015), *Misbehaving: The Making of Behavioral Economics*, New York, NY: W.W. Norton & Company.

Thaler, R.H. (2016), "Behavioral economics: Past, present, and future", *American Economic Review*, **106** (7), 1577–600.

Thaler, R.H. and S. Benartzi (2004), "Save more tomorrow: Using behavioral economics to increase employee saving", *Journal of Political Economy*, **112** (1), S164–87.

Thaler, R.H. and H. Shefrin (1981), "An economic theory of self-control", *Journal of Political Economy*, **89** (2), 392–406.

Thaler, R.H. and C.R. Sunstein (2008), *Nudge: Improving Decisions About Health, Wealth, and Happiness*, New Haven, CT: Yale University Press.

# 8. Evolutionary regulation and financial behavior

## Paolo Mottura

## 1. INTRODUCTION

Research and studies concerning bank regulation and supervision have rarely crossed paths with behavioral finance. Regulators set rules and supervisors apply them, after interpreting the factual situation and according to their judgment. Therefore regulators and supervisors modify economic agents' incentives, orient their expectations, and influence their beliefs. Bank customers' behavior is very much related to supposed bank liquidity and solvency and, basically, to bank reputation. Regulators and supervisors are major contributors to bank reputation. Bank deposits are believed to be liquid on creditors' call. Regulators and supervisors bear great responsibility in this since they provide a rationale for trust, because banks' balance-sheets are inherently opaque. Given that economic agents have a varying degree of financial education, the accountability of regulators and supervisors involves obvious problems of disclosure and communication.

## 2. HOW THINGS (THAT IS, REGULATION) CHANGED

The term "evolutionary", in our case applied to bank regulation, has at least a double meaning:

- *First*: banking regulation has changed since its inception and it is important to review briefly its original motivations, its objectives, its approaches and mechanisms, and to outline the different stages of its evolution.
- *Second*: the progressive change of bank regulation has gradually become evolutionary in the sense that it has become more interactive within the financial system and more dependent upon environmental change and political choices.

In principle, regulation has been and still is a response to bank crises. Bank crises destroy value, drain liquidity from the financial system, endanger the circulation of bank money, have high (and unacceptable) social costs, and – mostly – they delude the widespread, deep-rooted expectation and preference for liquidity. All economic agents want to have stable access to a substantial supply of safe financial assets that are immune both to the issuer's failure and to market risks. This expectation is legitimate and has great political relevance. Therefore bank crises must be promptly managed to avoid bank failures and must be prevented by effective regulation of bankers' behaviors. Please take note that bank money – that is, bank deposits providing monetary functions – are and should be a safe asset *par excellence*. Its convertibility at par value cannot be questioned.

The initial and original approach of bank regulation – that devised during the Great Depression of the 1930s – was eminently structural. It was principally motivated as a response to the risk of bank failures. According to the classic paradigm "structure–conduct–performance", the governance of banking industry structure was deemed essential to achieve bank stability. Banks' performance should be stable (low failure rate), therefore bankers' conduct should be disciplined by a strict regulation of banking activities, that is, of what banks could or could not do. The regulation of banking structure – that is, the supply-side – was the main concern of bank regulators. The structural approach of regulation was mostly exogenous and mechanistic.

The stability objective was attained at the cost of drastically limiting bank entrepreneurship, innovation and competition. This drawback of bank regulation became more and more evident during the 1960s and 1970s, when the development of capital markets driven by economic growth and diversification made clear that banks were inefficient and their intermediation role was not properly integrated within the overall financial system. Banks lagged a few steps behind the times and their competitive and entrepreneurial role had to be promoted and fostered.

The objective of stability having been attained, banks appeared sufficiently stable and their failure rate was practically marginal. Central Banks were always ready to provide liquidity, acting as lenders of last resort to banks experiencing liquidity shortages. Bankers were pressing and lobbying for more action freedom. Political and economic thinking was more and more convinced that competitive markets were the best form to organize and discipline economic and financial activity. Regulators became concerned with bank efficiency and were pressed by the spreading belief that efficiency could be improved only by a substantial liberalization of banking activities, by reducing existing restrictions, without jeopardizing the original objective of stability.

The regulatory reform that was gradually introduced was essentially prudential and subverted the previous interpretation of the "structure–conduct–performance" paradigm. The structure of the banking industry no longer had to be exogenously regulated but it had to be allowed to become organically endogenous to the market. The choice of banking activities and the scope of the banking services supply had to be restored to the bankers' entrepreneurship and strategies. The main focus of regulators became the new design of prudential and functional rules specifically concerning the management of the bank's financial structure, that is, its balance-sheet. Provided they complied with these rules, bankers could choose and manage their business models and organization and could diversify their corporate portfolio within a larger range of business areas. The new set of rules – mostly based on capital requirements related to risk-taking – was judged the best trade-off between the main objective of bank efficiency and the necessary condition of "sound and safe banking". Bank stability became a condition, whereas bank market efficiency became the leading objective. Capital adequacy was the basic inspiring principle of prudential regulation.

It is important to focus on two aspects underlying the turnaround from structural to prudential regulation:

- *First*: bank regulation became market-endogenous and its effective application required a robust and continuous supervision. It was no longer a matter of allowing or forbidding bank activities, but rather it was the new challenge of controlling and disciplining the bankers' compliance to functional rules (Llewellyn, 2011).
- *Second*: and perhaps more relevant for a correct interpretation of the regulatory evolution, the new prudential regulation was not intended to be a response to bank crises, which by then belonged to the past and to an outdated memory. Rather the regulator's aim was to design the rules under which banks could enter a wider range of competitive markets.

Careful attention should be given to the changing and growingly endogenous culture of regulators. In the evolutionary context, bank regulation – referring mostly to Basel 1 and 2 – became contingent, adaptive and not sufficiently reactive and resilient. Certainly, bank regulation – up to the great and global financial crisis of 2007–2009 – did not prove to be particularly reactive. Regulators were systematically preceded and outwitted by bankers, who quickly learnt how to side-step regulation, by crossing the boundaries of regulated financial structures (shadow banking has been the dominant example), by taking more risks, by variously placing these risks off the regulated financial-sheet, by discovering that risk is not only something to be hedged at a cost but it is also something which can be profitably traded, thanks to inventive financial engineering, driven by innovation, either legal or technological.

Light-touch and arm's-length prudential regulation could not keep up with successful and mutating banks. Bankers, driven by strong market incentives and by a much praised profitability performance, could not but push against capital ratios, liquidity reserves and leverage, which are the essential productivity levers of bank management. On this point Basel 2 is a pertinent example: the inclusion of trading book risks in the computation of required regulatory capital was certainly belated. By the end of 2006 a significant numbers of global banks (UBS, Barclays, BNP Paribas, Citigroup, RBS, Deutsche Bank, Société Générale, Credit Suisse, Fortis Bank, Wachovia, Lloyds TSB. . .) scored a return on equity (ROE) before taxes well above an impressive 30 percent, while registering a very low and decreasing return on assets (ROA). Increasing leverage was the key success factor. The ratio of market-value to book-value was increasing, attaining multiples of between two and three. By these standards, investors in bank capital could expect that paid-out profits would shortly amortize their original stakes. Risk-taking was apparently risk-free. Risk appetite had no counterweight. The bankers' art and craft of balancing between risky, profitable, mostly illiquid, long assets and, on the other side, short, liquid, mostly low-cost and low-risk liabilities was paying off generously. Regulation culture was not resilient enough to cope with the growing and successful bubble. Profitability was mistaken as a signal of sound, safe and expert management.

The ensuing crisis was initially dealt with and managed by strong public – that is Governments and Central Banks – interventions, mostly based upon a generous input of new liquidity. Potentially insolvent banks were made solvent. Failing banks were kept stable. Subsequently the fundamental challenges to bank regulators and supervisors were again how to make banks stable. Endogenous, prudential, adaptive regulation had been proven inadequate.

Prudential regulation, as a model, was not per se disclaimed, but it radically changed its stance. Regulators adopted a hands-on approach. With the Dodd–Frank Act and Basel 3, the liberal interlude of bank regulation came to an abrupt end. Regulators responded once more to the banking crises, as had happened in the 1930s, they gave priority to bank and systemic stability and started playing the game by anticipation. Stress-tests became routine and forward-looking. The new financial structure requirements – that is, higher capital ratios, new and high liquidity coverage and stable funding ratios – have been targeted to future time-horizons and aimed to more stringent future benchmarks . . . in other words, they were intended to play a leading role of forward guidance. Bankers were told which was the expected path they should follow from the "now and here" to the "future and there". Supervisors acted accordingly, assuming a heavy-touch approach and an over-the-shoulder control.

Despite the strengthening of regulation and supervision, in the aftermath of the recent crisis it must be acknowledged that regulators' and supervisors' credibility and reputation have been substantially eroded. According to a new line of research (Morrison and White, 2010) the distrust in bank regulators should be considered as a potential cause of further bank crises. The basic points to be stressed are: common people trust banks in so far as they trust regulators and supervisors; banks – as private firms engaging in market competition – are subject to failure and subsequent resolution; bank money – as any private debt – is subject to its issuer's failure; bank money unquestionably is a public good or public utility; notwithstanding their public status, regulators by themselves cannot guarantee the nominal value of bank money; therefore, banks and regulators alone cannot be entrusted with bank money's safety; the State – entitled with monetary sovereignty – cannot forfeit its final accountability to bank money holders. In fact people clearly expect that the state will always provide a backstop to bank money failure (King, 2013) and their belief openly contradicts the no-bailout policy recently declared by governments. In short, there is something wrong with the present set-up of public bank regulation if this last deceives people's legitimate expectations.

## 3.   CONCLUSIONS (AND QUESTIONS)

From this story we should draw a few practical lessons. No theory or model, based on past experience, can provide a sure and sufficient guidance to future decisions and actions, more than ever when and if measurable risks are displaced by pervading uncertainty. Behind the veil of theoretical underpinnings, which are the object of much debate, bank regulation remains the exercise of a balancing art and craft which requires a refined application of sound judgment, experienced rules of thumb and ground-based heuristics. Bank liquidity and solvency are de facto promises referred to future time-horizons and future states-of-the-world. Bankers' and regulators' correct behavior should keep their promises in line with actual expectations.

Should people believe that banks are there to provide safe assets? Should people trust that regulators make banks safe, despite them being private companies engaged in market competition? Regulators influence expectations. Do regulators know better? Common people – that is, bank creditors and customers – are induced to think so. Expectations drive behaviors. Should people be educated in view of bank default risk?

## REFERENCES

King, M. (2013), Mervyn King has lunch with the FT: interview transcript, *Financial Times*, 5 July.

Llewellyn, T.D. (2011), Post crisis regulatory strategy: a matrix approach, in F. Browne, D.T. Llewellyn and P. Molyneux (eds), *Regulation and Banking after the Crisis*, SUERF Study 2011/2, Larcier.

Morrison, A.D. and White, L. (2010), Reputational contagion and optimal regulatory forbearance, ECB Working Paper Series, No. 1196, May.

# 9. Recent advances in behavioural macroeconomics and lessons for policymakers

## Giordano Zevi*

Economic modelling as we practise it today is mostly based on some process of maximization by agents who are assumed to be self-interested and rational. Self-interest is the independence of each subject's preferences from those of the other individuals; rationality is broadly defined as the ability to compare all the available alternatives and to pin down the best one according to one's own preferences, regardless of the framing of the possible choices (DellaVigna, 2009).

Behavioural traits that challenge these assumptions and hence the conclusions of such economic models are nothing new (Simon, 1955; Allais, 1953; Ellsberg, 1961). In turn, Keynesian, Neoclassical and Neo-Keynesian models – the prevailing mainstream models from the 1960s onwards – have been confronted by this critique, which is more fundamental than the usual disagreements between economists.

Such challenges have been recognized and legitimized by academia. Herbert Simon received the Nobel Prize in Economics in 1978, Maurice Allais in 1988; Nobel prizes to critics of the mainstream were also awarded in 2002 to Daniel Kahneman and in 2017 to Richard Thaler. Their insights are part of the teaching of economics: textbooks routinely contain warnings that the *homo economicus* hypothesis is a mere "simplification that allows powerful theoretical models to be constructed" (from the motivation of Richard Thaler's Prize, 2017) but is not meant to be a realistic description of man. Along the lines of Friedman (1953), this simplification is generally viewed as a useful tool that allows real economic agents to be stripped of their less fundamental characteristics – from the point of view of their economic behaviour – and permits attention to be focused instead on their core traits, at least in the realm of production and

---

*  The views expressed in this chapter are those of the author and do not necessarily reflect those of Banca d'Italia nor is it responsible for those views.

exchange. Behavioural deviations from this simplification are considered as random disturbances, with no particular bias. In this way, an obviously bad description of a single real human agent turns out to be a good predictor of the average behaviour of many agents, be they households allocating their income to savings or consumption, or entrepreneurs deciding the amount of investment they will make in a given year in light of current expectations about the future stream of income and the present cost of capital.

Economics textbooks also mention that prominent critics, such as the Nobel prizewinners mentioned above, pointed out that these behavioural perturbations are in fact not random and that in the aggregate can have significant effects, big enough to contradict the results expected on the basis of the standard theory. However, any deeper learning about these effects is usually left to the students' goodwill or postponed to PhD-level classes.

From the point of view of policymaking, generally speaking these concerns have been considered scarcely operable. Policymakers were aware of behavioural theories, but generally did not rely on them as they were not considered comprehensive enough to form a coherent alternative system and were subject to the critique that "you cannot beat something with nothing" (Blaug, 1980).

Recently, all of this has changed: the Great Moderation (that is, a prolonged period of small economic shocks and low inflation) was followed by the Great Recession (a deep and lasting downturn in many advanced economies). There has been intensive talk of secular stagnation (Summers, 2013; Pagano and Sbracia, 2014). The forecasting models have failed systematically to predict future economic developments (Visco, 2009). This has led to much macroeconomic soul-searching (Haldane and Turrell, 2017; Vines and Willis, 2018), and to a larger interest in informing public policies by behavioural insights, drawing from positive past experiences (Poterba, 2009).

Theories addressing the possibility of large deviations from the standard models have finally become fashionable. However, being the renewed attention motivated by the perceived empirical failures of the models in use, the focus has now switched more towards practical implementation and less towards theoretical advances. In other words, there is greater interest on incremental results, less on scientific revolutions.

In practice, enrichments of the existing models, and consequently of the descending policy tools, have followed different patterns. This is because it is not easy to pin down key behavioural elements in a non-arbitrary way. As Driscoll and Holden (2014) noted, 'even if there is considerable microeconomic evidence from cognitive psychology or experimental economics for certain behavioural features, it is often difficult to know which features are most relevant for macroeconomic models'.

We can identify three, fairly distinctive, strands of research that pursue the implementation of behavioural elements in the theory and practice of economics.

The first one could be labelled 'piecewise implementation' and coincides with efforts to challenge key assumptions of models based on agents' full rationality one at a time. This has led to an extensive and rapidly growing body of literature in widely different sub-fields, some of them active for many years, for example, habit formation in consumption, that is, the idea that, contrary to the simplest version of the neoclassical rational choice model, consumption behaviour has a memory. If bygones are not bygones, then past consumption represents a state variable in the agents' maximization. Behavioural considerations can represent plausible micro-foundations of this common shortcut in macroeconomic models (Driscoll and Holden, 2014). These sub-fields stem from the recognition of specific agents' cognitive limitations, either on their way to processing information, or in forming expectations about the future, or in deriving utility. Early critiques that these additions to models were ad hoc have progressively subsided, as more and more advances in psychology have reinforced the general acceptance that these features are both extremely common among human beings and definitely relevant to their economic decision making.

Against the objection that 'everything becomes possible when we move into the territory of irrationality' (De Grauwe, 2012), it is possible to develop models based on a local notion of rationality that include some specific agents' limitation (for example a 'rule-of-thumb' forecasting rule). Results from these models can rationalize observed local deviations from full-rationality (that is, deviations that are empirically relevant only in some well-defined circumstances) and don't imply a challenge to all mainstream economics (that is, a global refutation of agents' full-rationality).

A second strand of research is the further development of a sound empirical behavioural economics, beyond the results found by experimental economics techniques in laboratories and based on increasingly available field data. This line of research reflects the changing focus of behavioural economists. Earlier contributions tended to be focused on the detection of a number of common behavioural traits such as self-control or endowment effects that provided counterexamples and implied significant deviations from at least one axiom of the neoclassical rationality. Once these traits have come to be commonly accepted, and increasingly empirically verified, much recent work has instead been based on the appraisal of behaviourally-informed empirical policies. Early examples include the analysis of the effect of the nudges implicitly involved in the Save More Tomorrow™ program (Thaler and Benartzi, 2004), while recent ones include the long list of references to 'social nudges' mentioned in Brandon et al. (2017).

The third and final strand is a more radical 'holistic' approach, as advocated for example by Camerer in his description of behavioural economics to biologists:

> Behavioral economics uses evidence from psychology and other social sciences to create a precise and fruitful alternative to traditional economic theories, which are based on optimization. [. . .] It shifts the basis for theories of economic choice away from logical calculation and maximization and toward biologically plausible mechanisms. [. . .] [it] is especially useful when decisions are complex and optimality is difficult to achieve. (Camerer, 2014)

Here the Rubicon is crossed, towards a 'new economics' that adopts realistic hypotheses about human behaviour and replaces the *homo oeconomicus* artefact, as theorists place more value on building plausible narratives about individual decision makers rather than constructing models whose results are valid in the aggregate.

Policymakers are most likely still unwilling to go as far as the third strand implies, replacing their habitual tools and practice with almost completely new ones. However, they are amenable to consider a number of lessons stemming from the findings of the first two strands of behavioural research as follows.

The first lesson is that deviations from full rationality can be implemented in otherwise standard models. This has three consequences: (1) in given circumstances, which would have been overlooked by the mainstream theory, policy prescriptions change; (2) it is in principle possible to describe a well-defined mapping between deviations and policy changes, so that the detection of deviations which are sufficiently commonplace among the agents brings certain policy changes as a logical consequence; (3) in partial connection with the two previous points, the presence of real agents' cognitive limitations could twist the trade-offs faced in practice by policymakers.

The most important *caveat* with respect to the behaviourally informed approach is that in many instances there is still considerable uncertainty about the behaviour of agents (Hyde et al., 2007). Consider for example the insights coming from behavioural finance, a field which has long since addressed the 'well-documented "anomalies" in financial markets which the standard intertemporal model fails to explain' (Hyde et al., 2007): notwithstanding all the recent advances, there could still be a discussion on which deviations are more salient, in the common case of the simultaneous presence of many of them (Rossi, 2018).

Directly deriving from these considerations, a second lesson is that theoretical models implementing many behavioural traits together are still very hard to formulate and call for caution in deriving policy implications. This holds true even if a reasonable, more tractable, subset of consolidated deviations could be defined. Rustichini (2009), for example, suggests switching from considering as the main subject of economics a two-dimensional rational man defined by risk propensity and time preferences, to a five-dimensional rational man. The additional three dimensions are loss aversion, cognitive skills and a notion of 'intelligence' (Rustichini, 2015). Failing to address these concerns could result in incomplete (and therefore potentially mistaken) policy advice.

A third lesson, strictly connected with empirical behavioural economics, is that nudging and other behavioural strategies are in fact powerful tools, but: (1) designing the nudging schemes effectively could prove extremely difficult (OECD, 2017); (2) the fields of application could be limited (DellaVigna, 2009), making them overall unsuitable for the macroeconomists' attention; and (3) the social gains deriving from their adoption could be extremely short-lived in some cases (Brandon et al., 2017).

A final 'meta' lesson is that, at long last, policymakers are willing to listen to behavioural economists. It is now up to them to rise to the challenge.

## REFERENCES

Allais, M. (1953), 'Le Comportement de l'Homme Rationnel devant le Risque: Critique des Postulats et Axiomes de l'Ecole Americaine', *Econometrica*, **21** (4), 503–46.

Blaug, Mark (1980), *The Methodology of Economics*, Cambridge: Cambridge University Press.

Brandon, A., P.J. Ferraro, J.A. List, R.D. Metcalfe, M.K. Price and F. Rundhammer (2017), 'Do the effects of social nudges persist? Theory and evidence from 38 natural field experiments', NBER Working Paper No. 23277.

Camerer, C. (2014), 'Behavioral economics', *Current Biology*, **24** (18), R867–R871.

De Grauwe, P. (2012), *Lectures on Behavioural Macroeconomics*, Princeton, NJ: Princeton University Press.

DellaVigna, S. (2009), 'Psychology and economics: Evidence from the field', *Journal of Economic Literature*, **47**, 315–72.

Driscoll, J.C. and S. Holden (2014), 'Behavioral economics and macroeconomic models', *Journal of Macroeconomics*, **41**, 133–47.

Ellsberg, D. (1961), 'Risk, ambiguity, and the savage axioms', *Quarterly Journal of Economics*, **75** (4), 643–69.

Friedman, M. (1953), 'The methodology of positive economics', in Milton Friedman, *Essays in Positive Economics*, Chicago, IL: University of Chicago Press, pp. 3–43.

Haldane, A. and A. Turrell (2017), 'An interdisciplinary model for macroeconomics', Bank of England Working Paper No. 696.

Hyde, S., K. Cuthbertson and D. Nitzsche (2007), 'Monetary policy and behavioral finance', *Journal of Economic Surveys*, **21** (5), 935–9.

OECD (2017), *Behavioural Insights and Public Policy: Lessons from Around the World*, Paris: OECD Publishing.

Pagano, G. and M. Sbracia (2014), 'The secular stagnation hypothesis: A review of the debate and some insights', Banca d'Italia, Questioni di Economia e Finanza (Occasional papers) No. 231.

Poterba, James M. (2009), 'Behavioral economics and public policy: Reflections on the past and lessons for the future', in Christopher L. Foote, Lorenz Goette and Stephan Meier (eds), *Policymaking Insights from Behavioral Economics*, Boston, MA: Federal Reserve Bank of Boston, pp. 369–77.

Rossi, Salvatore (2018), Opening remarks for the 'Behavioral finance revolution and the financial regulations and policies' workshop, Banca d'Italia, December 2017.

Rustichini, A. (2009), 'Neuroeconomics: What have we found, and what should we search for', *Current Opinion in Neurobiology*, **19**, 672–7.

Rustichini, A. (2015), 'The role of intelligence in economic decision making', *Current Opinion in Behavioral Sciences*, **5**, 32–6.

Simon, H.A. (1955), 'A behavioral model of rational choice', *Quarterly Journal of Economics*, **69** (1), 99–118.

Summers, L. (2013), 'IMF Economic Forum: Policy Responses to Crises', speech delivered at the IMF Annual Research Conference, 8 November.

Thaler, R.H. and S. Benartzi (2004), 'Save more tomorrow™: Using behavioral economics to increase employee saving', *Journal of Political Economy*, **112** (1, Part 2), S164–S187.

Vines, D. and S. Willis (2018), 'The rebuilding macroeconomic theory project: An analytical assessment', *Oxford Review of Economic Policy*, **34** (1–2), 1–42.

Visco, I. (2009), 'The financial crisis and economists' forecasts', *BIS Review*, no. 49.

PART 2

Finance from the viewpoint of psychology, banks, regulators and industry

# 10. The heuristics revolution: rethinking the role of uncertainty in finance

## Gerd Gigerenzer

Ants use heuristics to measure the area of a candidate nest cavity. Humans rely on elimination heuristics to choose a smartphone from hundreds of options. Animals, humans and machines may even use one and the same heuristic. The gaze heuristic is relied on by dogs to catch frisbees, by baseball outfielders to catch fly balls and by the Sidewinder air-to-air missile to intercept enemy planes (Hamlin, 2017). Scientific discovery has also been based on heuristics; the term appears in the title of Einstein's 1905 Nobel Prize winning paper on quantum physics.

The term *heuristic* is of Greek origin, meaning "serving to find out or discover". Heuristics and analysis are not contraries but instead tools for different problems. For the mathematician George Polya, heuristics are needed for finding a proof and analysis for checking it. The economist Frank Knight distinguished situations of risk, where probabilities are known by design or through long-run frequencies, from situations of uncertainty, where probabilities are not knowable. Jimmy Savage (1954), the "father" of Bayesian decision theory, limited the theory to problems where the full state space is known, such as when playing a lottery, and emphasized that it does not apply to situations where unexpected events may happen, such as planning a picnic (1954, p. 16). Finally, Herbert Simon introduced the term *satisficing* for decision making under uncertainty, where the assumptions of neoclassical economics do not hold.

In finance, however, the distinction between risk and uncertainty is rarely made. Following the portfolio allocation framework of Markowitz and Merton, the assumption is that problems can be treated as if they involved risk only. The behavioral finance revolution, as it is called, has not challenged this assumption; rather, it has largely accepted risk models as a universal norm and attributed deviating behavior to flaws in the human mind rather than in the risk model. In this chapter, I argue that finance might consider taking uncertainty and heuristics more seriously.

Specifically, I argue:

1.  *In situations of risk where the future state space is known, fine-tuned complex risk modeling is likely to succeed.* A state space is the exhaustive and mutually exclusive set of future states of the world, their consequences and their probabilities (Savage, 1954). Situations of risk do not require heuristics, except for saving time by attaining quick-and-dirty solutions.
2.  *In situations of uncertainty where the future state space is not known, fast and frugal heuristics are likely to succeed.* Under uncertainty, fine-tuned optimization models tend to be fragile, overfit noise and create illusions of certainty.

The aim of this chapter is to use some of the insights from the study of the ecological rationality of heuristics (for example, Gigerenzer et al., 2011; Gigerenzer and Selten, 2001a) to sketch a new framework for rethinking behavioral finance. This is not to say that fine-tuned models should be dispensed with, but that these should be understood as one tool in the toolbox, alongside heuristic tools. In reference to the "probabilistic revolution", I will call this program the "heuristics revolution" (Gigerenzer, 2014).

## THE PROBABILISTIC REVOLUTION

The probabilistic revolution differs from the scientific revolutions of Galileo, Darwin or Einstein. Unlike these, it did not revolutionize a specific discipline, but instead provided new intellectual tools – probability theory and statistics – that eventually transformed theories in many disciplines (Krüger et al., 1987). The probabilistic revolution replaced the determinism of Newtonian physics with the indeterminism of statistical mechanics and quantum mechanics while also revolutionizing genetics, evolutionary theory and scientific experimentation. The beginning of probability theory dates back to 1654, when the mathematicians Blaise Pascal and Pierre Fermat solved gambling problems. From the beginning, mathematical probability has had three interpretations: design, as of roulette tables; relative frequencies in the long run, as in mortality tables; and degrees of belief, as in the evaluation of eye witness testimony in court (Daston, 1988). Design and frequency became the definition of what Knight (1921) called "risk". Risk can be insured against, but not genuine uncertainty. Yet uncertainty, as opposed to risk, allows for profit. The probabilistic revolution also provided the mathematical tools for the central pillars of finance, such as the mean-variance model of Markowitz in the 1950s, the capital asset pricing model (CAPM) of the 1960s and the option theory of Black, Scholes and Merton. These tools have created an impressive body of theory tailored to situations of risk.

The problem with applying these tools to finance is that banks do not play roulette or lotteries; they act in an uncertain world. Under uncertainty, risk models can create illusions of certainty. For instance, in 2003, the distinguished macroeconomist Robert Lucas declared in his Presidential Address to the American Economic Association that economic theory had learned its lesson from the Great Depression and succeeded in protecting us from future disaster: "Its central problem of depression-prevention has been solved, for all practical purposes, and has in fact been solved for many decades" (Lucas, 2003, p. 1). Four years later, the precision of modern economic theory proved to be an illusion.

Behavioral finance emerged with the intention of eliminating the psychological blind spot in finance but ended up portraying psychology as the source of irrationality. Although it could have extended the risk models and systematically studied how people *should* make decisions under uncertainty, the dominant version did not. Rather, it mostly took risk models, or *Homo economicus*, as the benchmark for rational decisions and attributed deviations to shortcomings in people rather than in models. The result is a large catalogue of anomalies and cognitive biases (Thaler, 2015). These biases have attained the status of truisms, ignoring psychological research that cautions against this overly negative view of human nature. For example, what has been called gambler's fallacy, the hot-hand fallacy, overconfidence and framing errors have been shown to reflect realistic judgments, except under very specific situations (for example, Gigerenzer, 2015; Hahn and Warren, 2009; Miller and Sanjuro, 2018; Mousavi and Gigerenzer, 2011).

In the wake of designing ever more sophisticated mathematical models that assume risk, curiosity about how successful investors actually make decisions has been lost. As Soros (2008) put it,

> I contend that rational expectations theory totally misinterprets how financial markets operate. Although rational expectations theory is no longer taken seriously outside academic circles, the idea that financial markets are self-correcting and tend towards equilibrium remains the prevailing paradigm. [. . .] I contend that the prevailing paradigm is false and urgently needs to be replaced. (p. 6)

Behavioral finance would have gone in a very different direction had it followed Herbert Simon's lead to take uncertainty seriously, take heuristics seriously and study the heuristics that help make good decisions under uncertainty.

## THE HEURISTICS REVOLUTION

Like the probabilistic revolution, the heuristics revolution is not specific to a discipline but provides intellectual tools. The heuristics revolution complements the probabilistic revolution in three ways:

1. takes uncertainty seriously rather than generally assuming risk;
2. studies the heuristics in individuals' and organizations' toolbox of strategies; and
3. studies the ecological rationality of heuristics, that is, the environmental conditions under which heuristics can be expected to outperform more complex strategies.

### Taking Uncertainty Seriously

The former governor of the Bank of England, Mervin King, once said: "If only banks were playing in a casino, then we probably could calculate approximate risk weights."[1] So true. But even a casino has to face uncertainty. Taleb (2007) describes how the management of a Las Vegas casino handled their core business risk. They calculated gambling odds, diversified risk across tables and countered cheating. Nevertheless, they experienced their main losses outside these situations of risk. The worst loss occurred when their star artist, performing his famous tiger act, was attacked by the tiger. The second-worst loss occurred when a disgruntled former contractor tried to dynamite the casino. Next, a clerical employee failed to file tax reports over a long period, exposing the casino to a major fine and almost losing its license. Finally, the daughter of the owner was kidnapped and the owner violated gambling laws by using casino money to pay her ransom.

To an even greater extent than the world of a casino, the world of finance is largely one of uncertainty. Under uncertainty, fine-tuned risk models lead to overactive policy and modeling noise. In his Nobel lecture "The pretense of knowledge", Hayek (1974) spoke about the perils of assuming omniscience. Friedman (1960) proposed a k-percent policy heuristic in the absence of certainty and Simon (1989) called for a systematic study of how people make decisions when the assumptions of neoclassical theory are not met. Despite these calls, we do not yet have such a theory of finance under uncertainty.

---

[1]    http://www.bbc.co.uk/news/business-11624994.

## The Study of the Adaptive Toolbox

The adaptive toolbox of an individual or institution is the repertoire of heuristics at their disposal. The study of the adaptive toolbox is descriptive (as opposed to the prescriptive study of ecological rationality; see below) and models the heuristics people use, including their building blocks. Building blocks of heuristics include rules for how to search for information, when to stop searching and how to make a final choice. Recombining the building blocks enables heuristics to be adapted to new problems (Gigerenzer and Gaissmaier, 2011). In general, a heuristic is a strategy that uses only limited information, with the goal of making decisions faster, more frugal, more robust, more transparent and more accurate than would be the case with fine-tuned complex strategies. Consider a simple example.

One of the theoretical pillars of modern finance theory is the mean-variance optimization portfolio by Harry Markowitz. When Markowitz made his own investments for the time after his retirement, one would assume that he used his mean-variance method. What he did, however, was to rely on a fast and frugal heuristic known as the 1/N rule: invest your money equally across the N options. If N = 2, this means a 50:50 allocation, and so on. From the point of view of behavioral finance, 1/N is a behavioral bias, the so-called naïve diversification bias, which is attributed to people's cognitive limitations. This attribution clearly would not apply to Markowitz. DeMiguel et al. (2009) tested 1/N against the mean-variance method and reported that 1/N outperformed it in six out of seven allocation problems, as measured by the Sharpe ratio and other criteria. Under uncertainty, the asset weights for the mean-variance portfolio tend to be unstable over time and perform poorly out of sample. Moreover, none of a dozen more sophisticated allocation methods, such as Bayesian models and minimum variance with various constraints, could consistently outperform 1/N. The authors calculated that for N = 50, one would need 500 years of data before mean-variance might surpass the simple heuristic. Even this calculation requires the future to resemble the past, assuming that the same stocks – and the stock market itself – are still around in the year 2500. Thus, the real question is: can we identify the conditions under which heuristics such as 1/N can be expected to outperform more complex strategies? This challenge is the focus of the study of the ecological rationality of heuristics.

## The Study of Ecological Rationality

The study of ecological rationality is a normative discipline. Its results are conditions under which the performance of heuristics is expected to exceed that of more complex methods, and vice versa. Its tools are proof, computer simulation and principles of methodology.

**Methodological principles**
The study of ecological rationality is based on three principles:

1.  formal models of heuristics;
2.  competitive testing of heuristics against strong competitors; and
3.  testing of predictive accuracy instead of data fitting.

There is room for these principles in current behavioral finance and economics. First, the heuristics proposed to date are mostly vague labels rather than formal models. Prominent examples are the availability heuristic, representativeness, and the affect heuristic. These labels cannot predict behavior, but only "explain" almost every behavior after the fact. For instance, the meaning of *availability* is constantly changed in the literature, from ease of recall to the number of instances recalled to the vividness of instances recalled, and so on, even though these are not the same psychological processes and appear not even to be correlated (Sedlmeier et al., 1998). In contrast, heuristics such as 1/N, fast-and-frugal trees or the recognition heuristic make predictions that can be tested. Second, formal models of heuristics need to be tested against the strongest competitors in a field, such as machine learning algorithms (Brighton and Gigerenzer, 2015). Finally, prediction means that performance is evaluated in foresight (out-of-sample or out-of-population) rather than in hindsight by fitting parameters to known data. For Friedman (1953), prediction is the goal of economic models, not realism of assumptions. This maxim cautions against models with many free parameters, which can easily achieve a better fit than simpler models, whereas the simple models may achieve better prediction.

**Why less can be more**
A formal way to understand when and why heuristics can predict better than complex models with more free parameters is the bias-variance dilemma from machine learning (Brighton and Gigerenzer, 2015; Geman et al., 1992). Consider the problem of estimating the true value $\mu$ in a population on the basis of random samples. Each of $S$ samples ($s = 1, \ldots, S$) generates an estimate $x_s$. The variability of these estimates $x_s$ around their mean $\bar{x}$, which is called *variance* in machine learning, is another source of prediction error. The variance component reflects the sensitivity of the predictions to different samples drawn from the same population. Thus, the prediction error (the sum of squared error) can be captured in the equation:

$$\text{Prediction error} = \text{bias}^2 + \text{variance} + \varepsilon,$$

where bias $= \bar{x} - \mu$, that is, the average deviation of the mean of the sample estimates from the true value, and variance $= 1/s \, \Sigma(x_s - \bar{x})^2$, that is, the mean squared deviation of the sample estimates from their mean $\bar{x}$.

The term "bias-variance dilemma" refers to the empirical fact that by reducing bias one typically increases variance, and vice versa. For instance, one can reduce bias by adding free parameters, but this is likely to increase error due to variance. Or one can reduce variance by deleting free parameters, but that is likely to increase error due to bias.

Let us apply the bias-variance dilemma to understand the conditions under which 1/N can outperform mean-variance. The mean-variance method has both bias and variance as sources of error. Bias means that its modeling assumptions deviate from the unknown true state. Variance is the key factor in why its estimates are empirically unstable, because of overly fine-tuning from historical samples, where small changes in the estimated asset returns or correlations can have large effects on the estimates. In contrast, 1/N has no free parameters, that is, its allocation is not sensitive to the peculiarities of samples. Thus, 1/N has zero error due to variance. Yet this comes at the price that it is likely to have a larger bias than mean-variance.

Therefore, the question is whether the squared bias of the heuristic is larger than the sum of the squared bias and the variance of the mean-variance portfolio. The size of the bias can only be known if the true value is known. However, we know that the sample size and number of free parameters (which is a function of N) influence variance. This leads to the hypothesis that the smaller the sample size and the larger the number N of assets, the greater the advantage of 1/N over mean variance.

Note that the bias-variance analysis assumes repeated sampling from a stable population and thus represents only a minimal form of uncertainty due to sampling error. In contrast, the situation in investment rarely corresponds to sampling from a stable population, which means that other factors besides sample size and number of assets will determine whether the heuristic or mean-variance can be expected to lead to better returns. There are studies that report that 1/N is superior to complex methods and others that report the opposite. Typically, the debate is about whether the heuristic or the complex methods are better. That is the wrong question. The actual question concerns ecological rationality: what is the set of conditions under which we can expect 1/N to outperform mean-variance or similar fine-tuning methods, and what are the conditions under which we can expect fine-tuning to pay?

In sum, heuristics are reasonable tools for making decisions under uncertainty and not mental quirks, as often portrayed in behavioral economics and behavioral finance. In what follows, I sketch out a systematic program for analyzing heuristics in finance in three areas of application: financial literacy of the general public, professional investment and design of regulatory rules.

## FINANCIAL LITERACY FOR THE GENERAL PUBLIC

Literacy is the ability to read and write. Financial literacy is the ability to manage personal finances. In the Western world, we have taught almost everyone reading and writing, but not financial literacy. The Jump$tart Survey administered every two years to 12th-grade students demonstrates the lack of progress made in the US. Similarly, a representative study in Germany showed that 18 to 84-year-olds could correctly answer, on average, only 59 percent of questions measuring "minimal economic knowledge". People with a college or university degree performed 10 percentage points better than those without, readers of serious newspapers also performed 10 points better than readers of the yellow press and men 8 points better than women (Wobker et al., 2014). For every hour per day a person watched TV, his or her score dropped by 1.5 points. Most alarmingly, people who said they had taken an economics course performed no better than those who hadn't. Similar lack of financial literacy has been documented worldwide, and I will not attempt to provide an overview here (see Drexler et al., 2014).

But knowledge is not enough. In Germany, two-thirds of adults know that stocks and bonds result in higher returns yet prefer to invest their money in savings accounts and insurances (Ergo, 2018). Few studies have analyzed what people actually do when they invest. A study with customers in Italian cooperative banks is an exception. Cooperative banks are non-profit institutions whose aim is to support the economic development of people living in the area.

### What do Bank Customers Think about Risk?

Ninety-nine active bank customers at an Italian cooperative bank who had investments of at least 40000 euros were asked to list three associations that came to mind when they thought about risk (Monti et al., 2011). The most prevalent associations, in the order of their frequency, were: "loss", "equities", "investment", "fear", "attention: danger!", "Argentinian bonds", "bankruptcy", "negative" and "avoid".

Most of these associations were emotionally negative, and none corresponded to economic definitions of financial risk such as volatility. The advisors of the customers reported that it was very difficult to help them arrive at an appropriate understanding. Customers were also asked how highly they trusted the nation's bank system. On an 11-point Likert scale, with 11 indicating high trust, the majority of customers responded with 3 to 5 (Monti et al., 2014). That is, customers were fairly distrustful of the banking industry. Given this distrust, one might think that customers would take time to learn how to protect their money. However, more than 40 percent of the customers said that they spend less than one hour a month on thinking about their investments and insurances, despite (or because of) their lack of basic financial literacy.

## How do Bank Customers Invest?

How do bank customers make investment decisions given that they lack financial literacy, perceive risk-taking negatively, lack trust in the nation's banking system and spend little time thinking about how to invest? The answer is: they trust their personal advisor. The vast majority of the customers gave trust scores of 8 to 10 for their financial advisor, compared to only 3 to 5 for the nation's banking system (Monti et al., 2014). The average customer proceeds roughly in this way:

- *Step 1: Check trustworthiness.* Customers first check whether they can trust a financial advisor. This decision is made by social signals alone, not by matter-of-fact questions that test the advisor's competence. Psychological research suggests that in the absence of financial literacy, trust is inferred from interaction cues such as whether the advisor listens, smiles, nods and maintains eye contact. If these cues are in place, the customer finds the advisor trustworthy.
- *Step 2: Delegate decision.* If Step 1 results in trust, then customers delegate the decision about their investment to the advisor. As a result, the vast majority of bank customers do not play an active role in the management of their money. A common request is: "Please help me make this decision as if I were your mother (father)".
- *Step 3: Go with what you know and avoid risk.* If advisors suggest more than one option to invest in, customers rely on two elimination criteria to choose the final investment. The first is name recognition: investments from companies whose name the customer recognizes are preferred; others tend to be eliminated. The second criterion is risk: if an investment is said to have low risk, this is preferred; if it

is said to have moderate or high risk, it is likely eliminated (Monti et al., 2012).

The typical Italian bank customer is woefully unprepared to make an informed decision. The same appears to hold in most countries. There is also a striking similarity between financial and medical decision-making. As surveys have documented, few European citizens are health literate (Gigerenzer et al., 2009; Mata et al., 2014). In this situation, most patients go through Steps 1 and 2 outlined above and rely on the *white-coat heuristic*, that is, trust their doctor (Wegwarth and Gigerenzer, 2013). Step 3, in contrast, is specific to bank customers. Lack of health literacy exposes people to health risks, such as by not vaccinating children against MMR or exposing them to unnecessary CT scans with high doses of radiation. Lack of financial literacy exposes people to becoming victims of fraudulent activities, as the subprime crisis showed, which dealt with largely inexperienced and uninformed customers.

**Financial Heuristics for the General Public**

What can be done to improve the situation? Governments and non-governmental organizations across the world have begun to teach financial literacy. The operational definition of financial literacy in most programs is "knowledge of financial concepts and facts" such as compound interest, stocks and bonds, and product attributes. The problem we have to face is that these interventions to improve financial literacy explain only 0.1 percent of the variance in financial behavior, as a meta-analysis of 201 studies concluded (Fernandes et al., 2014). Larger effects reported in correlational studies appear to be due to lack of control of intervening factors. This result is consistent with the previously reported fact that economic courses did not improve minimal economic knowledge in Germany (Wobker et al., 2014). Is there an alternative to teaching facts?

I propose teaching not just financial concepts but heuristics. Financial heuristics are rules that specify what to do in a given situation. 1/N is an example, as is "invest 1/3 in stocks, 1/3 in bonds, and 1/3 in real estate" or "don't buy financial products you don't understand". Had the latter rule been observed before 2007 by everyone on both sides of the Atlantic, the financial crisis would probably not have happened on such a large scale. Teaching heuristics means teaching behavior, and it should be taught "just-in-time", that is, at a time when the behavior is relevant to an individual.

In a randomized study with more than 1000 micro-entrepreneurs in the Dominican Republic, one group received standard accounting training, a second training in financial heuristics and a third group served as control

(Drexler et al., 2014). The classes were offered in a weekly three-hour session for a period of five to six weeks. For example, the standard accounting training taught the participants how to separate business and personal accounts by calculating profits based on a typical accounting curriculum. In contrast, the heuristics training taught a concrete physical rule: to keep their money in two separate drawers or purses and only transfer money with an explicit IOU ("I owe you"). The authors reported that the accounting training failed to improve financial practices, while the heuristics training led to better practices: its participants were more likely to keep accounting records, calculate monthly revenues and separate their business and personal books. In addition, objective reporting quality improved and errors were reduced. Similarly, Shefrin and Nicols (2014) describe fast and frugal heuristics that help consumers make effective budgeting decisions when using credit cards.

We need a research program that systematically studies which heuristics are useful for the general public and which teaching methods can successfully add these heuristics to people's adaptive toolbox. Finally, we need to find out how to teach individuals about the ecological rationality of heuristics, that is, in what situation to use what heuristic.

## Financial Literacy versus Nudging

Teaching heuristics aims at making people competent and self-reliant. In contrast, the program of "nudging" relies on methods from marketing and advertising to steer people into behavior that is deemed desirable by government authorities (Thaler and Sunstein, 2008). This program of "libertarian paternalism" is based on the claim that because people have systematic cognitive biases that lead to harmful decisions and can hardly be educated out of these biases, governments should step in and steer people toward their own good. The claim that people can hardly learn how to deal with risk and uncertainty, however, is incorrect. Experiments have shown that people can learn quickly if they are taught in an adequate way (Bond, 2009; Gigerenzer, 2015). For instance, people are said to fall prey to the base rate fallacy, which means ignoring base rate information when making Bayesian-type inferences (Kahneman, 2011; Thaler and Sunstein, 2008). In contrast, psychological research has shown that people can learn in less than two hours to make correct Bayesian inferences (Sedlmeier and Gigerenzer, 2001) and even fourth-graders can reason the Bayesian way (Zhu and Gigerenzer, 2006). Nudging may be an effective short-term solution, but in the long term, it will not teach people to manage their personal finances, leaving them instead in the same state of ignorance as that of the Italian bank customers described above. Moreover, nudging may serve as an excuse for not protecting consumers from industry that markets unhealthy products. The House of Lords (2011) criticized the British government for nudging citizens rather than considering more efficient options such as prohibiting television advertising of products high in sugar, salt and fat.

A few centuries ago it was said that ordinary people would never learn to read and write. When finally schooling became mandatory for every child, as in many countries across the world, this assumption proved to be wrong. Today, it is said that the general public might never learn to take care of their personal finances. We need to repeat the same experiment, this time for financial literacy, with everyone, in school and beyond.

## HEURISTICS FOR INVESTMENT

Traders have always used trading rules that resemble heuristics, going back to the pioneers of "technical analysis" (Forbes et al., 2015; Lo and Hasanhodzic, 2010). A source for heuristics is Graham's *The Intelligent Investor* (1973 [2003]), which Warren Buffet praises as "by far the best book on investing ever written" (p. ix). Haug and Taleb (2011) argue that option traders use heuristics, not the Black–Scholes–Merton formula: "Option traders use (and evidently have used since 1902) sophisticated heuristics and tricks more compatible with the previous version of the formula of Louis Bachelier and Edward O. Thorp" (p. 1). For traders, hedging, pricing and trading are an extremely rich craft based on heuristics, with traders learning from traders or by copying successful traders. In the absence of probability theory, such rules have often been dismissed by academics. Finance theory has to some extent lost its curiosity about what successful investors actually do and instead teaches risk models that traders should allegedly use, thereby "lecturing birds how to fly" (Haug and Taleb, 2011).

Overviews on heuristics in business can be found in Gigerenzer et al. (2011) and Gigerenzer and Gaissmaier (2011). Here, I will illustrate professional decision making with a single class of heuristics: satisficing. Satisficing applies to situations where one has to choose one option among many, and where the state space is unknown or unknowable.

*Satisficing*: Set an aspiration level $\alpha$, and invest in the first object that meets $\alpha$.

Consider investment decisions in the real estate business. Berg (2014) studied entrepreneurs in the Dallas–Fort Worth greater metropolitan area who need to decide in which location to invest, that is, where to develop a commercial high-rise or a residential area. He reports that every single one of the 49 professionals relied on a version of the above satisficing heuristic:

If I believe I can get at least $x$ return within $y$ years, then I take the option.

The time horizon $y$ was typically one to three years, and $x$ a *prominent* number. Prominent numbers are powers of 10, their halves, and their doubles (that is, 1, 2, 5, 10, 20, 50, . . .). For instance, convenience store and gas station investors required at least 10 percent annual return on capital within one or two years. Most of the entrepreneurs considered only one, two or three options; not a single one tried to determine the point at which the marginal benefit of search equals its costs. Many expressed skepticism that such calculations could be made in one-off decisions in high-stakes and quickly changing environments.

Every heuristic can be adapted if it does not work. In the case of satisficing, the aspiration level can be adapted:

*Satisficing with aspiration level adaptation*: Set an aspiration level $\alpha$ and invest in the first object that meets $\alpha$. If no object meets $\alpha$ within time $\beta$, then lower alpha by $\gamma$ and start again.

A study of 628 BMW dealers offering 328 000 used cars showed that 97 percent of the dealers priced their used cars with aspiration-level adaptation, including 19 percent that relied on satisficing without adaptation (Artinger and Gigerenzer, 2016). The most frequent version was to set an initial price in the middle of the price range of similar cars, to keep the price constant for about four weeks and, if the car is not sold, then lower the price by 2 to 3 percent. Dealers adapted their choice of parameter values to the characteristics of the environment in which the dealership is located. Consider the duration $\beta$. With every additional competing dealer in the region, the duration the price was kept constant decreased by about 3 percent. For every 1000 euros in GDP per capita in the region, $\beta$ increased by 1 percent. There was no fine-tuning of prices to market conditions during the observation period, despite drastic changes of up to 50 percent in supply. Randomizing prices was also absent. A comparison with the best "mixed strategy" pricing model showed that the aspiration-level heuristics made substantially higher profit, in fact more than doubling the profit. Even the simple constant price satisficing strategy was superior.

Satisficing also provides a realistic alternative to the concept of "net present value" (Magni, 2009). To determine the net present value of a project or option, it needs to be compared to the return rate $r$ of the next-best option available, which is known as the opportunity cost of capital. That is, by investing in a project, one forgoes the opportunity to earn a rate of return on one's capital. Trying to maximize the net present value is an impossible task in many investment decisions, given the usually enormous number of options and ways to produce a given commodity, which rules out exhaustive search across all possibilities.

The satisficing rule replaces the return $r$ of the next-best option with the aspiration level $\alpha$. This spares the investor from wasting time on solving a task that is, by definition, not solvable under uncertainty. By satisficing, knowing and evaluating all future options are no longer necessary.

Besides satisficing, numerous other investment heuristics have been documented, some of which have been put to competitive testing in prediction. For instance, Peter Lynch (1994) suggested that a lack of name recognition is grounds for eliminating a stock from consideration. This rule is a version of the recognition heuristic "invest only in stocks you have heard of". The heuristic is ecologically rational if there is a relationship between recognition, market share and profitability of companies. Borges et al. (1999) tested the recognition heuristic with laypeople and business students in Chicago and Munich, measuring their recognition of hundreds of American and German stocks. Then they created eight "recognition portfolios", that is, portfolios containing the most recognized stocks (laypersons vs. students; Americans vs. Germans; US stocks vs. German stocks). The recognition portfolios outperformed randomly chosen portfolios, the Dow and Dax, the American Fidelity Blue Chip Growth Fund and the German Hypobank Investment Capital Fund. The recognition portfolios also outperformed control portfolios with the most unrecognized stocks. Ortmann et al. (2008) report similar results for a bear market (but see Boyd, 2001). The conditions under which the recognition heuristic can succeed are generally known (Goldstein and Gigerenzer, 2002), but no such analysis exists for financial investment.

In sum: under uncertainty, investors rely on satisficing and a rich repertoire of other heuristics. Finance can profit from extending its scope from risk models to uncertainty and to the study of the ecological rationality of heuristics under these conditions.

## COMPLEX OR SIMPLE REGULATION?

Although the Federal Reserve in Washington DC hosts some 300 PhD economists, they did not foresee the subprime crisis. Financial regulation, as embodied in Basel II and III, relies on complex models such as value at risk (VaR). To compute its value at risk, a large bank may have to estimate thousands of risk factors and, because these are dependent, additionally estimate the matrix of millions of correlations. Such a procedure might increase safety in a casino, but there is no evidence that it has done the same in the uncertain world of banking. For financial regulation, it may in fact have the opposite effect. Complex risk estimation increases the opportunities for gaming the system and creates new opportunities for excessive risk taking while following the rules. For instance, the requirement of estimating millions of risk factors offers many degrees of freedom and, by using internal models, banks can reduce their capital by picking the "right" estimates.

Complexity breeds complexity. When complex regulations fail, the idea is to make them more complex. The Basel Accord of 1988, the first genuinely international prudent regulatory agreement, was only 30 pages long. Basel II, agreed on in 2004, came in at 347 pages. A few years later the financial crisis hit. The revised framework from 2010, Basel III had grown to 616 pages.

Against this background, Andy Haldane, then Executive Director of Financial Stability of the Bank of England, gave a noteworthy Jackson Hole speech in 2012, entitled "The dog and the frisbee" (Haldane and Madouros, 2012). The title referred to the gaze heuristic, used by dogs to catch frisbees and baseball outfielders to catch fly balls (Gigerenzer and Selten, 2001b). Haldane began systematically to study the potential of heuristics in regulation in a collaborative project between the Bank of England and the Max Planck Institute for Human Development (Aikman et al., 2014). This research indicates that simple methods can dominate more complex modeling approaches for calculating banks' capital requirements, especially when data is limited and with fat-tailed distributions. It also showed that simple leverage ratios outperformed risk-weighted metrics in predicting individual bank failure in a sample of 100 large global banks at the end of 2006. Finally, fast-and-frugal trees – robust trees that rely on only a few indicators – can provide transparent alternatives to information-intensive regression techniques and are easier to communicate. Under conditions that are not yet understood, fast-and-frugal trees can be even better at prediction than the most sophisticated tools of machine learning (Katsikopoulos et al., 2017). The bias-variance dilemma provides a first approximation to understand why this is so.

In his 2005 Mais Lecture, Mervyn King, then governor of the Bank of England, made a similar case for using fast-and-frugal heuristics in central banking. Specifically, he suggests heuristics for setting interest rates and controlling inflation, depending on environmental conditions such as whether or not the economy has been hit by a large shock. The proposal to simplify the regulatory framework, however, requires a philosophical shift in regulators' thinking. In financial regulation, less may be more.

A systematic study of heuristics for regulation would also need to deal with the moral hazard problem. Taleb and Sandis (2013) describe the "skin in the game" heuristic for protection against tail events. They propose that everyone who makes financial decisions should have his or her own money in the game. J.P. Morgan, the preeminent financier of his time, operated his firm as a partnership with unlimited liability, which meant that with every deal, Morgan put his own personal wealth on the line (Dowd et al., 2011). This liability changes the focus from short-term to long-term profitability, reduces extensive risk taking to careful risk taking and makes gaming the system to get away with inadequate capital largely pointless. Personal liability can also reduce the practice of hiding risks in off-balance sheet vehicles that mask the true leverage ratio of banks. More generally, skin in the game can be considered as a heuristic for a safer and more just society. Implementing "skin in the game" together with other heuristics (Taleb, 2015) would be a promising move toward a safer world of finance. It also would free banks of much of the complicated paperwork, stress testing and supervision.

## TOWARD A SYSTEMATIC STUDY OF HEURISTICS IN FINANCE

Herbert Simon left us with an unfinished task: a theory of decision making under uncertainty. Such a theory should make two contributions. First, it should describe how individuals and institutions actually make decisions. This entails going beyond "as-if" theories of expected utility maximization. Second, the theory should be able to deal with situations of uncertainty where "the conditions for rationality postulated by the model of neoclassical economics are not met" (Simon, 1989, p. 377). In other words, it should extend beyond risk to realistic situations where the future state space is not knowable.

The world of finance is a prime candidate for Simon's program. This chapter provides only a sketch of how we could get there. This sketch can be worked out in more concrete detail. And it may help in rethinking the nature of behavioral finance.

# REFERENCES

Aikman, D., Galesic, M., Gigerenzer, G., Kapadia, S., Katsikopoulos, K.V., Kothiyal, A., Murphy, E. et al. (2014), 'Taking uncertainty seriously: Simplicity versus complexity in financial regulation', Bank of England Financial Stability Paper, No. 28, London: Bank of England.

Artinger, F.M. and Gigerenzer, G. (2016), 'The cheap twin: From the ecological rationality of heuristic pricing to the aggregate market', in J. Humphreys (ed.), *Proceedings of the Seventy-sixth Annual Meeting of the Academy of Management*, online ISSN: 2151-6561.

Berg, N. (2014), 'Success from satisficing and imitation: Entrepreneurs' location choice and implications of heuristics for local economic development', *Journal of Business Research*, **67**, 1700–709.

Bond, M. (2009), 'Risk school', *Nature*, **461**, 1189–92.

Borges, B., Goldstein, D.G., Ortmann, A. and Gigerenzer, G. (1999), 'Can ignorance beat the stock market?', in G. Gigerenzer, P.M. Todd and the ABC Research Group, *Simple Heuristics That Make Us Smart*, New York, NY: Oxford University Press, pp. 59–72.

Boyd, M. (2001), 'On ignorance, intuition and investing: A bear market test of the recognition heuristic', *Journal of Psychology and Financial Markets*, **2**, 150–56.

Brighton, H. and Gigerenzer, G. (2015), 'The bias bias', *Journal of Business Research*, **68**, 1772–84.

Daston, L. (1988), *Classical Probability in the Enlightenment*, Princeton, NJ: Princeton University Press.

DeMiguel, V., Garlappi, L. and Uppal, R. (2009), 'Optimal versus naive diversification: How inefficient is the 1/N portfolio strategy?', *Review of Financial Studies*, **22**, 1915–53.

Dowd, K., Hutchinson, M., Ashby, S. and Hinchcliffe, J.M. (2011), 'Capital inadequacies: The dismal failure of the Basel regime of bank capital regulation', *Policy Analysis*, **681**, 1–38.

Drexler, A., Fischer, G. and Schoar, A. (2014), 'Keeping it simple: Financial literacy and rules of thumb', *American Economic Journal: Applied Economics*, **6**, 1–31.

Ergo (2018), *Ergo Risiko-Report 2018: Über die Risikokompetenz und Eigenverantwortung der Deutschen.* Accessed at https://www.risikoreport.de/assets/files/ergo-risiko-report.pdf.

Fernandes, D., Lynch, J.G. Jr, and Netemeyer, R.G. (2014), 'Financial literacy, financial education, and downstream financial behaviors', *Management Science*, **60**, 1861–83.

Forbes, W., Hudson, R., Skerratt, L. and Soufian, M. (2015), 'Which heuristics can aid financial decision-making?', *International Review of Financial Analysis*, **42**, 199–210.

Friedman, M. (1953), *Essays in Positive Economics*, Chicago, IL: University of Chicago Press.

Friedman, M. (1960), *A Program for Monetary Stability*, New York, NY: Fordham University Press.

Geman, S., Bienenstock, E. and Doursat, R. (1992), 'Neural networks and the bias/variance dilemma', *Neural Computation*, **4**, 1–58.

Gigerenzer, G. (2014), *Risk Savvy: How to Make Good Decisions*, New York, NY: Viking.

Gigerenzer, G. (2015), 'On the supposed evidence for libertarian paternalism', *Review of Philosophy and Psychology*, **6**, 363–83.

Gigerenzer, G. and Gaissmaier, W. (2011), 'Heuristic decision making', *Annual Review of Psychology*, **62**, 451–82.

Gigerenzer, G., and Selten, R. (eds) (2001a), *Bounded Rationality: The Adaptive Toolbox*, Cambridge, MA: MIT Press.

Gigerenzer, G. and Selten, R. (2001b), 'Rethinking rationality', in G. Gigerenzer and R. Selten (eds), *Bounded Rationality: The Adaptive Toolbox*, Cambridge, MA: MIT Press, pp. 1–12.

Gigerenzer, G., Hertwig, R. and Pachur, T. (eds) (2011), *Heuristics: The Foundations of Adaptive Behavior*, New York, NY: Oxford University Press.

Gigerenzer, G., Mata, J. and Frank, R. (2009), 'Public knowledge of benefits of breast and prostate cancer screening in Europe', *Journal of the National Cancer Institute*, **101**, 1216–20.

Goldstein, D.G. and Gigerenzer, G. (2002), 'Models of ecological rationality: The recognition heuristic', *Psychological Review*, **109**, 75–90.

Graham, B. (1973 [2003]), *The Intelligent Investor* (revised edn), New York, NY: HarperBusiness Essentials.

Hahn, U. and Warren, P.A. (2009), 'Perceptions of randomness: Why three heads are better than four', *Psychological Review*, **116**, 454–61.

Haldane, A.G. and Madouros, V. (2012), 'The dog and the frisbee', 31 August, accessed at https://econpapers.repec.org/article/fipfedkpr, pp. 109–59.

Hamlin, R.P. (2017), '"The gaze heuristic:" Biography of an adaptively rational decision process', *Topics in Cognitive Science*, **9**, 264–88.

Haug, E.G. and Taleb, N.N. (2011), 'Option traders use (very) sophisticated heuristics, never the Black–Scholes–Merton formula', unpublished manuscript.

Hayek, F.A. (1974), 'The pretense of knowledge', Nobel Prize Lecture, accessed 12 April 2018 at https://www.nobelprize.org/nobel_prizes/economic-sciences/laureates/1974/hayek-lecture.html.

House of Lords: Science and Technology Select Committee (2011), *2nd Report of Session 2010–12: Behaviour Change*, London: Authority of the House of Lords.

Kahneman, D. (2011), *Thinking, Fast and Slow*, London: Allen Lane.

Katsikopoulos, K.V., Durbach, I.N. and Stewart, T.J. (2017), 'When should we use simple decision models? A synthesis of various research strands', *Omega*, advance online publication.

King, M. (2005), 'Monetary policy: Practice ahead of theory. The Mais Lecture 2005: Speech by the Governor', *Bank of England Quarterly Bulletin*, Summer, accessed at SSRN: https://ssrn.com/abstract=753989.

Knight, F.H. (1921), *Risk, Uncertainty and Profit*, Boston, MA: Houghton-Mifflin.

Krüger, L., Gigerenzer, G. and Morgan, M. (eds) (1987), *The Probabilistic Revolution: Vol. 2. Ideas in the Sciences*, Cambridge, MA: MIT Press.

Lo, A. and Hasanhodzic, J. (2010), *The Evolution of Technical Analysis*, Chichester: Wiley.

Lucas, R.E. (2003), 'Macroeconomic priorities', *American Economic Review*, **93**, 1–14.

Lynch, P. (1994), *Beating the Street*, New York, NY: Simon & Schuster.

Magni, C.A. (2009), 'Investment decisions, net present value and bounded rationality', *Quantitative Finance*, **9**, 967–79.

Mata, J., Frank, R. and Gigerenzer, G. (2014), 'Symptom recognition of heart attack and stroke in nine European countries: A representative study', *Health Expectations*, **17**, 376–87.

Miller, J.B. and Sanjuro, A. (2018), 'Surprised by the gambler's and hot hand fallacies? A truth in the law of small numbers', *Econometrica*, forthcoming.

Monti, M., Boero, R., Berg, N., Gigerenzer, G. and Martignon, L. (2012), 'How do common investors behave? Information search and portfolio choice among bank customers and university students', *Mind & Society*, **11**, 203–33.

Monti, M., Martignon, L., Pelligra, V. and Guglielmetti, C. (2011), 'The insurance by my side: Better risk assessment for smarter insurance decisions', CAREFIN Working Paper No. 3/2011, Milan: Universita Bocconi.

Monti, M., Pelligra, V., Martignon, L. and Berg, N. (2014), 'Retail investors and financial advisors: New evidence on trust and advice taking heuristics', *Journal of Business Research*, **67**, 1749–57.

Mousavi, S. and Gigerenzer, G. (2011), 'Revisiting the "error" in studies of cognitive errors', in D.A. Hofmann and M. Frese (eds), *Error in Organizations*, New York, NY: Taylor & Francis, pp. 97–112.

Ortmann, A., Gigerenzer, G., Borges, B. and Goldstein, D.G. (2008), 'The recognition heuristic: A fast and frugal way to investment choice?', in C.R. Plott and V.L. Smith (eds), *Handbook of Experimental Economics Results: Vol. 1 (Handbooks in Economics No. 28)*, Amsterdam: North-Holland, pp. 993–1003.

Savage, L.J. (1954), *The Foundations of Statistics*, New York, NY: Wiley.

Sedlmeier, P. and Gigerenzer, G. (2001), 'Teaching Bayesian reasoning in less than two hours', *Journal of Experimental Psychology: General*, **130**, 380–400.

Sedlmeier, P., Hertwig, R. and Gigerenzer, G. (1998), 'Are judgments of the positional frequencies of letters systematically biased due to availability?', *Journal of Experimental Psychology: Learning, Memory, and Cognition*, **24**, 754–70.

Shefrin, H. and Nicols, C.M. (2014), 'Credit card behavior, financial styles and heuristics', *Journal of Business Research*, **67**, 1679–87.

Simon, H.A. (1989), 'The scientist as problem solver', in D. Klahr and K. Kotovsky (eds), *Complex Information Processing: The Impact of Herbert A. Simon*, Hillsdale, NJ: Erlbaum, pp. 375–98.

Soros, G. (2008), *The Crash of 2008 and What it Means*, New York, NY: Public Affairs.

Taleb, N.N. (2007), *The Black Swan: The Impact of the Highly Improbable*, New York, NY: Random House.

Taleb, N.N. (2015), 'Ten principles for a Black Swan-proof world', *Financial Times*, 8 January, accessed 9 April 2018 at http://www.ft.com/cms/s/0/5d5aa24e-23a4-11de-996a-00144feabdc0.html#axzz3ODQQN9bc.

Taleb, N.N. and Sandis, C. (2013), 'The Skin In The Game heuristic for protection against tail events', *Review of Behavioral Economics*, **1**(1), 115–35.

Thaler, R. (2015), *Misbehaving: The Making of Behavioral Economics*, New York, NY: Norton.

Thaler, R.H. and Sunstein, C.R. (2008), *Nudge: Improving Decisions About Health, Wealth, and Happiness*, New Haven, CT: Yale University Press.

Wegwarth, O. and Gigerenzer, G. (2013), 'Trust-your-doctor: A simple heuristic in need of a proper social environment', in R. Hertwig, U. Hoffrage and the ABC Research Group, *Simple Heuristics in a Social World*, New York, NY: Oxford University Press, pp. 67–102.

Wobker, I., Kenning, P., Lehmann-Waffenschmidt, M. and Gigerenzer, G. (2014), 'What do consumers know about the economy? A test of minimal economic knowledge in Germany', *Journal für Verbraucherschutz und Lebensmittelsicherheit*, **9**, 231–42.

Zhu, L. and Gigerenzer, G. (2006), 'Children can solve Bayesian problems: The role of representation in mental computation', *Cognition*, **98**, 287–308.

# 11. The psychology of financial incompetence: past, present and future[†]

## Caroline Attia and Denis Hilton[*]

From 2007 through to 2015 there was an extended global financial crisis, which began with the subprime meltdown (provoking the collapse of major banks like Lehman Brothers in the US and the nationalization of others, like the Royal Bank of Scotland in the UK) and was prolonged through the Eurozone crisis (provoked by Greece's failure to meet her debt obligations). In this chapter, we examine how some well-known psychological biases may help explain some of the failures of judgment that contributed to these crises. As we shall see, these errors seem not only to have been present in members of the public who bought financial products such as subprime mortgages, but also in financial experts in both investment and central banks. They also help explain aspects of past financial crises, and if not corrected, will no doubt do the same for future ones.

It may well have seemed, as one economist working at the Federal Reserve Board wrote at the time, that "The forces that hit the financial markets in the United States in the summer of 2007 seemed like a force of nature, akin to a hurricane, something beyond human control" (Gorton, 2010, p. 61). But we do not agree with the then-president of the Federal Reserve Board, Alan Greenspan, when he wrote in 2009 that "Unless somebody can find a way to change human nature, we will have more crises". We find this approach unduly fatalistic, as it is a bit like saying that unless someone can find a way to change human biology, diseases will continue to occur. We will attempt to diagnose some of the underlying psychological causes of the 2007–12 financial crisis, suggest how economic models could be improved, and indicate directions for prevention and regulation. Our contribution is complementary to more conventional analyses of the crisis in terms of loss of confidence and panic (for example,

---

[†]   This chapter draws extensively on Chapter 18 of Attia and Hilton (2013).
[*]   We thank Andrew Hilton and Shabnam Mousavi for their comments on an earlier draft.

Gorton, 2010; 2015) which justify institutional responses (more substantial reserves, stress tests and so on). In addition to these financial measures, we believe that educating both consumers and finance professionals in the nature of judgmental biases will help them make their judgments more rational, and so render the financial system safer.

In this chapter we will review some well-known psychological biases in judgment (for example, judgmental overconfidence, undersampling, temporal discounting, positive illusions, the affect heuristic and groupthink) and show how each of these played a role in the 2007 subprime crisis. We will also show how some of these have contributed to other recent financial crises, thus illustrating their general nature.

## JUDGMENTAL OVERCONFIDENCE IN FINANCE

Psychologists have developed ways of measuring people's overconfidence in their judgment. One common technique is the interval estimation method. For example, I might ask you to set an interval with an upper and lower limit such that you are 90 percent sure that J.S. Bach's date of birth falls within that limit. If I ask you a hundred such questions (for example, about the weight of a Boeing 747 when loaded, about the circumference of the moon, about the gestation period for an elephant) you should normally have 90 responses that fall in the interval if your confidence level is well calibrated, and only 10 "surprises" that fall outside the intervals. The recurring finding in this field is that people are spectacularly miscalibrated in the direction of overconfidence in their judgment. For example, in three studies using general knowledge questions of the kind given above, Hilton et al. (2011) found that on average students only got 30–40 percent responses in their intervals when set a 90 percent confidence target.[1]

Judgmental overconfidence as measured by interval scales seems to be a very general finding that seems to be immune to expertise. For example, McKenzie et al. (2008) found that experts generated smaller confidence intervals but showed the same level of miscalibration as non-experts. In other words, experts were more precise than non-experts,

---

[1]   We note that miscalibration can also be measured by probability evaluation techniques, where a participant is asked to select one of two possible answers to a question and then give a probability between 50 and 100 percent that she expects this answer to be correct. This technique reliably produces overconfidence but to a lesser degree than obtained with the interval estimation technique (cf. the "format effect", Juslin et al., 2007). It also yields an ordering of individual differences in miscalibration that is only weakly related to that obtained with the interval estimation technique on the same set of questions (Hilton et al., 2011). In this chapter, we focus on miscalibration scores obtained with interval estimation techniques.

but still overestimated their accuracy to the same degree as non-experts. Importantly for present purposes, financial experts asked questions about their area of expertise (for example, experienced foreign exchange traders in a major bank who were asked to give 90 percent confidence intervals for currency exchange rates in one year's time) are highly overconfident. Stephan (1998) took 36 experienced participants (average time in job, 8.5 years) from a major German bank and asked for 90 percent confidence intervals for questions concerning general knowledge, share prices and exchange rates. As can be seen from Figure 11.1, the number of "correct" responses that fell within the predicted interval ranged between 15 and 30 percent. Another illustration of overconfidence in financial forecasts comes from Record Asset Management, who analysed the predictions about \$/£ exchange rates made every year between 1981 and 1996 by 40 financial experts for *Euromoney*. As can be seen from Figure 11.2, the actual \$/£ exchange rate one year after the predictions often fell outside the interval created by taking the highest and lowest forecast made by the group, and seldom fell near the middle of each year's interval. Intriguingly, this last observation suggests that correct predictions cannot always be obtained by aggregating judgments of experts and taking the mean (somewhat in the manner of Galton's method for arriving at the correct estimate of an ox's weight). It is of course possible that financial analysts

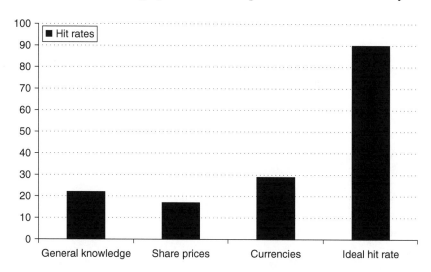

*Source:* Stephan (1998).

*Figure 11.1 Hit rates obtained with a 90 percent confidence interval by Stephan (1998) with a group of experienced currency traders*

## Is forecasting useful?

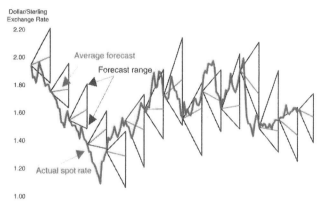

Every June Euromoney magazine surveys the top 40 professional foreign exchange forecasters for their forecasts of the $/£ spot rate at a twelve month horizon. The triangles on the chart illustrate the range of the forecasts, the green line the resulting average forecast and the red line the spot rate

REF:J:MKT_OPS\GENERAL\FORECAST

*Source:*   Record Currency Management.

*Figure 11.2    Predictions £/$ exchange rate by 40 professional foreign exchange forecasters between 1981 and 1996*

all read the same documents, meet each other in the same bars and so form a consensus based on being ensconced in the same informational bubble. Rather, as we shall see later, the risks of groupthink on Planet Finance are often high, and can be costly.

Does overconfidence in judgment matter? Yes, if you care about financial performance. For example, Biais et al. (2005) showed that players in an experimental financial market who were highly miscalibrated on general knowledge questions were more likely to do badly in an experimental asset trading game. These findings have been replicated by other researchers in experimental economics (for example, Deaves et al., 2008) and a field study found a similar relationship between judgmental overconfidence and real-life entrepreneurial failure (Hilton et al., unpublished data). Given the apparent importance of accurate forecasting for successful financial management, one would have expected that better calibrated individuals would be rewarded with promotions and be more likely to become senior figures in banks. However, an extensive study of US traders by Oberlechner and Osler (2012) did not find this to be the case: all the traders studied were highly miscalibrated, including the senior, higher-paid ones. These results suggest that major banks employ staff who not only widely (and wildly) overestimate the precision of their predictions but also do not seem to have self-correction or learning mechanisms for systematic misjudgment. Insights such as these of course help answer the Queen of England's question, posed just after the subprime crash in 2008 when opening a new building at the London School of Economics: *Why didn't anyone see it coming?*

## JUDGMENTAL CONFIDENCE AS UNDERSAMPLING: SOME HISTORICAL EXAMPLES

One way of conceptualizing judgmental overconfidence is to think of it as underestimating variability in the world. A specific source of this error may be "undersampling", whereby a judge does not sample enough of the available information about a class of event, and thereby underestimates the range of possible outcomes. Memory processes may play a role, as people with larger short-term memory capacity may be able to keep a wider range of events in mind when generating confidence intervals, and so be more likely to be aware of the potential variability of relevant events. In line with this reasoning, Juslin et al. (2007) found that people with greater short-term memory capacity were in fact less miscalibrated.

Of course, financial experts do not rely just on their short-term memory when making judgments. But there nevertheless seems to be a tendency to undersample available published information, for example in constructing models of price volatility in order to estimate VaR (Value at Risk). Consider the collapse of Long-Term Capital Management (LTCM) in 1998, which boasted two well-known economists on its staff (Black and Scholes) who had won the Nobel Prize the previous year. Their VaR model predicted that the maximum loss that the funds could suffer would be no more than $35 million in a day.[2] Nevertheless, on 21 August 1998, during the Russian default crisis they lost more than half a billion dollars in a single day. To add insult to injury, this then happened a second time.

How is such a catastrophic miscalculation possible? One problem is that the fundamental assumptions of VaR models are wrong. For example, a key assumption of VaR models is that fluctuations in market prices follow

---

[2]    VaR models enable calculation of the maximum daily loss of the trading positions of a bank, in general with a confidence level of 99 percent.

a normal distribution. However, according to Mandelbrot (1999) this is wrong: the movements of market prices follow a "fractal" process character-ized by "fat tails" in the distribution. Price movements are *discontinuous and concentrated in time* and a large number of small events and *some extreme events (black swans)* fall outside the ranges of a normal distribution.

A second related problem is that the relevant data for these models is often undersampled. For example, the mathematical models of VaR used by LTCM were based on five years of data, and did not even go back 11 years to the crash of 1987. As we shall see below, many financial analysts in the run-up to the 2007 subprime mortgage crisis used a mathematical model of HPA (House Price Appreciation) that only went back to 1998, even though earlier historical data was available (Gerardi et al., 2009). One way of characterizing the problem is that financial analysts incor-rectly believed in the *representativeness* of their sample with respect to the modeled population of events, and tended to reason according to avail-able stereotypes and extrapolate to the future from the recent, familiar past, based on a few well-known cases. By relying on the "Law of Small Numbers" (Tversky and Kahneman, 1971) they will overestimate the extent to which a small sample will represent the population from which it is drawn. The risk of undersampling available data thus seems to be evident, especially as the Basel 3 agreement only requires risk models to be based on an observation period of at least one year of historical data.[3]

## UNDERSAMPLING AND MISPREDICTION IN THE US HOUSING MARKET PRIOR TO THE SUBPRIME CRASH

Gerardi et al. (2009) collected information through analyzing reports written between 2004 and 2006 by analysts working in five of the biggest investment banks (Citibank, JPMorgan, Lehman, Morgan Stanley, UBS) operating in the credit markets, as well as rating agencies. What kinds of errors of prediction did they make?

First of all, we should note that according to contemporary observers it was the drop in house prices beginning in Spring 2006 (see Figure 11.3) that constituted the deep root of the subprime mortgage crisis. Allen and Carletti (2008, p.27) wrote that "The deep cause of the crisis was the spectacular collapse in property prices", and Dell'Ariccia et al. (2008, p.27) considered that "Lenders in some sense bet on a continuous 'boom'

---

[3]   Directives of the Basel commission on bank controls concerning the management of risks under the aegis of the Bank for International Settlements.

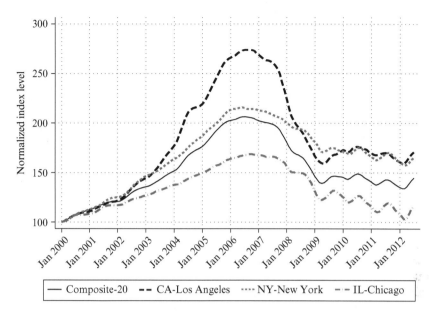

*Figure 11.3* *The evolution of US house price indices from 2000 to 2012*

in property, relying on the fact that borrowers who defaulted could always liquidate their collateral (their house) and pay back the loan."

So why did analysts fail to predict the drop in property prices and the consequences? The market participants studied well understood the role played by house prices and the major risk constituted by a possible fall. These analysts used an index: HPA = *"House Price Appreciation"*, which required estimation of *two elements*: (1) the *probability distribution* associated with different scenarios of changes in house prices (in particular the scenarios of negative HPA, that is, fall in house prices); and (2) the *resulting consequences* in terms of losses.

Gerardi et al. (2009) analyzed how the analysts of the abovementioned banks approached each task, naming them as Banks A, B, C, D and E in order to preserve anonymity. Concerning the first task (estimation of the *probability distribution* associated with different scenarios in movements of house prices) analysts of Bank A wrote that "the risk of a national decline in house prices seems infinitesimal. The annual HPA has never been negative in the United States since at least 1992" (Gerardi et al., 2009, p. 34). Bank

B described a future scenario in which "house prices would drop but not collapse". Bank C centered its subjective probability distribution around the value of HPA at that period in a conservative scenario. Their second task was to estimate the "Loss in case of default" should houses decline in price. Credit analysts and rating agencies used sophisticated tools to do this but:

> They were greatly hindered by the absence of episodes of drops in prices [of houses] in their data. The majority of analysts appeared to be aware of the fact that the lack of examples of negative HPA was not ideal. [. . .] And they knew that this constituted a problem [. . .] Certain analysts simply focused on the study of cases of HPA for which they had data. (Gerardi et al., 2009)

In an illustrative example, Bank C's analysts ended up by assigning probabilities to five different scenarios (see Table 11.1).

The majority of analysts used a database (First American LoanPerformance) that just went back to 1998, and therefore did not correctly examine the consequences of a scenario of a drop in house prices. And yet, just such a database existed, collected by the Warren Group on Massachusetts homeowners in the early 1990s. Although this database was (theoretically) available, it seems that market participants did not make the effort to get it. The consequence of using the First American LoanPerformance database is that it led to a low probability being assigned to the negative HPA scenario, which in turn seems to have interfered with the search for information and evaluation of the consequences of negative HPA. For example, even though it appeared clearly from the calculations and tables featuring in the report of Bank C's analysts that their "meltdown" scenario would result in generalized defaults in payment, they did not devote time to discussing the consequences of this scenario, presumably because they thought a "meltdown" to be unlikely.

Interestingly, the rating agency Standard & Poor's was obliged by the

*Table 11.1*  *Estimated scenario probabilities concerning House Price Appreciation (HPA) by Bank C's financial analysts*

| Name of scenario | Description of scenario | Probability |
| --- | --- | --- |
| Aggressive | HPA = 11% in the remaining years | 15% |
| [No name] | HPA = 8% in the remaining years | 15% |
| Base | HPA slows to 5% from now to end 2005 | 50% |
| Pessimistic | HPA = 0% in the next 3 years; 5% afterwards | 15% |
| Meltdown | HPA = −5% in the next 3 years | 5% |

*Source:*  Gerardi et al. (2009).

nature of its methodology to consider the worst case scenario, and indeed contemplated one that was very similar to the one that actually happened:

- a 30 percent house price decline over two years for 50 percent of the pool;
- a 10 percent house price decline over two years for 50 percent of the pool;
- an economy that was "slowing but not recessionary";
- a cut in Fed Funds rate to 2.75 percent;
- a strong recovery in 2008.

However, Standard & Poor's considered that this scenario would only have a modest impact on loan defaults. Consequently, like the bank financial analysts they were bullish in 2005–06 but for different reasons. Whereas the analysts believed that negative HPA was unlikely, the ratings agency underestimated its effect on defaults. To complete the judgmental debacle, when things turned sour, analysts were slow to react, showing the kind of confirmation bias characteristic of groupthink (see below). As Gerardi et al. (2009) note, the titles of a series of analyst reports entitled "HPA Update" from Bank C tell the story (see Table 11.2).

*Table 11.2   Updates on Housing Price Appreciation (HPA) in 2006–2007 by Bank C*

| Date of data | Title |
| --- | --- |
| 12/8/06 10/06 | "More widespread declines with early stabilization signs" |
| 1/10/07 11/06 | "Continuing declines with stronger stabilization signs" |
| 2/6/07 12/06 | "Tentative stabilization in HPA" |
| 3/12/07 1/07 | "Continued stabilization in HPA" |
| 9/20/07 7/07 | "Near bottom on HPA" |
| 11/2/07 9/07 | "UGLY! Double digit declines in August and September" |

*Source:*   From Gerardi et al. (2009).

## CLIENT PSYCHOLOGY: POSITIVE ILLUSIONS, TEMPORAL DISCOUNTING AND "PREDATORY" MORTGAGES

In the present section, we discuss two further kinds of psychological bias that help explain why subprime homeowners accepted loans that later led them into default. The first is self-overconfidence (or hubris) which has motivational origins, such as the desire to have a positive, flattering self-image. This kind of hubris is characterized by a constellation of "positive illusions" about the self, such as illusion of control, overestimation of one's ability relative to others, belief that good things are more likely to happen to oneself and misfortunes to happen to others, and so on. We distinguish this from the judgmental overconfidence discussed above, which we suggest has principally cognitive origins, such as the tendency to undersample. People who have one form of overconfidence do not necessarily have the other, as they are uncorrelated (Hilton et al., 2011) and predict different things. For example, Glaser and Weber (2007) found that the belief that one was better than average predicted amount of trading, whereas miscalibration did not. The second kind of psychological bias that helps explain subprime borrowers' behavior is *temporal discounting*, a well-established tendency in humans and other animals to underweight the importance of outcomes the further away they are in the future (Read et al., 2018).

Cognitive biases provide a fertile ground for overstretch in committing to mortgages. Banks all round the world know this, and therefore set limits on how much a client can borrow against their income in order to protect against their clients' overconfidence in their ability to pay off a mortgage, or beliefs that misfortunes such as having one's home repossessed are more likely to happen to others. However, many subprime mortgages in the USA in this period were sold with "teaser" interest rates that were fixed at a very low level for the first two or three years, but which reset to a higher variable rate after the initial period. In the early 2000s, variable interest rates were low and stayed low. After January 2001 and following the 9/11 attacks in September, there were 13 consecutive reductions of interest rates. The Federal funds rate (which directly influences mortgage rates) stayed fixed at 1 percent, between June 2003 and June 2004. However, things changed thereafter, as the rate rose from 1 to 5.25 percent between June 2004 and June 2006. Even if homeowners were still paying the lower fixed "teaser" rate by 2006, many would have known that their monthly interest repayments would soon rise sharply and that they would struggle to keep up.

It seems quite plausible that when these subprime mortgages were sold to homeowners, they would have discounted the possibility of having to make higher repayments in what may have seemed a relatively distant future and focused on the attractively low rates offered in the immediate 2 to 3-year time window. Ashcraft and Schuermann (2008) argued that a major factor that helps in understanding the collapse of the *subprime* mortgage market is that many products offered to *subprime* borrowers are very complex and subject to misunderstandings, errors of comprehension and/or of representation. Financially inexperienced borrowers may have their attention focused on the attractive interest rates of the initial period and have had difficulty understanding or properly weighting the longer-term implications of the contracts that they have just signed. In addition, their evaluation of the future variable rates may have been "anchored" by the attractively low teaser rates. In contrast, it is hard to believe that the financial institutions who sold these "predatory" mortgages were not aware of what they were doing. Otherwise why would they have offered such "teaser" rates in the first place?

In Ashcraft and Schuermann's (2008) view, households could not but find themselves asphyxiated by this type of loan which in turn raises the question as to why such a loan was granted in the first place. These authors believe that "The probable answer is that the lenders expected that the borrower would be able to *refinance* at the moment of adjustment". Put another way: the lenders thought that at the moment of adjustment property prices – the assets that were their guarantee – would have continued to rise, and that they could still recover their loan because the borrower would always have the possibility to sell his/her house and repay the loan. However, as we have seen, this assumption by the financial institutions was mistaken, and based on a VaR model that insufficiently sampled US house price behavior. Some homeowners effectively preferred to return homes which had dropped in value to the bank rather than pay off a loan which had become increasingly costly to service, while others simply could not meet the higher monthly instalments.

## GROUPTHINK AMONG US SECURITIZATION PROFESSIONALS AND FINANCIAL ANALYSTS IN 2007

We now return to an additional factor that can help explain how Planet Finance got it so wrong in 2007, and why the champions of austerity got the upper hand in the debate about how to handle the later Eurozone crisis. The concept of *groupthink* was originally proposed by Janis (1982) to explain US foreign policy fiascos, such as the decision to invade the Bay of Pigs in Cuba in 1961, and is based on a mix of psychoanalytic insight (groups collectively erect a shell to "repress" unwelcome thoughts that menace the group's sense of security and self-esteem) and experimental research on group functioning. Symptoms of groupthink include: a belief in the moral righteousness and invulnerability of the group; exclusion of dissenters; failure to analyse all possible alternatives: failure to collect information that contradicts favored alternatives; failure to question and test assumptions other than those favored by the majority; and failure to have a back-up plan.

When we look at the subprime credit markets in the early 2000s, we find plenty of evidence of symptoms of groupthink in financial institutions. Gerardi et al. (2009) examined financial analysts' reports and concluded that:

> Credit establishments, so analysts thought, were capable of overcoming a hurricane. [. . .] If financial markets came to be affected by turbulence, the market players would be in a much better position than before to overcome this [. . .] Another way in which the financial market had improved was the use of data bases.

The increased use of databases and modern statistical techniques may have contributed to a collective sense of security and invulnerability. Financial analysts of Bank B (see above) expressed a widely held view in 2006 when they wrote that they had observed: "A rise in the degree of sophistication of all market participants, from lenders to rating agencies and including brokers and investors. All these participants now have access to quantitative models that analyse a complete range of data in order to evaluate their risks". As Gerardi et al. (2009) observed, rating agencies used what seemed to be sophisticated models of credit performance, relying on databases and up-to-date statistical techniques. All this may have led banks to continue lending money, in the mistaken belief that the risks had been correctly analyzed.

Telling evidence that securitization professionals in the housing and mortgage sector had fallen prey to groupthink comes from comparison of sales of their own homes in this period with that of lawyers, another wealthy group. Figure 11.4 from Cheng et al. (2014) shows that lawyers increasingly sold second homes each year from 2000 to 2005 whereas securitization professionals overall sold these homes less, as did a third group, financial equity analysts (Panel A). In the same period securitization professionals increasingly swapped up existing homes for more expensive ones and bought more second homes (Panel B). Only after the bubble burst in 2006 did securitization professionals increase the sales of their second homes.

The verdict seems quite clear: the securitization professionals and equity analysts did not see the crash coming (and suffered the financial consequences) whereas the lawyers did and appear to have got out of the market in time. The pattern in securitization professionals is consistent with the phenomenon of group polarization, whereby groups over time take stronger collective views about a topic due to members mutually reinforcing shared views. Thus securitization professionals presumably discussed their (generally upbeat) perspectives on the market with other colleagues (leading to informational influence) and saw those colleagues holding on to their second homes (leading to normative influence). These

Panel A

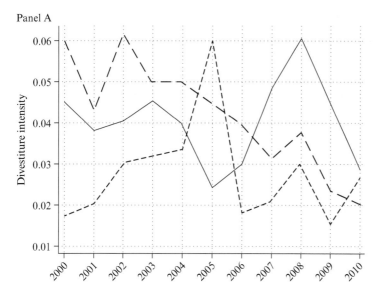

Panel B

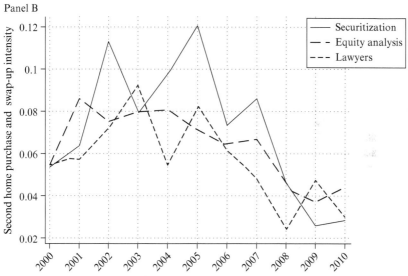

*Source:* Cheng et al. (2014). Copyright American Economic Association.

*Figure 11.4* *Home divestitures (Panel A) and purchases (swap ups and second home purchases, Panel B) by US securitization professionals, equity analysts and lawyers between 2000 and 2010*

factors would have prompted them to hold on to second homes over this period. In contrast, the lawyers (who did not specialize in real estate law) may not have been subject to such influence.

## ASYMMETRIC REWARDS IN THE FINANCE INDUSTRY AND THE CULTURE OF RISK

The striking divergence between the finance professionals and the lawyers reviewed above invites some reflection as to why there was such a difference. As we have seen, part of the answer may lie in the way that finance professionals as a group formed incorrect beliefs about the risks associated with subprime mortgages. It may well be that lawyers have a "culture of prudence" whereas modern bankers have a "culture of risk". In this vein, it is worthwhile noting that – whatever their personal beliefs – market participants in the run-up to the subprime crisis were rewarded for taking risks and protected against losses. In some cases, simple greed may have led banks to sell dubious products. According to Calomiris (2008), Gorton described the behavior of Citibank, Merrill Lynch and UBS as "shocking" as they continued to issue financial derivatives backed by subprime mortgages even when the problems with these products had begun to emerge in 2006 and 2007. Further down the line, fund managers may have understated the risks associated with subprime mortgages as their clients would have asked for their money back if they had stated the truth. But as the variable part of remuneration packages of these managers depended on the amount of money they managed, they clearly had an incentive to talk up the attractiveness of these investments (Calomiris, 2008). However, when the market crashed and their institutions made massive losses, neither the bankers who originated the derivatives nor the fund managers who sold them on these participated in these losses. A related point is that reward schemes in the finance industry were strongly oriented to rewarding profitability in the short term. Hence risky ventures that brought immediate profitability and yearly bonuses that would be pocketed by bank employees would naturally be favored, whatever their longer-term implications for the bank.

Ultimately, it was often the taxpayer who footed the bill: Citibank suffered $40bn losses due to its subprime business, and had to be refloated through the US government buying a part of it. A similar pattern of privatization of gains and socialization of losses was observed throughout the world, for example through the bailout of the Royal Bank of Scotland, the UK's biggest bank. The government's injection of £37bn into the bank in October 2008 was equivalent to £613 per UK citizen. One imagines that many of those responsible for the crash that necessitated the bailout were still able to keep their yachts in Marbella and Newport.

## RELAXING CREDIT STANDARDS AND MISPRICING RISK: MAKING ROOM FOR THE AFFECT HEURISTIC

When financial derivatives such as collateral debt obligations (CDOs) and credit default swaps (CDSs) backed with subprime mortgages were first sold, much was made of their innovative and complex nature as the latest word in financial engineering. For example, the way that the collateral debt was sliced up into different tranches meant that risk was being distributed, according to classic financial precepts. But the downside was opacity – it was difficult for the buyers of these products to know what exactly it was that they were holding and where the risks were. In the view of the President's Working Group on financial markets (March 2008), fund managers, rating agencies, traders, and so on failed to do due diligence and examine the actual risks involved in buying such derivative products, tending to rely on simulations based on risk models. One can summarize by saying that credit standards were relaxed and investment decisions were no longer based on careful risk–benefit analyses, but were made on the basis of impressions formed in other ways. What does psychology have to say about how these impressions might be formed?

A substantial body of research has revealed that people's reasoning about risk often diverges from normative analyses. In particular, they may evaluate the risks associated with something not only on the basis of their beliefs or information about a product or activity but also on the basis of their feelings towards it. This can lead to a sort of "halo" effect, as positive feelings towards an object lead to the generalized attribution of positive attributes to that object. For example, MacGregor et al. (2000) showed that US business students expressed greater preferences for investing in financial products associated with "glamorous" industries (such as high tech) than in unglamorous ones (such as railways), even though the financial ratios were the same.

One notable implication of such affective processing is that it may lead people to believe that the risks associated with an activity are low and the benefits great, whereas negative feelings may lead people to believe that the risks are high and the benefits low. Slovic et al. (2005) illustrate how this "affect heuristic" can explain the pattern or results observed by Alhakami and Slovic (1994) with respect to attitudes to nuclear power: those with favorable attitudes to nuclear power believed it to be both

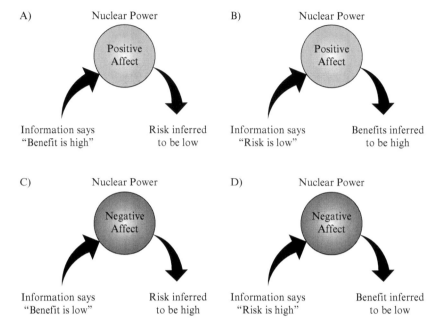

*Source:* From Slovic et al. (2005). Copyright American Psychological Association.

*Figure 11.5* *Diagrammatic model of the relation between affective processing and perceived risks and benefits of nuclear power*

safe and beneficial, whereas those with unfavorable attitudes believed it to be unsafe and of little benefit (see Figure 11.5). This perception of an inverse relation between risk and benefit was found in 32 out of 33 hazards studied, and was statistically significant in 30 of these cases. A second set of findings that suggest that people naturally think about risk in this way comes from findings on the effect of time pressure on judgment: given the ease with which people can use their feelings to make a judgment, one may expect them to be more reliant on the affect heuristic when under pressure to arrive at a judgment quickly. The findings of Finucane et al. (2000) exactly fit this pattern, as the perceived inverse correlation between risk and benefit was strongest in participants asked to make judgments under time pressure about a series of targets (alcoholic drinks, cigarettes, natural gas, pesticides, and so on). As may be noted, this inverse relation between risk and benefit appears to contradict basic precepts of risk analysis, yet seems to be quite generalized in human risk perception.

We may then ask: when are people likely to use an affect heuristic in judgment? Research has shown that the less familiar, the more complex and the more atypical the target, the more likely that affect is likely to be infused into judgment (Forgas, 1995). These are exactly the characteristics that characterized financial derivative products in the early 2000s. They were unfamiliar, complex and atypical financial products, and their opacity rendered traditional financial analysis of their actual potential risks and benefits (due diligence) difficult. So in addition to overreliance on simulations based on risk models, it seems quite plausible that financial analysts and others would have come to rely on affective processing in the absence of analytic frameworks for evaluating these products. Such processing based on an affect heuristic is likely to become even stronger and exacerbate perception of an inverse relation between risk and benefit. Moreover, in the early days when derivatives had a positive image this affective processing was likely to exaggerate the attractiveness of these products, thus contributing their mispricing before the bubble burst.

## AUSTERITY AND THE EUROZONE CRISIS: GROUPTHINK AND COGNITIVE BIASES IN POLICY MAKING

A final example of how psychological biases may have predictably contributed to mishandling of the financial crisis comes from the management of the Eurozone crisis that arose in part from the subprime crisis. In order to avoid complete collapse of the global financial system, nation states were obliged to bail out banks and insurers that had become overexposed due to the years of easy credit and overexposure to subprimes. The debate of the period (c.2008–09) revolved around the "austerity" approach (which broadly argues that states will get out of economic difficulty by cutting public spending) and the "stimulus" approach, which argues that states get out of economic difficulty by increasing public spending. Once again, it illustrates that the risk of undersampling and groupthink can be found in prestigious universities, central banks and parliaments. It can also be used to suggest a new (and perhaps more scientific) way to do financial analysis.

In 2008, an influential academic paper appeared, which was later published in the *American Economic Review* (Reinhart and Rogoff, 2010). This paper implied that it would be best for states not to borrow more than 90 percent of their GDP because it would inhibit growth and was used by prominent political figures to justify austerity policies in the Eurozone (Olli Rehn, EU Commissioner for Economic Affairs), the UK (George Osborne, later Chancellor of the Exchequer) and USA (Paul Ryan, presidential candidate and later Speaker of the House). Their conclusion is based on data which appears to show a neat inverse linear relation between level of public debt in advanced countries and growth.

However, there were numerous problems with the data analysis in this paper (Herndon et al., 2013). The first is that data were excluded (without explanation) from countries whose behavior did not fit the claimed pattern (for example, postwar Australia, Canada and New Zealand), whereas data from other countries from the same period that fit the authors' claim were included (for example, United States). Second, some other countries (Austria, Belgium and Denmark) were omitted due to an alphabetical coding error. Third, weights were used such that one year of data from New Zealand (1951) that support their claims (–7.6 percent negative growth) was weighted equally to the United Kingdom, which was also in the highest debt category but averaged 2.4 percent growth over 19 years. When these errors were eliminated or controlled for, the sample showed that countries with over 90 percent debt averaged 2.2 percent growth, not the –0.1 percent growth claimed by Reinhart and Rogoff (2010). In fact, when the initial errors were corrected, the data set had very different implications for austerity policies.

The question then rises as to how such poor scholarship could pass muster and be published in the *American Economic Review*? The probable explanation is to be found in a combination of causes. The first is a "decidedly empirical" approach (authors' words), unconstrained by a well-specified guiding theory about how debt constrains growth. A second is cognitive biases, such as undersampling (again) and confirmation bias (it is clear that the conclusions drawn from this flawed data set fit the authors' preconceptions). And there was probably a good dose of groupthink, as the authors' preconceptions about what constitutes a valid data set and what can be concluded from these data sets must have fit preconceptions shared by the editor and reviewers of the article for the *American Economic Review*.

## HOW TO CORRECT ERRORS IN STATISTICAL THINKING: WILL CAUSAL MODELS HELP?

More generally, the continuing inability of economics to make successful predictions means questions must be raised about the scientific maturity of the discipline. A starting point is the observation that Reinhart and Rogoff's argument was only based on correlations, and as everyone knows, correlation does not prove causation. After all, it is quite possible that extended periods of low growth will lead public debt to rise, as happened in Japan in the 1990s. One can imagine that had Reinhart and Rogoff had a well-specified causal model (in the sense of Pearl, 2000) of how public debt influences a nation's growth, they might have noticed anomalies in their data analysis sooner. In related vein, one can wonder whether financial analysts' over-reliance on a simplified statistical (VaR) model in the years leading up to the subprime crisis blinded them to the causal processes that led to the subprime meltdown.

Our perception is that economists do not use causal analysis in the way that, say, biologists do when constructing models of ecosystems, because they are not encouraged to build causal models with ontological assumptions about how the world works as they have a predominantly statistical approach to modeling the problems that interest them. As an anecdotal example, in a collaboration which involved analyzing data about how media predictions affect share-buying behavior (Galy et al., 2014), the communication scientist among us expected that we would start with a model of how financial information is obtained and flows, who gets it first, when it is communicated to which media, and drew a flow chart to represent his model of how the system works in Germany (where the data came from). In contrast, the economists favored a model that was much more statistical in nature with minimal assumptions about causal relationships in the media and finance world, which shocked my communication scientist colleague. Indeed, he wondered whether we should continue the collaboration. But as the economists were taking the lead on this paper, we used their approach. It was actually informative, and incidentally disproved the communication scientist's assumption that share prices were strongly influenced by media announcements (share prices did move strongly, but mostly just before the announcement was made).

But there may be cases where having a causal model will yield significant scientific advantages, for example by facilitating accurate predictions and enabling appropriate measures to be taken. To give a flavor of how this can be done, let us return to summer 2007. At that time, there were *two* looming global crises, one being the subprime crisis and the other being a health crisis due to Mexican swine flu, which had infected humans. When the swine flu crisis hit, epidemiologists had a clear idea of how the flu was likely to spread and correctly predicted that the next two zones of infection would be New York and Madrid, and then London. This is because they were able to construct a causal model of the flu's propagation, based on knowledge of vectors such as the amount of passenger travel between the cities concerned, and latencies based on knowledge of incubation times. They were also able to determine what preparations needed to be made should there be an epidemic, and vaccines were ordered in bulk in many countries such as France in preparation for the following winter (even

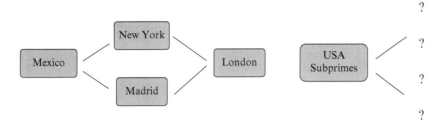

*Figure 11.6    Causal models of contagion for the Mexican swine flu and
financial subprime crises of 2007*

though, in the end, these were not needed). In contrast, when the subprime
crisis hit, no one knew what would happen next and which banks would
be affected because they held subprime-backed derivatives. In addition,
it took some time for the causes of the crisis to be understood and for
appropriate (and costly) measures to restore confidence to be taken to stop
what was essentially a bank run (Gorton, 2010).

Why did the biologists have a relevant causal model (on the left, see
Figure 11.6), whereas the economists did not (on the right)? We do not
think that an answer that requirements of moral hazard, namely that
information about who lends what to whom must be kept private, is a sufficient answer to this question. If it were, we would expect to see economists
constructing causal models in other domains where such issues are not of
concern. However, a recent review of econometrics textbooks (Chen and
Pearl, 2013) suggests that econometricians are not taking full advantage of
the recent causal modeling revolution in Bayesian statistics (Pearl, 2000).

## SOME CONCLUSIONS

The recent (and some would say continuing) financial crisis is rich with
examples of how well-known psychological biases may have contributed
to major financial catastrophes. These biases are to be found not only in
"naïve" consumers (who for example bought subprime mortgages) but
also in the financial experts whose analyses guided banks' policies. In
addition, we have reviewed examples of how dangerous errors can creep
into the analyses proposed by leading academic economists, which in
turn influence central bankers' and governments' policy decisions. No
one seems to be immune, and groupthink often leads errors induced by
psychological biases to be exacerbated (rather than corrected). We also
noted how the affect heuristic could have led financial experts to misprice

the risk associated with derivate products that were innovative, complex, atypical and opaque. At the very least this litany of examples of individual and collective irrationality suggests that, in general, a prudent attitude to financial regulation should be adopted.

In addition, the analysis of how specific biases have influenced financial decision-making in the past may prompt specific, targeted regulations. People discount over time, and the subprime mortgage crisis does suggest that governments should give thought to regulating (or "nudging") against mortgage deals that rely too much on initial "teasers". However, it should not be thought that temporal discounting induces unwise decision-making only in house-owners. For example, the popularity of PPPs (public–private partnerships) in public procurement may in part be due to the political attractiveness of only paying later for services that are enjoyed immediately. In general people (including financial analysts) seem to be systematically overconfident, under-sample and underestimate volatility. In view of this, the Basel stipulation that risk models must rely on at least one year of historical data seems woefully inadequate. Moreover, we are left with the impression that regulators themselves underestimate the risks of undersampling for their own practice. For example, the liquidity ratio (LCR) being discussed under the Basel III Rules only covers a 30-day period, which seems to us to risk undersampling cash outflows in a stressed bank.

We have also touched on issues to do with "corporate culture". For example, in the run-up to the 2007 subprime crisis it seemed likely that bankers would get immediate bonuses for contracting subprime loans (and hence a share in the profits generated for the bank) but would be insulated from the accrued losses when the crisis hit. At worst they would lose their job at the bank and get a new one somewhere else. Clearly, such a "bonus culture" is likely to encourage an appetite for risk when an agent is likely to obtain significantly higher rewards than losses. For these reasons, the person who stands to pick up the tab after a crash (that is, the taxpayer) has an interest in ensuring that these bonus schemes are properly regulated.

One merit of the recent financial crisis is that it definitively gives the lie to the hypothesis that markets composed of human beings are invariably efficient and can be left to regulate themselves. It gives the lie to the belief that crowds (or markets) are always more intelligent than individuals (aka the Hayek hypothesis), as groupthink processes can sometimes exacerbate shared delusions rather than correct them. We have tried to show how recent events in financial history can be understood in terms of psychological processes that can be systematically demonstrated under controlled laboratory conditions, much in the manner of Irving Janis' (1982) use of experimental work on group dynamics to illustrate fiascoes in US foreign policy decision-making. There are of course many other psychological biases that can impact financial decision-making (see Attia and Hilton, 2011; 2013; Hilton, 2001; Montier, 2007). Unless corrected by regulation and by education, they are likely to strike time and time again.

# REFERENCES

Alhakami, A.S. and Slovic, P. (1994). A psychological study of the inverse relationship between perceived risk and perceived benefit. *Risk Analysis*, **14**, 1085–96.

Allen, F. and Carletti, E. (2008). The role of liquidity in the financial crisis. Paper prepared for the 2008 Jackson Hole Symposium on Maintaining Stability in a Changing Financial System, 21–23 August. Accessed at http://www.kansascity fed.org/publicat/sympos/2008/AllenandCarletti.08.04.08.pdf.

Ashcraft, A.B. and Schuermann, T. (2008). Understanding the securitization of subprime mortgage credit. Federal Reserve Board of New York Staff Reports No. 318. Accessed at SSRN: http://ssrn.com/abstract=1071189.

Attia, C. and Hilton, D.J. (2011). *Decidere in Finanza*. Milan: Il Sole 24 Ore.

Attia, C. and Hilton, D.J. (2013). *Financiers sur le Divan*. Paris: Optraken Editions.

Biais, B., Hilton, D.J., Pouget, S. and Mazurier, K. (2005). Judgmental overconfidence, self-monitoring and trading performance in an experimental financial market. *Review of Economic Studies*, **72**, 297–312.

Calomiris, C. (2008). The subprime turmoil: What's old, what's new, and what's next. Paper presented at the Federal Reserve Bank of Kansas City Symposium, "Maintaining stability in a changing financial system", Jackson Hole, Wyoming, August.

Chen, B. and Pearl, J. (2013). Regression and causation: A critical examination of six econometrics textbooks. *Real-World Economics Review*, No. 65, 2–20.

Cheng, I-H., Raina, S. and Xiong, W. (2014). Wall Street and the housing bubble. *American Economic Review*, **104**(9), 2797–829.

Deaves, R., Lüders, E. and Luo, G.Y. (2008). An experimental test of the impact of overconfidence and gender on trading activity. *Review of Finance*, **13**(3), 555–75.

Dell'Ariccia, G., Igan, D. and Laeven, L. (2008). Credit booms and lending standards: Evidence from the subprime mortgage market. CEPR Discussion Paper No. 6683.

Finucane, M.L., Alhakami, A., Slovic, P. and Johnson, S.M. (2000). The affect heuristic in judgments of risks and benefits. *Journal of Behavioral Decision Making*, **13**, 1–17.

Forgas, J.P. (1995). Mood and judgment: The affect infusion model (AIM). *Psychological Bulletin*, **117**, 39–66.

Galy, N., Germain, L., Hilton, D. and Mathes, R. (2014). In which media are analysts' recommendations most followed? *Bankers, Markets & Investors*, No. 133, 34–46.

Gerardi, K., Lehnert, A., Sherlund, S.M. and Willen, P. (2009). Making sense of the subprime crisis. Federal Reserve Bank of Atlanta Working Paper No. 2009-2.

Glaser, M. and Weber, M. (2007). Overconfidence and trading volume. *The Geneva Risk and Insurance Review*, **32**(1), 1–36.

Gorton, G.B. (2010). *Slapped by the Invisible Hand: The Panic of 2007*. New York, NY: Oxford University Press.

Gorton, G. (2015). Stress for success: A review of Timothy Geithner's Financial Crisis Memoir. *Journal of Economic Literature*, **53**(4), 975–95.

Herndon, T., Ash, M. and Pollin, R. (2013). Does high public debt consistently stifle economic growth? A critique of Reinhart and Rogoff. *Cambridge Journal of Economics*, **38**(2), 257–79.

Hilton, D.J. (2001). Psychology and the financial markets: Applications to trading, dealing and investment analysis. *Journal of Psychology and Financial Markets*, **2**, 37–53.

Hilton, D.J., Régner, I., Cabantous, L., Charalambides, L. and Vautier, S. (2011). Do positive illusions predict overconfidence in judgment? A test using interval production and probability evaluation measures of miscalibration. *Journal of Behavioral Decision Making*, **24**, 117–39.

Hilton et al. (n.d.). Judgmental overconfidence and entrepreneurial performance. Unpublished data.

Janis, I. (1982). *Groupthink* (2nd edn). Boston, MA: Houghton-Mifflin.

Juslin, P., Winman, A. and Hansson, P. (2007). The naïve intuitive statistician: A naïve sampling model of intuitive confidence intervals. *Psychological Review*, **114**, 678–803.

MacGregor, D.G., Slovic, P., Dreman, D. and Berry, M. (2000). Imagery, affect and financial judgment. *Psychology and the Financial Markets*, **1**(2), 104–10.

Mandelbrot, B. (1999). A multifractal walk down Wall Street. *Scientific American*, **280**(2), 50–53.

McKenzie, C.R.M., Liersch, M.J. and Yaniv, I. (2008). Overconfidence in interval estimates: What does expertise buy you? *Organizational Behavior and Human Decision Processes*, **107**, 179–91.

Montier, J. (2007). *Behavioural Investing*. Chichester: John Wiley & Sons.

Oberlechner, T. and Osler, C. (2012). Survival of overconfidence in currency markets. *Journal of Financial and Quantitative Analysis*, **47**(1), 91–113.

Pearl, J. (2000). *Causality*. Cambridge: Cambridge University Press.

President's Working Group on Financial Markets (2008). Policy statements on financial market developments, March. Accessed at http://www.ustreas.gov/press/releases/hp871.htm.

Read, D., McDonald, C. and He, L. (2018). Intertemporal choice: Choosing for the future. In A. Lewis (ed.), *The Cambridge Handbook of Psychology and Economic Behaviour* (2nd edn). Cambridge: Cambridge University Press.

Reinhart, C.M. and Rogoff, K.S. (2010). Growth in a time of debt. *American Economic Review*, **100**(2), 573–8.

Slovic, P., Peters, E., Finucane, M.L and MacGregor, D.G. (2005). Affect, risk, and decision making. *Health Psychology*, **24**(4), S35–S40.

Stephan, E. (1998). Anchoring and adjustment in economic forecasts: The role of incentives, ability and expertise. Paper presented at the Conference on Judgemental Inputs to the Forecasting Process, University College, London, November.

Tversky, A. and Kahneman, D.E. (1971). Belief in the law of small numbers. *Psychological Bulletin*, **76**, 105–10.

# 12. Behavioral finance: from financial consumer protection to financial education

**Magda Bianco and Francesco Franceschi**

## 1. INTRODUCTION

In the real world, economic decisions are almost never made as economic theory prescribes. This implies that competition cannot be relied on as the unique instrument to ensure efficient results.

In what follows we first provide new evidence on financial literacy in Italy and on some biases affecting financial consumers (section 2). Compared to other countries, this evidence reinforces the need to ensure consumer protection with a set of tools, which are described in sections 3 and 4: on the one hand are public polices, which should include laws, effective public enforcement and mechanisms for private enforcement; on the other hand are financial education programs, to empower consumers and ensure greater awareness. Both should be developed and implemented considering behavioral issues in order to produce effective and longstanding results.

## 2. NEW EVIDENCE ON FINANCIAL LITERACY IN ITALY

As stated, individual (economic) decisions are almost never made as economic theory prescribes in the real world. Nonetheless, theory is useful in a normative sense, making the relevant factors influencing economic decisions explicit in a coherent representation and providing the fundamental elements for sound choices. For instance, the Markovitz portfolio theory suggests the importance for risk-averse agents of diversification even if estimating the efficient frontier is most of the time unfeasible.

In practice, sound financial decisions are at minimum rooted in some basic level of financial literacy, on cautious behavior, and on adequate choice rules. Together, these three elements represent the foundation of financial competencies. Accordingly, the OECD-INFE has developed a conceptual framework describing financial literacy along three dimensions: knowledge, good behavior, attitude towards the long term. To assess the individual level of financial competencies, the OECD-INFE developed a survey in which each of the three dimensions is measured through a set of questions (OECD, 2015).

Within the OECD-INFE survey, the variables used to define good behavior and attitudes towards the long term are sometimes difficult to reconcile with standard neoclassical consumer theory, but they always imply cautious behavior and rules of thumb that are normally correlated with sensible economic decisions in real life. For instance, having positive savings is always assessed as good behavior, regardless of the consumer's preferences, age and other relevant characteristics. This is hardly justifiable within the neoclassical framework but it may be a reasonable approach when over-indebtedness is one of the most frequently observed symptoms of low financial competencies.

At the beginning of 2017, the Bank of Italy conducted a harmonized survey based on the OECD-INFE methodology (IACOFI, *Indagine sull'Alfabetizzazione e le Competenze Finanziarie degli Italiani*) for Italy. Compared with other OECD countries[1] the level of competencies among Italian adults is low. Combining together indicators of basic knowledge, good behavior and long-term attitude, Italy is ranked last among the G20 countries (Figure 12.1; see OECD, 2017).

About two-thirds of Italians do not achieve a sufficiently high level on financial knowledge, compared with an average of about one third in other OECD countries (Banca d'Italia, 2017). In particular, Italian adults struggle with understanding basic concepts such as simple and compound interest, and they are rarely aware of the advantages of portfolio diversification. Italian adults also score very low on the behavior indicator. This is mainly because there is a lack of financial assets in Italian households' portfolios and because they seldom use budgets as a device to manage family resources. The long-term attitude of Italian adults is close to the OECD average.

Interestingly, the IACOFI survey also provides an assessment of overconfidence, one of the most well acknowledged behavioral biases. According

---

[1]   The comparison with OECD countries is made based on OECD, *OECD/INFE International Survey of Adult Financial Literacy Competencies*, 2016. The OECD countries considered are, in descending order of financial competency: France, Finland, Norway, Canada, New Zealand, South Korea, Belgium, Austria, Portugal, the Netherlands, Estonia, Latvia, the United Kingdom, the Czech Republic, Turkey, Hungary and Poland.

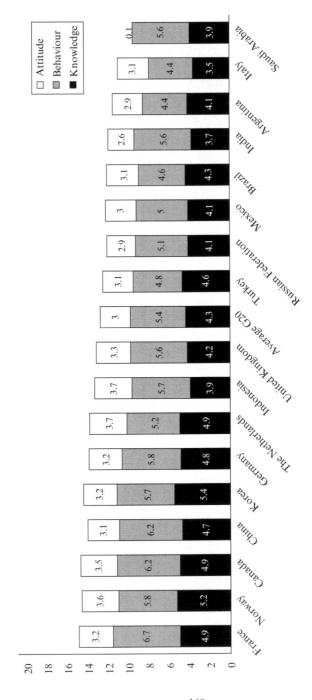

Source: Di Salvatore et al. (2018).

Figure 12.1 Financial knowledge, attitudes and behavior (averages; weighted data)

to a general definition, an agent is overconfident when he/she overestimates his/her own ability to successfully perform a particular task or to make an accurate judgment. The specific form of overconfidence that can be studied exploiting the IACOFI survey is that of individuals believing that their financial knowledge is average or above average when it is actually below average.

Italians are particularly cautious in the self-assessment of their own level of financial literacy: more than 50 percent of them believe that it is below average, compared with about 20 percent in the OECD countries average. However, 22 percent of Italians are overconfident. Men, the self-employed, those resident in Southern Italy and those with a medium-high level of education are at higher risk of overestimating their level of financial literacy. According to the same definition, the share of overconfident individuals is much higher in other countries, such as Germany, the UK and the Netherlands, where it is close to or above 40 percent (panel (a) in Figure 12.2).

We should, however, bear in mind that being overconfident might be more of a problem in countries where the average level on knowledge is really low. In fact, what really matters is not whether people are able to assess their level of knowledge correctly, but whether a wrong self-assessment (overconfidence) increases the probability of making wrong financial choices. This seems actually to be the case in Italy, where overconfident individuals face a higher risk of making bad investments, being victims of phishing or of unauthorized use of their payment cards (panel (b) in Figure 12.2).

The share of underconfident consumers, those who underestimate their actual financial competencies, is in Italy close to 25 percent, whereas in the average OECD comparison countries it is below 10 percent (Di Salvatore et al., 2018). Underconfidence can be a problem as well as overconfidence, since consumers with low self-assessment are more likely not to participate in financial markets, which means they are less likely to hold investment products, to use debt instruments, or to have private pension plans.

While the financial competencies of adults in Italy are much lower than in other developed countries, the picture is definitely more encouraging when focusing on young students. Data from the latest edition of the *OECD's Programme for International Student Assessment* (PISA) show in fact that the financial literacy of 15-year-old students in Italy has increased since 2012, and in 2015 it was not too far from the OECD average (Panel (a) of Figure 12.3).

Among the elements of concern in Italy there is the persistent evidence that males perform significantly better than females (Panel (b) of Figure 12.3). Italy is the only country where this happens; in most of the

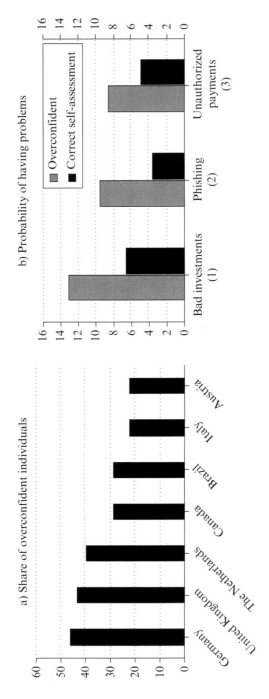

a) Share of overconfident individuals

b) Probability of having problems

Notes:
(1) Respondents declaring they accepted suggestions to invest in something that proved to be worthless.
(2) Respondents declaring they gave out financial and banking details in response to an email or a phone call that proved to be dishonest.
(3) Respondents declaring unauthorized use of their debit or credit cards.

Source: Panel (a): authors' calculations based on the Italian Literacy and Financial Competence Survey (IACOFI) and other countries' surveys based on the OECD/INFE Toolkit for Measuring Financial Literacy and Financial Inclusion (2015). Panel (b): Bank of Italy, Annual Report for 2016.

Figure 12.2   Overconfidence and risk to consumers (percentages)

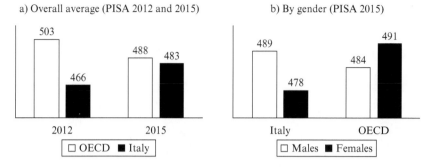

a) Overall average (PISA 2012 and 2015)          b) By gender (PISA 2015)

*Source:*    Bracale and Franceschi (2018).

*Figure 12.3    OECD-PISA: financial literacy of 15-year-old students*

other countries there is not a significant difference between boys' and girls' scores; in a few cases the gender gap is in favor of females.

In line with the OECD-INFE methodology for measuring financial competencies of adults, and according with the idea that knowledge is not enough to take good financial decisions, Bracale and Franceschi (2018) propose a novel indicator of good behavior for students. This indicator is the result of the sum of two components: attitude toward savings and ability to deal responsibly with the desire of buying something that cannot currently be afforded. Bracale and Franceschi (2018) show that 15-year-old students in Italy have a significantly lower good behavior indicator than their OECD peers. Moreover, in OECD countries higher literacy (knowledge) is positively correlated with better behavior, while in Italy this relation does not hold.

The role of parents in shaping financial behavior seems, however, to be important. Students who often discuss economic and financial matters with their parents obtain a much higher behavioral score.

## 3.    FINANCIAL CONSUMER PROTECTION: THE POLICY MAKER'S CHALLENGES

The evidence on Italian consumers' weaknesses presented above is the starting point for sound policies.

In principle, (especially financial) consumer protection has been recognized as necessary due to market failures that do not allow competition to ensure an optimal allocation of resources. Asymmetric information (and bargaining power) in (financial) markets imply that customers cannot easily choose among different products, driving down prices for a given quality. Banking and financial products and services are typically credence goods.

Some kind of public intervention is therefore deemed necessary.

It is widely recognized that policies should take two parallel avenues: (a) on the one hand, they should develop instruments to ensure effective consumer protection through laws and their enforcement; (b) on the other hand, they should invest in consumer financial education. Neither, alone, is probably able to ensure satisfactory results, that is, that consumers are able to benefit from participating in the financial markets by comparing products and services effectively, avoiding traps and mistakes, and planning carefully for the long term. But the combination of the two avenues might produce relevant synergies.

Both avenues present important challenges, and must take into account behavioral issues (Lefevre and Chapman, 2017). Let us start with consumer protection.

At an early stage, the main instrument developed to ensure consumer protection was to introduce strong and pervasive transparency requirements. European Directives and national laws were imposed to provide consumers with detailed information on product and services, conditions imposed, prices and commissions, both before signing contracts and during the entire contractual life. Full disclosure was the response to information asymmetry.

Only recently has attention focused on the recognition of consumers' behavioral weakness and their difficulty in processing a vast amount of information. As discussed in FCA (2013), in financial markets many products are inherently complex for most people and involve trade-offs between present and future, decisions may require assessing risk and uncertainty, and some products permit little learning from past mistakes. Difficulties are associated with the multiplicity of prices and the presence of percentages and compounding, which many consumers have trouble understanding. The biases that affect consumers refer to preferences (present bias, reference dependence and loss aversion, regret), to beliefs (overconfidence, over-extrapolation, projection bias), to decision-making short-cuts (framing, salience, limited attention, mental accounting and narrow framing, decision-making rules of thumb). Firms may exploit these difficulties and biases, for example by increasing non-salient prices and decreasing salient prices. Evidence of this difficulty with reference to Italian checking accounts is presented in Branzoli (2016), who shows that consumers keep on paying high costs on their bank accounts even when cheaper options become available within the same bank.

As a result of the awareness of consumers' behavioral weaknesses, which add to information asymmetry, the desirable policy approach has been reoriented. What is needed is a combination of regulation, effective public enforcement and private enforcement, all somehow taking into account behavioral issues.

## Regulation

The production of a great amount of information is not helpful in protecting consumers, but some information is essential; what is recognized is that information should be salient: summary disclosure, the engagement of consumers, a correct presentation of product information may be effective in making consumers aware of actual costs and benefits of products.[2]

Furthermore, since even salient information production might not ensure sufficient consumer awareness, regulation is now moving towards requiring fairness of behavior to producers. This is obtained by imposing organizational requirements aimed at making producers develop products and services that are in the interest of consumers themselves (see, for example, requirements introduced in MiFID II and EBA Guidelines on Product Oversight and Governance), and ensuring that remuneration policies do not create incentives to sell products that are not in the interest of customers (see, for example, EBA Guidelines on remuneration policies for sales staff).

## Public Enforcement

At the same time also public enforcement by supervision authorities needs to adapt and move from ensuring that contracts include all the information prescribed to a more substantial approach, ensuring fairness of behavior of producers.

This may take different routes: reducing the uncertainty in interpretation of norms, by offering examples of fair interpretation; providing producers with supervisory expectations, including best practices available on the market; introducing benchmarking exercises allowing producers to rank themselves in terms of consumers' friendliness. This might induce producers to compete also for customer satisfaction.

But taking into account potential behavioral biases in organizations themselves (see FCA, 2016) suggests an evolution of instruments that might be used. It might be important to recognize that preferences, beliefs

---

[2]  See the experiment on payday loans by Bertrand and Morse (2011), who show that presenting borrowers with information in dollars (rather than through interest rates) on the costs of payday loans compared with other financial instruments reduces the amount of debt taken.

and decision-making processes can make rule breaking acceptable: firms themselves and regulators could exploit biases to change the perception of detection and punishment, exploiting the relevance of group behavior and hence social norms and corporate culture within firms. People like to think of themselves as "moral" and their actions determine the extent to which they can maintain this view; a number of factors might affect their perceptions: for example, the salience of ethics (making people recall moral codes when they engage in an activity); the distance from rule breaking (the distance between the decision and the impact on consumers); the effect of small steps (increasing the magnitude of rule breaking little by little may lead to more severe infringements being acceptable); ambiguity and complexity (unclear rules allow self-serving interpretations). The response of the supervisor should be, on the one hand, to make detection and punishment more salient, and on the other hand, to publicize and share good practices, avoiding ambiguous rules or tick-box approaches.

**Private Enforcement**

Since public enforcement might not cover all possible cases of mis-selling, sometimes due to the uncertain interpretation of norms or to the difficulty of identifying wrongdoing, ensuring that consumers may access an *ex-post* redress mechanism increases trust in the financial system and may enlarge the market.

Private enforcement may be obtained through ordinary justice, but given costs and length of civil procedures, recourse to alternative dispute resolution (ADR) procedures has become more appealing and more effective in protecting consumers.

ADRs may vary in nature: mediation, conciliation, decisions (with no strong evidence of a superior performance of one model over others); and typically perform various functions: they solve disputes but also produce aggregate information on the reasons of the disputes (which might feed back into public enforcement mechanisms); they provide some pressure on firms to solve disputes by improving their relationships with customers. Hence they are strongly complementary to the other consumer protection instruments.

In concluding this section, we should observe that also public policy, and hence regulators, might themselves be subject to biases (see Hirshleifer, 2008). They might react more strongly to salient events (cases of misbehavior) than to (less salient) costs of regulation. They might refrain from giving indications that might appear to be placing the burden on those perceived as potential victims (for example, suggesting to diversify investments) and instead prohibit some type of investments. A greater awareness of these biases is important in evaluating the appropriateness of policies before their implementation.

## 4.  FINANCIAL EDUCATION WITH ADULTS: THE NEED FOR A PORTFOLIO OF APPROACHES AND TOOLS

Let us turn to the second avenue, that is, promoting financial education. In the practice of policy making, it is common to distinguish two different macro-targets of financial education programs: students and adults. Here we briefly focus on the main challenges encountered when dealing with adults; we argue that there is no so-called silver bullet providing an immediate and effective solution to their lack of ability to make sound financial decisions, and we suggest that a portfolio of initiatives, with bias-specific resources and tools, should be developed to tackle the problem with some chances of success.

As we already mentioned, financial education can represent the fourth pillar of the overall system of protection for the financial consumer. The experience of policy making and the academic research show that teaching adults financial concepts is a hard task. Adults are most of time reluctant learners and they are keen on acquiring new information only just prior to making a financial decision (the so-called teachable moments). Providing consumers with knowledge is, however, not enough in many cases, because financial decisions are commonly affected by behavioral and cognitive biases. To increase the effectiveness of consumer protection, and more in general to augment financial well-being, financial education should not only increase people's awareness and knowledge, but it should also provide consumers with cognitive tools useful to make decisions consistent with their needs and wants.

In 2014 the OECD report on *Regulatory Policy and Behavioural Economics* (Lunn, 2014) outlined that improved knowledge of consumers' psychological traits and of the decision-making process is the basis to shape the policy vision and strategy in several areas of intervention. A behaviorally inspired approach is not, however, an alternative to regulation; it is an additional ingredient in designing efficient (and effective) regulation.

A one-size-fits-all approach is really unlikely to work with a target as heterogeneous as the general public of adults. The behavioral finance literature has identified a large number of biases, each of them impacting economic and financial choices in a different manner. To put it simply, economic theory basically prescribes only one way of being a rational consumer, whereas the forms of irrationality are many. Therefore, initiatives of financial education dealing with wrong choices and aiming to induce consumers to better behavior cannot be generic.

Financial education with adults requires the implementation of a diversified portfolio of tools, some for the general public and others calibrated on the needs of specific targets. Wide initiatives to raise the general public's awareness on the relevance of financial literacy for achieving financial well-being are essential to sow the seeds for an effective strategy of financial education. Initiatives to increase the knowledge of basic concepts or of financial products/services aim at supporting those economic choices that consumers make very frequently (for example opening and managing a bank account). These kinds of resources also represent the prerequisite for developing more focused and detailed programs.

More targeted initiatives are the needed complement to the general ones since they can better deal with specific needs of adults and with clearly identified behavioral and cognitive biases. This is the approach undertaken by the most active institutions on the field, which often organize their resources by life events (for example, buying a home, having a baby, retiring) and by target groups (for example women, the elderly, immigrants, the unemployed).

Targeted initiatives need to be tailored to specific mistakes and they require a precise identification of the roots of such mistakes (lack of knowledge, cognitive or behavioral bias). This approach seems to be in line with the one adopted by the UK Financial Conduct Authority (FCA) on the more general ground of consumer protection. The FCA has identified three steps that a regulator should follow to implement policies benefiting from behavioral insight: (1) identifying and prioritizing issues; (2) identifying root causes of problems (regulation, consumers' awareness/knowledge, consumers' behavioral biases); (3) designing effective (specific) interventions.

At its core, a behaviorally oriented financial education approach requires a thorough understanding of the individual decision process. Following Loerwald and Stemmann (2016), the decision process can be broken down into three phases: information perception; information processing and evaluation; decision making. The phase of information perception allows the consumer to reduce uncertainty by selecting the relevant information for the decision to be made. During the second phase, the consumer exploits (processes) the relevant information to come up with a choice. The phase of decision making occurs at the moment the choice is actually made. Even though this is just a simplified representation of the decision process, it turns out to be a useful conceptual tool since it makes the identification of biases easier. In fact, different biases act at different stages of the decision process. For instance, framing and selective perception can blur information perception; anchoring, heuristics and overconfidence impact on information processing and evaluation; loss aversion and self-control bias can still push consumers who correctly perceived and processed information into wrong behavior. In line with the idea that biases need to be tackled with specific remedies, De Meza et al. (2008) provides a detailed taxonomy of cognitive and behavioral biases and for many of them they also propose possible debiasing techniques or tools.

## 5. CONCLUSIONS

We have documented the low level of financial competencies of adults in Italy, showing also that the lack of knowledge is not the only factor reducing consumers' ability to make sound financial decisions. We have documented that behavioral biases, overconfidence in particular, are common among investors and can have relevant negative consequences.

Financial consumer protection authorities should recognize that consumers are often affected by behavioral and cognitive biases, and should take these biases into account when they implement their policies. In particular, financial consumer protection should take two parallel avenues: regulation (laws and their enforcement), and financial education. Neither, alone, is probably able to ensure satisfactory results, but the experience of the most active authorities on the field of consumer protection suggests that a combination of the two set of tools has a higher chance to be effective.

We argue that an approach to financial education that takes into account behavioral insights requires the development of a rich set of bias-specific (and target-specific) resources, in particular when dealing with adults.

An integrated and behaviorally-oriented approach to financial consumer protection requires a multi-disciplinary line of attack. The skills of economists are not enough and need to be complemented by those of psychologists, experts in adult learning and in communication. All these competencies are, however, very unlikely to be found in just one institution. For instance, central banks, which are often active in the field of financial education, may easily lack psychologists and experts in adult learning.

National strategies on financial education explicitly recognize the importance of a close cooperation between public and private players, and aim, among other goals, to stimulate a multi-disciplinary approach to develop resources able to improve consumers' actual financial behavior.

# REFERENCES

Banca d'Italia (2017), Annual Report for 2016, pp. 84–7.

Bertrand, M. and A. Morse (2011), Information disclosure, cognitive biases, and payday borrowing, *Journal of Finance*, **66**(6), 1865–93.

Bracale, A. and F. Franceschi (2018), Le competenze finanziarie dei ragazzi in Italia: Conoscenze e comportamenti, Mimeo.

Branzoli, N. (2016), Price dispersion and consumer inattention: Evidence from the market of bank accounts, Bank of Italy Working Papers No. 1082.

De Meza, D., B. Irlenbusch and D. Reyniers (2008), Financial capability: A behavioural economics perspective. Consumer Research, No. 69. The Financial Services Authority, London.

Di Salvatore, A., F. Franceschi, A. Neri and F. Zanichelli (2018), Measuring the financial literacy of the adult population: The experience of Banca D'Italia, questioni di economia e finanza, Occasional Papers 435, Bank of Italy, Economic Research and International Relations Area.

Financial Conduct Authority (FCA) (2013), Applying behavioral economics at the Financial Conduct Authority, April, Occasional Paper no. 1.

Financial Conduct Authority (FCA) (2016), Behavior and compliance in organizations, December, Occasional Paper no. 24.

Hirshleifer, D. (2008), Psychological bias as a driver of financial regulation, *European Financial Management*, **14**(5), 856–74.

Lefevre, A.F. and M. Chapman (2017), Behavioural economics and financial consumer protection, OECD Working Papers on Finance, Insurance and Private Pensions no. 42, Paris: OECD.

Loerwald, D. and A. Stemmann (2016), Behavioral finance and financial literacy: Educational implications of biases in financial decision making. In C. Aprea, E. Wuttke, K. Breuer, N. Koh, P. Davies, B. Greimel-Fuhrmann and J. Lopus (eds), *International Handbook of Financial Literacy*, Singapore: Springer, pp. 25–38.

Lunn, P. (2014), *Regulatory Policy and Behavioural Economics*, Paris: OECD Publishing.

OECD (2015), 2015 OECD/INFE Toolkit for measuring financial literacy and financial inclusion, Paris: OECD.

OECD (2017), G20/OECD INFE Report on adult financial literacy in G20 countries, Paris: OECD.

# 13. Behavioral impact of policies for the start-up and Venture Capital ecosystem

**Giampio Bracchi**

New technological companies and Venture Capital funds are at the center of much attention in Europe, and particularly in Italy, in order to regenerate the industrial and economic system after the long crisis, to support innovation, job creation, productivity and economic growth, and to promote sustainable smart development.

Governments at the national, regional and local levels play an important role in deciding on suitable legal and fiscal frameworks for boosting new entrepreneurship as well as in filling market gaps. Governments can also support and orientate entrepreneurial attitudes and behavior inside academic research and education, by providing systematic strategic goals and by developing an integrated policy framework to cover the entire spectrum of activities, from basic research to spin-offs (Audretsch et al., 2007).

This chapter will briefly review some of the existing public policies for academic spin-offs, start-ups and Venture Capital funds in Italy, and will discuss the empirical evidence of their effects on the behavior of the actors and stakeholders in the technological ecosystem.

## 1. THE ITALIAN INNOVATION ANOMALY

Start-ups, in order to succeed, need a strong technological ecosystem with easy access to Venture Capital finance (Hwang and Horowitt, 2012). Venture Capital and start-ups in Italy – and in some other countries in Europe – differently from the US, up to now have been substantially a case of market failure. The numerical evidence of the significant lack of Venture Capital and start-ups in Italy in comparison with European countries like the UK, France or Germany, and Switzerland or Spain, has led to a number of new specific regulations and laws in order to reduce the existing gap. The aim of this legal framework is to create a favorable environment, gradually introducing tax exemptions and incentives, guarantees on loans, specific rules in the case of failure or bankruptcy, easy employment regulations, dedicated funds, incentives for patents, and so on.

However, in spite of those measures, an evident anomaly remains in the Italian ecosystem, as Figure 13.1 shows. Italy ranks 11th worldwide for the number of researchers, while coming 7th for the number of scientific publications. However, looking to the economic exploitation of research results, Italy falls to 12th position for the number of patents, to 18th (in Europe only) for high-tech exports, and again falls to an unacceptable 24th position for Venture Capital investments worldwide (Varaldo, 2014).

A part of this anomaly is a consequence of the specific content and application of the public policies and of the opportunistic behavior of the actors of the technological and financial ecosystem. The rest of this chapter will briefly discuss some relevant issues.

## 2.   VALUATION CRITERIA OF UNIVERSITIES AND INDUCED ACADEMIC BEHAVIOR

The technical innovations at the basis of successful start-ups frequently originate from academic research. Academic institutions can assume a critical role as intellectual hubs by serving as pre-incubators for the exploitation of research results, as well as focal points for collaboration between researchers, companies and start-ups. Furthermore, universities are required to take specific action to serve as catalysts for sustainable innovation systems, involving various actors and stakeholders, activating a virtuous cycle of creativity, research and development, knowledge generation, application and innovation (Passiante and Romano, 2016).

However, traditionally in Italy the valuation of university researchers essentially considers the number of papers they publish in international journals and their bibliographic citations. As a result, researchers prefer to address theoretical research, which can be developed and completed in a shorter time span and requires fewer resources and simpler structures with respect to applied and experimental work. Therefore, professors and researchers produce many papers that are not immediately useful in generating new patents and spin-offs or start-ups. The result is a quantity of papers, but not an important contribution to technical innovation and, in general, to turning ideas into action.

More recently, in order to promote the industrial and economic exploitation of research, the valuation – and funding – of universities and research centers also considers the number of the patents they register

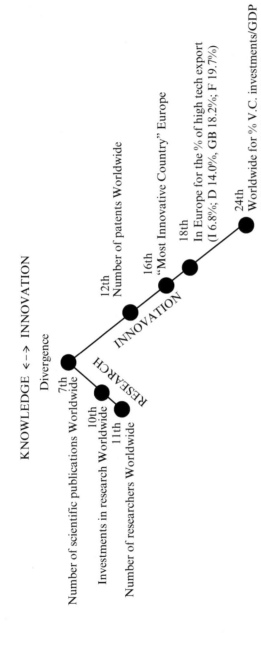

*Source:* Varaldo (2014).

*Figure 13.1   The Italian innovation anomaly*

and the number of spin-offs of research. However, the Key Performance Indicator for patents, for example, is their number, and not the value of the royalties obtained from the market. The result has been that universities have structured small and local Technology Transfer Offices and Incubators of spin-offs and start-ups, producing an increasing number of patents and small entrepreneurial initiatives (Ramaciotti and Daniele, 2016). Such initiatives frequently remain isolated and fragmented, lacking an integrative and systemic approach that could have the potential to cultivate successful entrepreneurial mechanisms.

In this critical environment, most universities were not able to provide an effective support, in terms of professional competences, structures and capital, for obtaining market value from patents or for fostering the growth and the economic success of spin-offs (Piccaluga et al., 2012).

Also the capability, and will, of government agencies to select the best performers among universities and to concentrate the small amount of available resources was limited. Therefore, the result of the new policies was again the quantity of small initiatives and not economic value.

Problems of governance have thus emerged in terms of understanding the factors that affect entrepreneurial behaviors of individual researchers and academic organizations, and introducing and managing motivational systems that spur individuals and departments to act in an entrepreneurial way (Gemmel et al., 2012).

## 3.  FISCAL INCENTIVES, PERFORMANCE OF THE START-UP ECOSYSTEM AND BEHAVIOR OF INVESTORS

In a wider context, in order to sustain the creation of new technological companies and their attractiveness in raising funds, government agencies in Europe introduced a number of tax exemptions, incentives and regulatory simplifications for both start-ups and Venture Capital funds (European Commission, 2013). In Italy and in some other European countries, however, start-ups and Venture Capital funds, at least in recent years, have not been able to produce significant profits. Consequently, those tax incentives were useful only to initially foster the creation of a number of weak entrepreneurial initiatives and small VC funds, but in the absence of profits, the tax exemptions could not really be applied and exploited. The result was that the new measures failed to produce a significant outcome in attracting important private investments to Venture Capital funds and to fast-growing start-ups. The result also in this case was more quantity than quality.

Rules that are more recent have been automatic and generous tax rebates and incentives directly in favor of the investors – and not only of target funds or companies – and larger public funds (and funds of funds) for investing in start-ups and Venture Capital. However, this has produced once again only a limited improvement in the capability of attracting private investments, since a problem of skepticism or underconfidence remains in the investors, due to the scarcity of previous success histories or inspiring champions. The capitalism of start-ups has not yet reached a market structure.

Finally, there is also a very limited number of spin-offs originated by existing large technological or media companies, which usually, in other countries, are the best candidates to become successful initiatives. This relates also to a different behavioral factor, that is, the existing overprotection of employees and managers in Italy, by virtue of labor regulations that are very rigid and favorable to the workers: consequently, they develop an aversion to taking entrepreneurial risks in leaving the original company and starting a new autonomous initiative.

## 4.   CONCLUDING REMARKS

A large number of important public measures and regulations have been gradually introduced, and Italy is probably now at a turning point, but is still far from transforming the start-up ecosystem into an effective platform. An integrated and flexible motivational framework should stand at the basis of any policy or action plan focusing on new technology-driven idea generation and the translation of such ideas into business opportunities (Viale, 2008).

A change, or at least a tuning, of many policies is necessary, with a more pragmatic and goal-oriented approach that overcomes dispersion and localism. More courage is necessary to select the best performers, even when making somebody unhappy. This will help to induce more appropriate behavior on the part of the different actors, and to generate valuable and fast-growing start-ups that are able to attract important private investments to the Venture Capital industry.

## REFERENCES

Audretsch, D.B., I. Grilo and A.R. Thurik (eds) (2007), *Handbook of Research on Entrepreneurship Policy*, Cheltenham, UK and Northampton, MA, USA: Edward Elgar Publishing.

European Commission (2013), Entrepreneurship 2020 Action Plan: Reigniting the Entrepreneurial Spirit in Europe, EU DG Enterprise and Industry, Brussels.

Gemmel, R.M., R.J. Boland and D.A. Kolb (2012), The socio-cognitive dynamics of entrepreneurial ideation, *Entrepreneurship Theory and Practice*, **36** (5), 1053–73.

Hwang, V.W. and G. Horowitt (2012), *The Rainforest: The Secret to Building the Next Silicon Valley*, Los Altos Hills, CA: Regenwald.

Passiante, G. and A. Romano (eds) (2016), *Creating Technology-Driven Entrepreneurship*, London: Palgrave Macmillan.

Piccaluga, A., C. Balderi and C. Daniele (2012), *The ProTon Europe*. Ninth Annual Survey Report, Brussels: ProTon Europe.

Ramaciotti, L. and C. Daniele (eds) (2016), *XIII Report on Exploitation of Italian Public Research*, Pavia: Netval.

Varaldo, R. (2014), *The New Game of Innovation* [in Italian], Bologna: Edizioni Il Mulino.

Viale, R. (ed.) (2008), *The Culture of Innovation* [in Italian], Milan: Edizioni Il Sole 24 Ore.

# 14. Investors' inconsistencies and the need for better financial literacy

## Gregorio De Felice

This chapter examines some apparent inconsistencies in the attitude of Italian savers towards investment. The figures discussed are drawn from the 2017 edition of the *Survey on Italian Saving and Financial Choices*.[1] The survey is carried out yearly by Centro Einaudi (Turin) and Intesa Sanpaolo and is based on interviews (conducted by Doxa, the market research company) to a sample of over 1000 households holding a bank or a postal account.

The first inconsistency refers to the households' approach to portfolio selection.

Generally, Italian households show a very prudent attitude (see Table 14.1). When asked: "What do you think people should first consider when investing?", around 62 per cent of respondents cite: "Safety" (that is, "Confidence that capital is not eroded significantly in the case of a crisis"). Indeed, capital protection stands out as the single most relevant concern for Italian investors, as the second choice in the ranking (namely: "The yield you can gain in the short run, i.e. less than 1 year") is cited by only 14.7 per cent of respondents. Third in the rank is "Liquidity" (that is: "The possibility to divest rapidly, at low costs and without incurring capital losses"), which is mentioned by 13.4 per cent of the sample.

According to this approach, householders show high risk aversion. If asked to rank their propensity to bear risk in a scale that goes from 1 ("I am completely uninterested") to 5 ("I am extremely interested"), around 65 per cent of respondents choose "1" or "2". Only 11 per cent select "4" or "5" (which correspond to a high or very high propensity to bear risk). Of course, differences emerge between categories: risk propensity is comparatively higher when the participant is an entrepreneur (21 per cent) or a "great saver" (that is, she/he saves 20 per cent or more of her/his disposable income). Interestingly, among very young people (aged between

---

[1] Intesa Sanpaolo and Centro di Ricerca e Documentazione Luigi Einaudi (2017).

*Table 14.1  What do you think people should first consider when investing? (First choice, percentage of total)*

| | Years | | | Gender | | Age | | | | | |
| --- | --- | --- | --- | --- | --- | --- | --- | --- | --- | --- | --- |
| | 2017 | 2016 | 2015 | Men | Women | 18–24 | 25–34 | 35–44 | 45–54 | 55–64 | 65 over |
| Yield (less than 1 year) | 14.7 | 14.9 | 17.5 | 14.1 | 15.9 | 43.5 | 7.8 | 15.0 | 14.9 | 17.6 | 13.5 |
| Safety | 61.9 | 58.3 | 52.0 | 63.6 | 58.1 | 42.4 | 67.2 | 64.0 | 60.7 | 58.8 | 62.6 |
| Liquidity | 13.4 | 13.6 | 13.0 | 12.2 | 16.0 | – | 18.6 | 12.6 | 13.2 | 14.0 | 12.6 |
| Yield (5 years and over) | 6.1 | 7.0 | 10.6 | 6.6 | 5.1 | 14.2 | 4.9 | 3.4 | 5.5 | 6.7 | 7.8 |
| No answer | 3.9 | 6.1 | 6.9 | 3.5 | 4.9 | – | 1.5 | 4.9 | 5.6 | 2.8 | 3.5 |

*Source:*  Intesa Sanpaolo and Centro Einaudi (2017).

18 and 24) answers are somewhat "polarized" between 1 ("I don't want to bear any risk", 42 per cent) and 4 ("I'm interested in risking", 36 per cent).

All these data notwithstanding, very few people diversify their investments: here is the first inconsistency. Over 52 per cent of the respondents say they have highly concentrated portfolios (that is, more than two-thirds of the portfolio is allocated to a single financial instrument), while only 5 per cent declare a "high diversification" (less than 10 per cent of the portfolio is allocated to a single financial instrument). To sum up: Italians prefer safety to returns, but they evidently ignore the fact that diversification is the most basic strategy to minimize risk.

The second inconsistency refers to the comprehension of risk and the role of information. According to around 56 per cent of the sample, understanding the degree of risk inherent in different investment proposals is the single most difficult task for a saver (see Table 14.2). Ranked second is the choice of the appropriate "time-to-market", which is cited by 43 per cent of the respondents; other areas of concern are the selection of specific bonds or shares (32 per cent) and the choice of the most appropriate allocation of savings among the different asset classes (31.4 per cent).

Even though recognizing that the comprehension of risk could be a major problem, people do not devote time and effort to gain financial information. Around 50 per cent of respondents say they are "uninterested" or "not particularly interested" in topics related to economics or finance. More than 80 per cent spend less than one hour per week reading financial newspapers, watching TV programmes or consulting the Internet; only 1.5 per cent had the opportunity to attend a course of finance, for example at high school, at university or in the workplace.

Around 30 per cent of respondents, on average, had gained some basic notion of finance from the family. The percentage is not particularly encouraging in itself, but the good news is that it is inversely correlated with age: it is 26.1 per cent for respondents over the age of 65, but reaches 57.4 per cent for those in the 18 to 24 age bracket.

These two "inconsistencies" emphasize, in my opinion, a very basic fact: although initiatives are already underway in Italy in the field of financial education, greater effort is needed. In order to look in greater depth at the problem, the Survey on Italian Saving and Financial Choices devotes a special section of the 2017 edition to financial education, prepared with a contribution from the Center for Economic and Policy Research (CEPR).

Financial literacy is measured using the so-called "big three" created by Annamaria Lusardi and Olivia Mitchell in 2011, namely: three questions designed to assess whether people correctly understand what interest rates, inflation and risk diversification are, and how they work.

Table 14.2   What is the single most difficult task a saver must perform when investing? (Percentage of total)

| | Years | | | Gender | | Age | | | | | |
|---|---|---|---|---|---|---|---|---|---|---|---|
| | 2017 | 2016 | 2015 | Men | Women | 18–24 | 25–34 | 35–44 | 45–54 | 45–54 | 65 over |
| Choice of the right asset allocation | 31.4 | 42.8 | 45.2 | 30.9 | 32.4 | 21.3 | 32.3 | 32.4 | 29.2 | 32.1 | 31.9 |
| Selection of specific financial instruments | 32.0 | 37.2 | 35.7 | 33.7 | 28.3 | 56.8 | 29.5 | 31.5 | 35.0 | 31.1 | 31.0 |
| Comprehension of risk | 55.9 | 43.7 | 37.5 | 56.0 | 55.7 | 58.4 | 52.4 | 58.2 | 55.4 | 51.4 | 58.3 |
| Time to market | 42.9 | 41.4 | 43.8 | 43.6 | 41.3 | 42.4 | 50.0 | 42.7 | 45.4 | 44.1 | 39.3 |
| Other | 0.7 | 0.6 | 0.8 | 0.5 | 1.0 | – | 1.1 | 1.0 | – | – | 1.2 |
| Don't know | 14.1 | 14.3 | 16.2 | 13.0 | 16.5 | – | 10.9 | 13.8 | 13.7 | 15.8 | 14.4 |

Source:   Intesa Sanpaolo and Centro Einaudi (2017).

*Table 14.3   Statistics on financial literacy (percentage of total)*

|  | Total | Men | Women | 18–54 | 55 and over |
|---|---|---|---|---|---|
| Comprehension of interest rates | 65 | 68 | 63 | 64 | 66 |
| Comprehension of inflation | 51 | 54 | 49 | 52 | 49 |
| Comprehension of risk diversification | 50 | 53 | 48 | 55 | 47 |
| Correct answers: 3 | 22 | 28 | 18 | 25 | 20 |
| Correct answers: 2 | 58 | 58 | 57 | 59 | 57 |
| Correct answers: 1 | 86 | 88 | 85 | 87 | 85 |
| Correct answers: 0 | 14 | 12 | 15 | 13 | 15 |
| Average number of correct answers | 1.66 | 1.75 | 1.60 | 1.71 | 1.62 |

*Source:*   CEPR elaborations on Survey on Italian Saving and Financial Choices.

Very briefly, the survey reveals (see Table 14.3) that 65 per cent of the participants correctly understand interest rates, 51 per cent understand inflation (and how it influences real interest rates and the purchasing power of money) and 50 per cent understand risk diversification (that is, that concentrating the portfolio on a single stock or bond could be riskier than buying, for example, a mutual fund). Unfortunately, only 22 per cent of the sample correctly understand all three variables jointly (which is not exactly encouraging).

Additional questions have also been included in the questionnaire to gain deeper insight into the ability of Italian households to deal with more complex economic problems. The questions are centred on the comprehension of: (1) volatility (percentage of correct answers: 51 per cent); (2) the relation between the duration of mortgages and the flow of interest payments (55 per cent); (3) the correlation between interest rates and the price of bonds (a modest 27 per cent); (4) respondents' computing abilities (61 per cent). Taking both batteries of questions together, respondents give 3.6 correct answers out of 7, on average. However, people aged between 18 and 24 show comparatively higher financial competence: they can correctly answer 4 questions out of 7, against 3.3 in for respondents aged 65 and over. This information is worth noting, as it could represent a promising indication for the future.

# REFERENCES

Intesa Sanpaolo and Centro di Ricerca e Documentazione Luigi Einaudi (2017), "Indagine sul Risparmio e le scelte finanziarie degli italiani 2017 – Consapevolezza, fiducia, crescita: le sfide dell'educazione finanziaria" ["Survey on Italian saving and financial choices, 2017 – Awareness, confidence, growth: the challenges of financial education"], ed. Giuseppe Russo, July.
Lusardi, Annamaria and Mitchell, Olivia S. (2011), "Financial literacy around the world: an overview", NBER Working Paper No. 17107.

# 15. How behavioural finance can reshape financial consumer protection: Consob's first steps in the European framework

**Nadia Linciano***

## 1. INTRODUCTION

The latest financial crisis has challenged the standard paradigm underlining financial regulation as well as the approach traditionally underpinning financial consumer protection.

To empower financial consumers, regulators and supervisors have long relied on information disclosure, rules of conduct and financial education. Broadly speaking, transparency rules mandate issuers to disclose the characteristics of their own financial instruments in terms of expected return, risks and costs. Intermediaries must act in the best interest of their clients and, in this perspective, comply with both transparency and conduct obligations. Finally, financial education should complement transparency and conduct rules by enabling consumers to understand the characteristics of financial products, properly interact with the intermediaries and claim for compensation in case of misconduct, frauds and scams.

This setting is rooted in the rationality hypothesis. Individuals making decisions under uncertainty are deemed to be able to process all the information available, to figure out all the alternative scenarios and to optimally choose one of the options available, given their (stable) set of preferences and their financial constraints.

Within this framework, the more information the better, as complete information triggers awareness and empowers consumers. Information in financial documents, both in narrative and quantitative formats, has therefore proliferated with little regard to its presentation and salience.

---

* Opinions expressed in this chapter are exclusively the author's and do not necessarily reflect those of Consob.

Rules of conduct themselves have increasingly relied on information flows from intermediaries to individuals both at the point of sale and on an ongoing basis.

Since the 2000s, several scandals across the world have highlighted that investors do purchase unsuitable financial products in spite of the information available to them. A rising number of policy makers have become interested in understanding why this could happen, while delving deeper in the individual decision-making process has increasingly been regarded as an important precondition for successful policy actions. Since then, international institutions and national jurisdictions have been launching behaviourally informed initiatives and policies.[1] Also Consob (the Italian Authority for Securities Markets) has increasingly been investigating the topic in order to improve the effectiveness of its supervision.

This chapter focuses on Consob's first steps towards behaviourally informed policies within the European framework. Section 2 recalls the engagement of the European Commission on one side, and of the European Securities Markets Authority (ESMA) on the other side, translating increasingly to a reference to behavioural insights as a background to regulation and supervision. Section 3 reviews behavioural research in Consob and its applications to financial disclosure, rules of conduct and investor education. Section 4 concludes.

## 2. ASCERTAINING THE ROLE OF COGNITIVE SCIENCES: THE ENGAGEMENT OF THE EUROPEAN INSTITUTIONS

The European Commission is among the first European institutions to foster the inclusion in the regulatory cycle of the theoretical background and the empirical toolbox built on cognitive sciences. Its Joint Research Centre (JRC) aims to support EU policy making by raising awareness

---

[1]  See, among others, the OECD, whose initiatives are detailed at http://www.oecd. org/gov/regulatory-policy/behavioural-insights.htm (accessed 1 April 2018). The European Commission is engaged in the dissemination of the behavioural approach through the Joint Research Centre (for a review of policy initiatives either explicitly or implicitly informed by behavioural insights as well as related institutional developments in EU and EFTA countries, see JRC, 2016a and 2016b). With reference to financial regulation and supervision, see IOSCO (2013), stating the board members' agreement to embed behavioural economics in the regulatory approach, and IOSCO (2014), discussing application of behavioural economics to financial education. As for national initiatives in the financial sector, see, among others, the UK Financial Conduct Authority at https://www.fca.org.uk/search-results?search_term=work%20in%20the%20Behavioural%20Economics&start=1 (accessed 1 April 2018), and the Autoriteit Financiële Markten as reviewed in AFM (2016).

and training EU policy makers in the use of behavioural insights. In detail, the JRC provides scientific advice and methodological support to the behavioural studies and market studies undertaken by the European Commission, fosters networking and knowledge sharing between Member States and conducts behavioural research (JRC, 2013; 2015). Beyond behavioural economics, the JRC draws from various disciplines such as social psychology, cognitive psychology, anthropology and experimental economics.

In 2010 the European Commission marked its interest in the behavioural approach through the publication of a Report on consumer decision-making in retail investment services (2010 EC Report, henceforth), gathering survey data and experimental evidence on the process of researching, choosing and purchasing retail investment products. As detailed in the following, the Report touched on several facets of the design of disclosure regulation and rules of conduct.

## 2.1   Financial Disclosure

Based on the survey and experimental evidence gathered across EU countries, the 2010 EC Report acknowledged that presentation of financial information does affect retail investors' decision-making process. In fact, not only financial illiteracy, but also information overload, heuristic decision-making and framing effects were found to severely impair individual choices, especially when disclosure is complex and/or perceived as such.[2] Simplification and standardization of product information were therefore claimed as necessary policy actions.

These findings subsequently informed the design of the Key Investor Information Document (KIID) on Undertakings for Collective Investment in Transferable Securities (UCITS).[3] The KIID initiated the delivery of information on UCITS to investors and replaced the formerly envisaged Simplified Prospectus. The content and format of the KIID were detailed on the basis of a consumer testing, run on a sample of consumers and intermediaries across some Member States and exploring preferences on a number of disclosure options. The test showed that the majority of consumers were not willing to read documents that were too long and that included information hidden in small print or detailed in large blocks of

---

[2]   By way of example, subjects were found to have trouble in identifying the optimal choice when fees on financial products were framed as percentages or when annual returns were not compounded over the duration of the investment.

[3]   The KIID was envisaged by the revised UCITS Directive (2009/65/EU, so-called UCITS IV), and the implementing Regulation (EU) No. 583/2010, detailed in the CESR (now ESMA) Guidelines issued at the end of 2010.

text, whereas visual formats, such as graphs, were more engaging. As for risk representation, on average consumers preferred a synthetic indicator to a narrative description. Finally, financial knowledge and investment experience were found to be the main factors prompting the use of the KIID by financial consumers.

Building on this approach, the 2014 legislation on Packaged Retail and Insurance-based Investment Products (PRIIPs) envisaged a standardized Key Investor Document (KID),[4] that is, a maximum three A4-format-page document, setting out information in a manner that is 'fair, clear and not misleading' and restricted to what the investors need (basically, risks, return and costs). The Joint Committee of the European Supervisory Authorities (JC ESAs) defined regulatory technical standards (RTS) detailing the presentation and the contents of the KID, as well as the methodology for calculation of risks, return and costs (JC ESAs, 2016).[5] The ESAs fulfilled their mandate also by building on the insights of the research on consumer behaviour. Indeed, they highlighted that:

> a traditional approach to disclosures focused solely on information and with little regard to its presentation, is in being superseded in policy making by an approach that is more informed by insights into consumer behaviours. For instance, the framing of information can be considered, so as to counter cognitive biases which may distort perceptions and provide information in a way that is both simple to understand but also salient for the consumer (i.e. capable of drawing the consumers' attention and appearing important for the decision to be made). (JC ESAs, 2014, p. 17)

## 2.2　Rules of Conduct

Individuals' behavioural biases may also interfere with the effectiveness of rules of conduct directed to intermediaries. The 2010 EC Report focused on this issue by gathering experimental and survey evidence on investors' response to disclosure of conflicts of interests between financial advisors and customers in terms of willingness to place trust in advisors and to pay up-front fees for information and advice.

Subjects' reaction to the declaration of conflicts of interest turned out to be context dependent. When interacting via online platforms, individuals hardly showed any reaction unless they were warned with

---

[4]　See Regulation (EU) No. 1286/2014 of the European Parliament and of the Council of 26 November 2014.
[5]　The RTS build on discussion and consultation papers (respectively, JC/DP/2014/02, JC/DP/2015/01 and JC/CP/2015/073) as well as on the evidence of a consumer testing (European Commission, 2015).

flagged and highlighted messages. In contrast, direct communication between advisors and advisee triggered a strong response of mistrust, with potentially adverse impact on the investment decision-making process (indeed, subjects lost trust even when advisors could not deceive them). Finally, narrow framing and loss aversion turned out to make people disproportionally averse to paying up-front fees for advisory services.

A further step towards the application of behavioural insights to the rules of conduct for investment firms was made by the European Securities Markets Authority (ESMA). ESMA has recently referred to behavioural economics in the revision of its 2012 Guidelines on suitability assessment obligation, a rule of conduct marking one of the most important stages of the relationship between the intermediary and the investor (ESMA, 2017).[6] The suitability assessment obligation was first envisaged by the Directive on markets and financial instruments (MiFID I) and then confirmed by the so-called MiFID II. This relates to the obligation for the advisor and the portfolio manager to check whether, respectively, the recommended financial product and the investment choice made on behalf of the clients are suitable to the financial profile of the clients themselves. The efficacy of the profiling heavily depends on the reliability and the validity of the tools (that is, the so-called MiFID questionnaires) used to gather information on customers' financial knowledge and experience, investment objectives and time horizon. In its 2017 revision, ESMA warned about cognitive distortions (first of all, framing effects) that need to be accounted for when structuring questionnaires and recommended paying special attention to the recognition of behavioural attitudes affecting the investor's financial profile (such as risk tolerance), particularly those sensitive to psychological and emotional factors. Upon these considerations, the new ESMA Guidelines include examples providing practical guidance for the development of questionnaires 'robust' to behavioural biases.

## 3.   DELVING DEEPER INTO THE APPLICATION OF COGNITIVE SCIENCES IN CONSOB

Consob has been engaged since 2010 in the investigation of how financial regulation and supervision can benefit from cognitive sciences. The trigger was a mis-selling case. A bank distributed its own bonds to its clients after deceitfully changing their financial profile at the point of sale. The bank

---

[6]   The new guidelines build on those already issued under MiFID I and are augmented to reflect the results of national supervisory activity, recent studies on behavioural finance and developments in automated advice tools.

had duly informed its customers that they might have lost almost half their capital with a probability higher than 60 per cent. Nevertheless, several investors had purchased the risky bonds (Consob, 2013, p. 43). This event evidently signalled the need to go beyond standard disclosure. It also made clear that the exploration of alternative avenues could best be undertaken on an evidence-based approach.

As a first step, Consob published a research paper reviewing studies in behavioural finance, cognitive psychology and experimental evidence on observed anomalies in individual investment choices, with the aim of stimulating the debate on the potential applications of behavioural analysis to financial regulation and supervision.

Second, an observatory was set up in order to gather data on consumers' financial knowledge, attitudes and investment choices. Since 2015, the data have been published in the annual report on the investment choices of Italian households.

Third, Consob started to review key pillars of investors' protection, such as financial disclosure and suitability assessment, through behavioural lenses.

### 3.1   Financial Disclosure

In 2015 Consob, in collaboration with Università Politecnica delle Marche, ran a consumer testing in order to gain insight into the extent to which subjective understanding and perception may challenge the effectiveness of disclosure on financial instruments (Gentile et al., 2015). A sample of 254 Italian investors were given different templates, each delivering in different modes the same information on risks, return and costs of four financial instruments (that is, two Italian listed stocks and two structured bonds – one outstanding and the other newly issued – negotiated on the Italian retail bond market). Risks were alternatively disclosed through four formats, mirroring those delivered by firms to investors, also pursuant to information obligations (that is, a synthetic indicator, a series of indicators gauging different financial risk dimensions, what-if scenarios and probabilistic modelling of expected returns). The test aimed to explore: (1) how different representation formats of the risk/return characteristics of a financial product are appraised in terms of complexity, usefulness and information content; (2) how different formats influence risk perception; (3) how different formats affect the willingness to invest. Consistently with the experimental literature, risk perception was found to be context-dependent and mainly driven by the way financial information was disclosed. Moreover, the higher the perceived complexity, the lower was the willingness to invest. However, perceived complexity declined (and willingness to invest rose) when investors were able to identify one or more pieces of information as salient, that is, relevant to the decision to be made. The study also pointed out that simplifying financial disclosure might not be sufficient to ensure correct risk perception and unbiased investment choices as both investors' heterogeneity and behavioural biases might hinder a 'one-size-fits-all' approach. In this perspective, the communication of risk should rely on more than one representation format, as fostered by some scholars (Diacon and Hasseldine, 2007) as well as by the European legislator in the KIID and KID regulations.

## 3.2 Rules of Conduct: Suitability Assessment and the Demand for Financial Advice

As for rules of conduct, Consob's economic research devoted special attention to the suitability assessment that, as mentioned above, firms are mandated to administer when recommending the purchase of a financial product or offering the portfolio management service. Specifically, Consob reviewed the MiFID questionnaires used by a representative sample of Italian banks with respect to both their contents and the procedures adopted for structuring and administering them (Linciano and Soccorso, 2012). Although overall compliant with MiFID I, most questionnaires were not aligned with the insights of the economic and psychological literature. In addition, several inappropriate linguistic and textual features hampered clarity and comprehensibility of the tool. Moreover, questions very often relied on clients' self-evaluation, thus potentially invalidating the elicitation of reliable information on their financial knowledge, financial capability and risk preferences. The assessment of risk tolerance was among the most defective item, as it was elicited jointly with preferences on the time horizon and investment objectives, neglecting the fact that each of these variables may be driven by different factors. Moreover, the wording of the questions on risk attitude lacked the stylistic and lexical precautions that, according to the psychometric literature, are key to the elicitation of valid and reliable answers. All told, only two questionnaires out of 20 turned out to be effective and valid. This evidence was shared with ESMA as Consob's contribution to the new Guidelines on suitability obligations mentioned in the previous paragraph.

An additional stream of Consob's investigation concerned the relationship between the demand for financial advice and overconfidence. Professional and unbiased support is usually deemed as key to investor protection, as it may guide illiterate individuals towards suitable financial choices. This opinion, however, rests on the hypothesis that consumers' willingness to ask for professional advice is independent of their financial knowledge or personal traits, such as overconfidence. In fact, Consob's investigation on the relationship between the propensity to seek for advice and financial knowledge and overconfidence showed the opposite (Gentile et al., 2016). The demand for financial advice was found to be positively related to financial knowledge and negatively related to overconfidence (as measured by the mismatch between perceived and actual knowledge). Moreover, high self-assessment of one's own competence turned out to be significantly and negatively associated with high levels of financial knowledge, which in turn resulted in being higher among male, wealthier and more risk averse individuals.

These findings highlighted the fact that financial advice may act as a complement rather than as a substitute of financial capability. To trigger demand by less sophisticated investors additional initiatives might be necessary, such as financial education campaigns highlighting the added value of professional support.

There is no doubt, however, that many retail investors' unwillingness to demand financial advice is also due to low accessibility to the service in terms of costs and wealth. This is the so-called advice gap, which is becoming a major concern of financial regulators.

Robo advice (that is, automated, online provision of financial recommendations) has been touted as an answer to the advice gap as it is less costly than the traditional service to both providers and consumers. However, digitalization may trigger new risks. Research on online shopping shows, for instance, that online and offline decision-making processes may differ along several dimensions, such as information search and trust placed upon the provider (Laudon and Traver, 2017; Lim and Dubinsky, 2004; Katawetawaraks and Wang, 2011). Information overload and impulsivity might be exacerbated. Further investigation is needed to understand to what extent these differences may impact on consumers' financial risk perception and behaviours. To this purpose, Consob is working together with academia to evaluate, through experiments and focus groups, first how risk perception, trust and choices may differ across human and robo advice, and secondly whether robo advice may enhance investors' willingness to ask for professional support.

### 3.3 Investor Education

Consob behavioural research on investors' choices and attitudes has also provided important insights for education initiatives. It is increasingly clear that traditional financial education, meant as delivery of notions and data, may be pointless because it neglects cognitive and non-cognitive processes underlying personal engagement and learning. Paradoxically, standard financial education might even produce undesired side-effects, for instance by fostering an unmotivated confidence in one's own skills and, as a consequence, by triggering excessive risk-taking behaviour (Willis, 2008). Consob has been gradually departing from the standard investor education approach. The collective work titled 'Challenges in ensuring financial competencies. Essays on how to measure financial knowledge, target beneficiaries and deliver educational programmes' (edited by Linciano and Soccorso, 2017), is a first step towards a renewed, multidisciplinary methodological setting that could inform financial education. The work, occasioned by Consob's participation in the World Investor Week (WIW), a week-long, global campaign promoted by the International Organization of Securities Commissions (IOSCO), gathers the views of several researchers engaged in the field of behavioural economics, neuroscience, sociology, psychology and pedagogy on how to gauge financial knowledge, elicit personal attitudes, target beneficiaries and deliver educational programmes. Among other things, it provides food for thought on the relationship among emotional status and personal motivations (such as financial anxiety and personal interest)[7] on one hand, and personal engagement and learning processes on the other hand. In addition, it suggests how behavioural finance and neuroscience may help in the development of effective communication channels and interactive tools (such as games and simulations) leveraging on experiential learning processes. This work is not conclusive, of course, nor does it cover key topics such as the assessment of educational initiatives, which are crucial to the design of effective actions and plans and to public accountability. Consob is committed to promoting further behaviourally informed investigation, also to the benefit of the implementation of the National Strategy for Financial Education, issued by the recently established National Committee for Financial Education.

## 4.   FUTURE STEPS

The behavioural research undertaken so far in Consob is in line with the attention that securities regulators and supervisors are increasingly paying to cognitive sciences worldwide and provides some examples of how traditional protection tools may be refined through behavioural lenses.

At the same time, it is becoming clearer that an effective integration of cognitive insights into financial consumer protection requires the

---

[7]   On these points, see also Consob (2017).

definition of a comprehensive methodological setting, well grounded in the regulatory and supervisory cycles, supporting both data analysis and decision-making processes. Data on investors' behaviour are key to *ex-ante* cost–benefit analysis and *ex-post* evaluation of policy interventions. Evidence on decision-making in organizations may help to promote compliance. Understanding of regulatory and supervisory processes also needs to be examined in order to identify areas of improvement. In this respect, the so-called 'fast-and-frugal' approach[8] is a promising starting point, which might allow regulators and supervisors to make decisions effectively and efficiently in spite of time, knowledge and computational limitations.

Much remains to be done, also in cooperation with market participants, who may benefit from the regulators' improved understanding of problems in the market, and academia, whose contribution is vital to keep track of the latest developments in the theoretical and applied literature.

## REFERENCES

AFM (2016), 'AFM and the application of behavioral insights', accessed 31 March 2018 at https://www.afm.nl/. . ./application-behavioural-insights.ashx?la=nl-nl.

Consob (2013), 'Annual Report', accessed 31 March 2018 at http://www.consob.it/documents/46180/46181/rel2013.pdf/21e050fc-da05-4e37-8ae4-5e16fc6c1684.

Consob (2017), 'Report on the investment choices of Italian households', accessed 31 March 2018 at http://www.consob.it/web/consob-and-its-activities/report-on-investments-households.

Diacon, S. and J. Hasseldine (2007), 'Framing effects and risk perception: The effect of prior performance presentation format on investment fund choice', *Journal of Economic Psychology*, **28** (1), 31–52.

ESMA (2017), 'Consultation paper on guidelines on certain aspects of the MiFID II suitability requirements', accessed 15 March 2018 at 2017-esma35-43-748_-_cp_on_draft_guidelines_on_suitability.pdf.

European Commission (2010), 'Report on consumer decision-making in retail investment services: a behavioural economics perspective', accessed 28 February 2018 at https://www.wiwi.uni-frankfurt.de/fileadmin/user_upload/dateien_abteilungen/abt_fin/Dokumente/PDFs/Allgemeine_Dokumente/Inderst_Downloads/POLICY_PAPERS_and_POLICY_RELATED_REPORTS/consumer_decision-making_in_retail_investment_services_-_final_report_en.pdf.

European Commission (2015), 'Consumer testing studies of the possible new format and content for retail disclosures of Packaged Retail and Insurance-based Investment Products, Final Report', accessed 1 April 2018 at https://ec.europa.eu/info/publications/consumer-testing-study-key-information-documents-priips_en.

Gentile, M., N. Linciano, C. Lucarelli and P. Soccorso (2015), 'Financial risk disclosure and investment decisions. Evidence from a consumer testing exer-

---

[8] See, among others, Gigerenzer et al. (1999).

cise', WP No. 82, May, accessed 1 April 2018 at http://www.consob.it/docu
ments/11973/204072/qdf82.pdf/86e8ba58-b421-40d7-8ed8-8cf765837b86.

Gentile, M., N. Linciano and P. Soccorso (2016), 'Financial advice seeking, financial
knowledge and overconfidence. Evidence from the Italian market', WP No. 83,
March, accessed 1 April 2018 at http://www.consob.it/documents/11973/204072/
Quaderno+di+finanza+n.+83/c91497dd-9971-49df-a481-a205c389b9f6.

Gigerenzer, G., P.M. Todd and the ABC Research Group (1999), *Simple Heuristics
that Make Us Smart*, New York, NY: Oxford University Press.

IOSCO (2013), 'IOSCO Board focuses on behavioral economics and social media',
accessed 31 March 2018 at http://www.iosco.org/news/pdf/IOSCONEWS286.
pdf.

IOSCO (2014), 'Strategic framework for investor education and financial literacy,
Final Report', accessed 31 March 2018 at http://www.iosco.org/library/pubdocs/
pdf/IOSCOPD462.pdf.

JC ESAs (2014), 'Discussion Paper: Key Information Documents for Packaged Retail
and Insurance-based Investment Products (PRIIPs)', accessed 10 March 2018 at
https://esas-joint-committee.europa.eu/Publications/Consultations/20141117_JC
_DP_2014_02_-_DP_PRIIPs_KID.pdf.

JC ESAs (2016), 'Final draft regulatory technical standards with regard to presentation, content, review and provision of the key information document, including
the methodologies underpinning the risk, reward and costs information in accordance with Regulation (EU) No. 1286/2014 of the European Parliament and of
the Council', accessed 15 February 2018 at https://eiopa.europa.eu/Publications/
Technical%20Standards/JC%202016%2021%20%28Final%20draft%20RTS%20
PRIIPs%20KID%20report%29.pdf.

JRC (Joint Research Center) (2013), 'Applying behavioural sciences to EU policymaking', accessed 31 January 2018 at https://ec.europa.eu/jrc/en/publication/
eur-scientific-and-technical-research-reports/applying-behavioural-science-eu-po
licy-making.

JRC (Joint Research Centre) (2015), 'Seven points to remember when conducting
behavioural studies in support of EU policy-making', accessed 31 January 2018
at https://ec.europa.eu/jrc/en/publication/eur-scientific-and-technical-research-
reports/seven-points-remember-when-conducting-behavioural-studies-support-
eu-policy-making.

JRC (Joint Research Centre) (2016a), 'Behavioural insights applied to policy –
European report 2016', accessed 1 April 2018 at https://ec.europa.eu/jrc/
en/publication/eur-scientific-and-technical-research-reports/behavioural-insights-
applied-policy-european-report-2016.

JRC (Joint Research Centre) (2016b), 'Behavioural insights applied to policy –
country overviews 2016', accessed 1 April 2018 at https://ec.europa.eu/jrc/
en/publication/thematic-reports/behavioural-insights-applied-policy-country-
overviews-2016.

Katawetawaraks, C. and C.L. Wang (2011), 'Online shopper behavior: Influences
of online shopping decision', *Asian Journal of Business Research*, **1** (2), 66–74.

Laudon, K.C. and C.G. Traver (2017), *E-Commerce 2016: Business, Technology,
Society*, 12th edn, Harlow: Pearson.

Lim, H. and A.J. Dubinsky (2004), 'Consumers' perceptions of e-shopping characteristics: An expectancy-value approach', *The Journal of Services Marketing*,
**18** (6), 500–13.

Linciano, N. (2010), 'Cognitive biases and instability of preferences in the portfolio choices of retail investors. Policy implications of behavioural finance', WP No. 66, January, accessed 1 April 2018 at http://www.consob.it/mainen/documenti/english/papers/index.html?symblink=/mainen/consob/publications/papers/index.html.

Linciano, N. and P. Soccorso (2012), 'Assessing investors' risk tolerance through a questionnaire', DP No. 4, July, accessed 1 April 2018 at http://www.consob.it/mainen/documenti/english/papers/index.html?symblink=/mainen/consob/publications/papers/index.html.

Linciano, N. and P. Soccorso (eds) (2017), 'Challenges in ensuring financial competencies: Essays on how to measure financial knowledge, target beneficiaries and deliver educational programmes', accessed 1 April 2018 at http://www.consob.it/documents/46180/46181/wp84.pdf/c369a6db-3b30-4c1a-8a90-d3f2d384ec4f.

Willis, L.E. (2008), 'Against financial literacy education', *Iowa Law Review*, **94** (1), 197–285.

# 16. When central bankers become humans: behavioral economics and monetary policy decisions

**Donato Masciandaro**

## 1. INTRODUCTION

The evolution of both the economics and the political economy of monetary policy in the last three decades is a story of two intertwined tales: on the one side the tale of how to govern money and interest rates in the short run, on the other side the tale of how to design central bank governance in a longer horizon, that is, the rules that govern central banker decisions.[1] In other words, monetary policy strategy and central bank governance are two sides of the same coin.

In practice the two tales are told separately, where academic scholars preferred to focus essentially on the first perspective while only central bankers and partly policymakers were also sensitive to the engineering of institutional monetary settings. The big innovation in modern monetary policy was the progressive merger of the analysis of the macroeconomic effects of public choices in the monetary games played day by day (monetary policy) with the study of the structural features that characterized both the monetary players – governments and central bankers – as well as the rules and institutions that shape goals and incentives of such as players.

But now, after the Great Crisis of 2008, the scenario is changing. It is evident that the pillars of monetary policy action must be reconsidered. But how should that be done? Here the interest in exploring the potential of the behavioral insights comes in. This chapter discusses how a well identified behavioral insight – the possibility of loss aversion in central bankers – can shape monetary policy decisions, triggering a well-known effect: interest rate inertia. In the chain that links behavioral economics to monetary inertia, the first link is loss aversion, which shapes the

---

[1]    Masciandaro (1995), Eijffinger and Masciandaro (2014).

decisions of the central banker in preferring the status quo in interest rate setting.

The relevance of interest rate inertia can be highlighted by just mentioning frequent mottos such as "too little, too late", or "wait and see"; these are usually the comments that the media use in observing the central bank's tendency to postpone and/or delay interest rate decisions. In these years such remarks have been commonly used in analyzing the behavior of both the Federal Reserve System (FED) and the European Central Bank (ECB), among others.

In the aftermath of the severest recession since the Second World War, the FED has faced extraordinary challenges in designing and implementing monetary policy. The overall result has been massive monetary accommodation with interest rates close to zero, coupled with an exceptional expansion of the Fed's balance sheet. The so-called Great Recession ended in June 2009, but seven years afterwards, the Fed is still delaying the process of getting back to normal. Expansionary monetary policy has been implemented long after the recession ended, raising questions on the drivers and consequences of monetary inertia, that is, in this case reluctance in leaving the ultra-expansionary monetary status quo to start a policy of interest rate normalization.

But the discussion over the (delayed) lift-off in US monetary policy is just the latest episode in a long-lasting debate: how can inertia in monetary policy be explained? In the last two decades in several cases central banks have shown reluctance in leaving the monetary status quo, raising questions on the rationale that can justify such a stance. As has been insightfully pointed out (Orphanides, 2015) at least in the case of the US monetary policy, a period of monetary inertia after the end of a recession is not uncommon. At the same time, cases of monetary inertia have been registered for some time after the end of an expansion; further this inertial feature of central bank behavior has been especially noted in the case of the Fed, but it characterized many other central banks (Goodhart, 1996 and 1998; Woodford, 1999 and 2003).

So far the economics literature has offered two different explanations: information inertia and governance inertia. In a recent study article (Favaretto and Masciandaro, 2016), a new driver of inertia has been introduced, independent of frictions and central bank governance settings: loss aversion. The introduction of a behavioral explanation offers a novel tale, besides the existing two, to explain the central banker motivations in retaining or changing monetary policies.

The chapter is organized as follows. Section 2 reviews the general and recent evolution of the economic thought on monetary policymaking as a story of two intertwined tales, that is, how to manage monetary policy in the short run and how to design central bank governance over a longer time horizon. Section 3 highlights a specific relevant monetary policy phenomenon – interest rate inertia – discussing its explanation when central bankers are considered "Econs", that is, rational players in the sense of the traditional economic mainstream. Then section 4 offers a behavioral explanation, showing how inertia can occur when the central bankers are humans, and precisely loss aversion can distort their decisions. Section 5 concludes, summing up the main results of the chapter.

## 2. MONETARY POLICYMAKING: THE COMPOSITION OF COMMITTEES

The recent literature on monetary policy (MP) acknowledges that monetary policy is conducted by committees.

It is a matter of fact that nowadays monetary policymaking is designed and implemented using committees. Fry et al. (2000), Pollard (2004) and Lybek and Morris (2004) documented that the large majority of central banks use committees. This feature of central bank governance deeply affects the definition of the MP stance. Ultimately, MP decisions become the endogenous result of a – sometimes complex – interaction between the rules of the monetary game and the preferences of the players, that is, the board members and the politicians.

The existing literature that looks at the link between monetary policy decisions and board members' diversity essentially focuses on two issues (Masciandaro and Eijffinger, 2018): (1) how monetary policy committees work, and (2) how the specific composition of committees can shape monetary policy outcomes, where the more disputed issue is related to the degree of activism, that is, the preferences of the central bankers toward an anticyclical interest rate policy. The conclusions of this body of literature are rather heterogeneous.

Using an experimental approach, Blinder (2007) and Blinder and Morgan (2005; 2008) have argued that committees can take more efficient monetary policy decisions via heterogeneity and diversity. Moving beyond this, Besley et al. (2008), Hansen and McMahon (2008), Gerlach-Kristen (2009), Hix et al. (2010) and Eijffinger et al. (2013a; 2013b; 2015) have claimed that heterogeneity can even trigger regularities in monetary policy actions, making it theoretically possible to alter a board's composition in order to drive different future monetary policy decisions.

As a result, the evaluation of monetary policy through a board's composition has mostly become a political economy issue, taking into account the role of preferences in defining the stance of the monetary policy. Therefore, the relevant preferences that have to be investigated are both political (that is, the choices of the policymakers) and bureaucratic (that is, the decisions adopted by the board members), together with their possible interconnections.

In a seminal paper, Chappell et al. (1993) suggested how the appointment process of committee members was the primary mechanism to generate partisan implications in monetary policy. Thereafter, it has become quite usual in the monetary policy field to apply political economy tools, using either spatial voting models or the study of reaction functions. Spatial voting patterns mostly differentiate between internally and externally appointed members (Hansen and McMahon, 2008; Bhattacharjee and Holly, 2010) and assign significant importance to the stages of committee design and monetary policy conduct. Harris and Spencer (2009) obtain similar results via reactions functions, showing that outsiders of the Bank of England staff reacted differently to forecasts of inflation and output than insiders.

All these results are reinforced by the findings that insiders are more likely to vote as a block, choose higher interest rates and are often featured on the winning side of policy decisions. Harris and Spencer's (2009) work also supports the idea that board heterogeneity matters. At the same time, Patra and Samantaraya (2007) create an index of monetary policy committee (MPC) empowerment. The index of MPC empowerment summarized ten different attributes, namely: separate entity; decision making role; legal mandate; absence of government override; presence of external members; absence of part-time members; attribution of individual votes to specific members; absence of government voting members; decision by voting (as against consensus); and publication of minutes. Higher empowerment seems to be associated with better inflation results. However they do not focus on personal characteristics.

Board composition has also been associated with monetary policy performance. Göhlmann and Vaubel (2007) test the hypothesis that inflation preferences of central bankers depend on their educational and occupational background. Performing a panel data analysis for the Eurozone and another eleven countries since 1973, they find that former members of the central bank staff are more prone to lower inflation rates than former politicians. Farvaque et al. (2006), on the other hand, link inflation records in a selected sample of countries with the biographical features of the board members. They use a well-structured panel data comprising 13 countries and a five-year period, from 1999 to 2003, and find that the age of board members appears to be the most important factor. More recently, Farvaque et al. (2014) perform a similar analysis focused on inflation and output volatility. They find that the size of the board matters, except in crisis times, while personal background influences the performances, with a positive role for board members coming from academia, central banks and the financial sector (the analysis considered six categories: public sector, private sector, financial sector, academics, central bankers, and others).

It is worth noting that against this background Harris et al. (2011) reshaped some of these previous findings. They first showed how the effects of members' career backgrounds and the political influence on voting behavior were negligible. Moreover, they suggested that the entire literature on voting behavior based on members' internal or external status was overly simplistic, laying the groundwork of accounting for possible unobserved heterogeneity.

Notwithstanding this contingency, the general insight from this literature highlighted the importance of the relationships between board composition and monetary policy decisions. More precisely, the role of preferences has been explored by focusing on the degree of activism in designing and implementing monetary policy actions. High inflation performances are usually correlated with active (Keynesian) monetary policies (Eijffinger and Masciandaro, 2014). Policymakers tend to use monetary tools with an anti-cyclical perspective, using the inflation tax to smooth different kinds of macroeconomic shocks – that is, real (Barro and Gordon, 1983) and/or fiscal (Sargent and Wallace, 1981) unbalances – thus trying to exploit the trade-off between real gains and nominal (inflationary) costs.

In this literature, a specific jargon has been coined: a "dove" is a policymaker who likes to implement active monetary policies, while a "hawk" is a policymaker who dislikes them (Chappell et al., 1993; Jung, 2013; Jung and Kiss, 2012; Jung and Latsos, 2014; Eijffinger et al., 2013a; 2013b; 2015; Neuenkirch and Neumeier, 2013; Wilson, 2014). The degree of activism is related to the role of interest rate policy as an anticyclical role, that is, to smooth the business cycle: the doves claim that activism improves the overall macroeconomic performances, exploiting from time to time the trade-off between inflation and output growth, while the hawks assume that interest rate policy is more effective the more it is focused on monetary stability only. Throughout time, the dovish/hawkish attitude has probably become a main focus of the analysis of monetary policy board decisions.

## 3. INTEREST RATE INERTIA: WHEN THE CENTRAL BANKERS ARE ECONS

A specific and relevant outcome of the general evolution of monetary policymaking analysis has been the discussion on interest rate inertia. In such a discussion the central bankers act as Econs, using the jargon coined by Alex Leijonhufvud (Leijonhufvud, 1973).

Originally, monetary inertia was motivated by observing that the central bank decisions depend on information on the state of the economy, as well as on the recognition of the long and variable lags in the transmission of monetary policies. In such a framework the agent expectations are considered rational in the Muth–Lucas sense (Muth, 1961; Lucas, 1972): all the players use the available knowledge on how the economic system works. Monetary inertia can be considered a rational strategy in order to avoid tough stop-and-go policies and their consequences in terms of negative macroeconomic spillovers. The tendency of central banks to adjust interest rates only gradually in response to changes in economic conditions can thus be considered optimal (Woodford, 1999; Driffill and Rotondi, 2007; Consolo and Favero, 2009). More recently, optimal monetary policy has been derived by departing from the rational expectations hypothesis, that is, by assuming that individual agents follow adaptive learning (Molnar and Santoro, 2014).

Under a different perspective, monetary policy inertia has been analyzed by exploring the role of central bank governance. In this respect two studies focusing on Monetary Policy Committees (MPCs) seem particularly interesting: Dal Bo (2006) and Riboni and Ruge-Murcia (2010).

Dal Bo (2006) shows that the voting procedure requiring a supermajority, that is, a so-called consensus setting, leads the MPC to behave as a conservative central banker *à la* Rogoff (1985). The supermajority rule mitigates issues of time-inconsistency and introduces a status-quo bias in monetary policy decisions.

Riboni and Ruge-Murcia (2010) analyze four different frameworks in central banking governance, comparing the simple majority (median voter) model, the consensus model, the agenda-setting model (where the chairman controls the board agenda), and the dictator model (case of influential chairman).

While the simple majority model and the dictator model are observationally equivalent to a one-man central bank, the consensus model and the agenda-setting model are different, creating something like a persistent status quo monetary policy. In the first two models, the MPC adjusts the interest rate taking into account the value preferred by the key members – respectively the median voter and the chairman – regardless of the initial status quo. In the other two models the MPC can keep the interest rate unchanged in the so-called inaction region, that is, monetary inertia can occur. Further, the agenda-setting model predicts larger interest rate increases than the consensus model, when the chairman is more hawkish than the median member. In other words, inertia in the interest rate decisions can be associated with features of central bank governance, aka *governance inertia.*

## 4. INTEREST RATE INERTIA: WHEN THE CENTRAL BANKERS BECOME HUMANS

But what happens if we assume that psychological drivers can influence the decisions of the central bankers? Recently Favaretto and Masciandaro (2016) simulated a monetary policy setting with three different kind of central banker.

By using a standard macroeconomic model it is possible to introduce a novel perspective to analyze monetary (interest rate) inertia, discussing issues that are becoming increasingly relevant in the real world: how important are behavioral drivers in explaining the monetary policy decisions? What are the consequences – if any – for monetary policy strategies and the design of central bank governance rules?

Consider an economy with nominal price rigidities and rational expectations, where a Monetary Policy Committee (MPC) makes decisions on interest rates using a majority rule. The central bankers are assumed to be the top bureaucrats that care about their careers and can be divided into three groups, depending on their monetary policy conservativeness: doves, pigeons and hawks, where pigeons fall in the middle, preferring the status quo, instead of moving up or down the interest rates.

It is worth noting that while the degree of conservatism per se doesn't necessarily produce monetary inertia, the Favaretto and Masciandaro model shows that introducing loss aversion in individual behavior influences the stance of monetary policy.

In analysis of monetary policymaking, the principal–agent perspective has been adopted in a more general and simple way, that is, the individual central banker is supposed to incorporate social gains and costs in implementing via monetary action successful stabilization policies, taking into account her personal conservativeness. But then the less central bankers are rational individuals in the traditional meaning, the more the design of governance procedures must take into account the possibility of behavioral biases. In calculating benefits and costs of different monetary policies, behaviorally viewed, central bankers can make choices that are quite different compared with the standard formal view of central bankers.

Therefore, given the degree of conservativeness of each central banker, it is possible to show that the introduction of loss aversion in individual behavior influences the monetary policy stance under three different but convergent perspectives.

First, a *Moderation Effect* can emerge, that is, the number of pigeons increases. More loss aversion among MPC members reduces the distance between their monetary policy positions. On the one side the doves overestimate the losses due to an inflationary choice, so they limit their dovishness. On the other side the hawks overestimate the losses due to a conservative choice, and therefore their hawkishness is dampened. As the central bankers become more loss averse, pigeons increase in number and inertia in setting the interest rate is likely to increase.

At the same time a *Hysteresis Effect* can become relevant: both doves and hawks smooth their attitudes. Given the existing monetary policy stance, if loss aversion characterizes the central bankers' behavior, the status quo is more likely to remain; any central banker – either a dove or a hawk – will overestimate any losses due to a change in strategy.

Finally a *Smoothing Effect* tends to stabilize the number of pigeons: in the event of a shock to the level of conservativeness among central bankers, only large shocks can trigger a change in the monetary policy stance.

The three effects consistently trigger higher monetary inertia. Therefore loss aversion can explain delays and lags in changing the monetary policy stance, including the so-called fear of lift-offs after recessions.

## 5.   CONCLUSION

Central bankers are individuals who can be subjected to the same source of behavioral biases all individuals face. In the presence of a behavioral bias, the outcome of considering different information sets or different governance rules can be quite different compared to the outcome from the standard analysis.

Usually, monetary inertia can emerge in a standard setting, where the central banker aims to design and implement the best monetary policy considering the possible macroeconomic trade-offs. At the same time governance rules are defined assuming the existence of a principal–agent relationship that characterizes citizens versus central bankers as bureaucrats, where the bureaucrats are rational players. Solving the governance problem involves designing rules of the game that can produce optimal interest alignment between society and central bankers.

However, one more perspective needs to be explored, namely to assume that central bankers can act consistently in the presence of behavioral biases. It is possible to show that loss aversion can explain delays and lags in changing the monetary policy stance.

In other words, central bankers can justify their lack of active choices using informational reasoning – "we adopted a data dependent strategy" –

or governance drivers – "we need to reach a larger consensus" – but being both bureaucrats – that is, career concerned players – and humans, other elements are at play, namely that central bankers can act based on behavioral biases. Such a perspective deserves attention also in designing and implementing central bank governance rules.

It is worth noting that loss aversion is just one source of behavioral bias. As has been correctly pointed out (Orphanides, 2015), in general the cognitive psychology perspective can be usefully employed in understanding the intertemporal challenges embedded in monetary policy analysis.

Therefore the analysis of central bank governance must take into account the potential relevance of behavioral biases. Future research will devote additional effort to uncovering the relationship between behavioral biases and alternative governance settings.

All in all behavioral economics deserves increasing attention. Monetary policy analysis should account for the fact that central bankers are individuals and prone to biases and temptations that can sensibly influence their ultimate choices in a setting of macroeconomics and interest rate targets. Theoretically, institutional and empirical studies are also needed to address in a systematic way the intrinsic difficulty in disentangling case by case when a monetary stance reflects a case of information, governance or behavioral phenomena.

# REFERENCES

Barro, R. and Gordon, D.B. 1983, Rules, discretion and reputation in a model of monetary policy. *Journal of Monetary Economics*, **12**, 101–21.
Besley, T., Meads, N. and Surico, P. 2008, Insiders versus outsiders in monetary policymaking. *The American Economic Review*, **98**(2), 218–23.
Bhattacharjee, A. and Holly, S. 2010, Rational partisan theory, uncertainty, and spatial voting: Evidence for the Bank of England's MPC. *Economics & Politics*, **22**(2), 151–79.
Blinder, A.S. 2007, Monetary policy by committee: Why and how? *European Journal of Political Economy*, **23**(1), 106–23.
Blinder, A.S. and Morgan, J. 2005, Are two heads better than one? Monetary policy by committee. *Journal of Money, Credit and Banking*, **37**(5), 789–811.
Blinder, A.S. and Morgan, J. 2008, Do monetary policy committees need leaders? A report on an experiment. *The American Economic Review*, **98**(2), 224–9.
Chappell Jr, H.W.M. and McGregor, R.R. 1993, Partisan monetary policies: Presidential influence through the power of appointment. *The Quarterly Journal of Economics*, **108**(1), 185–218.
Consolo, A. and Favero, C.A. 2009, Monetary policy inertia: More a fiction than a fact? *Journal of Monetary Economics*, **56**(6), 900–906.
Dal Bo, E. 2006, Committees with super majority voting yield commitment with flexibility. *Journal of Public Economics*, **90**(4), 573–99.

Driffil, J. and Rotondi, Z. 2007, Inertia in Taylor Rules, CEPR Discussion Paper Series, no. 6570.

Eijffinger, S.C. and Masciandaro, D. (eds) 2014, *Modern Monetary Policy and Central Bank Governance*, Cheltenham, UK and Northampton, MA, USA: Edward Elgar Publishing.

Eijffinger, S.C., Mahieu, R. and Raes, L. 2013a, *Inferring Hawks and Doves from Voting Records*, CEPR Discussion Paper Series, no. 9418.

Eijffinger, S.C., Mahieu, R. and Raes, L. 2013b, *Estimating the Preferences of Central Bankers: an Analysis of four Voting Records*, CEPR Discussion Paper Series, no. 9602.

Eijffinger, S.C., Mahieu, R. and Raes, L. 2015, *Hawks and Doves in the FOMC*, CEPR Discussion Paper Series, no. 10442.

Farvaque, E., Hammadou, H. and Stanek, P. 2006, Central bank committees' composition and inflation performances: Evidence from OECD and the enlarged EU. Unpublished manuscript, Université de Lille.

Farvaque, E., Stanek, P. and Vigeant, S. 2014, On the performance of monetary policy committees. *Kyklos*, **67**(2), 177–203.

Favaretto, F. and Masciandaro, D. 2016, Doves, hawks and pigeons: Behavioral monetary policy and interest rate inertia. *Journal of Financial Stability*, **27**(4), 50–58.

Fry, M., Julius, D., Mahadeva, L., Roger, S. and Sterne, G. 2000, Key issues in the choice of monetary policy framework, in L. Mahadeva and G. Sterne eds, *Monetary Policy Frameworks in a Global Context*, London: Routledge, pp. 1–216.

Gerlach-Kristen, P. 2009, Outsiders at the Bank of England's MPC. *Journal of Money, Credit and Banking*, **41**(6), 1099–115.

Göhlmann, S. and Vaubel, R. 2007, The educational and occupational background of central bankers and its effect on inflation: An empirical analysis. *European Economic Review*, **51**(4), 925–41.

Goodhart, C.A.E. 1996, *Why Do the Monetary Authorities Smooth Interest Rates?*, LSE Financial Market Group, Special Papers, no. 81.

Goodhart, C.A.E. 1998, *Central Bankers and Uncertainty*, LSE Financial Market Group, Special Papers, no. 106.

Hansen, S. and McMahon, M. 2008, *Delayed Doves: MPC Voting Behaviour of Externals*. Centre for Economic Performance, London School of Economics and Political Science.

Harris, M.N. and Spencer, C. 2009, The policy choices and reaction functions of Bank of England MPC members. *Southern Economic Journal*, **76**(2), 482–99.

Harris, M.N., Levine, P. and Spencer, C. 2011, A decade of dissent: Explaining the dissent voting behavior of Bank of England MPC members. *Public Choice*, **146**(3–4), 413–42.

Hix, S., Høyland, B. and Vivyan, N. 2010, From doves to hawks: A spatial analysis of voting in the Monetary Policy Committee of the Bank of England. *European Journal of Political Research*, **49**(6), 731–58.

Jung, A. 2013, Policy makers' interest rate preferences: Recent evidence for three monetary policy committees. *International Journal of Central Banking*, **9**(3), 45–192.

Jung, A. and Kiss, G. 2012, *Voting by Monetary Policy Committees: Evidence from the CEE Inflation Targeting Countries*, MNB Working Paper Series, no. 2.

Jung, A. and Latsos, S. 2014, *Do Federal Reserve Bank Presidents Have a Regional Bias?* ECB Working Paper Series, no. 1731.

Leijonhufvud, A. 1973, Life among the Econ. *Economy Inquiry*, **11**(3), 327–37.

Lucas, R.E. 1972, Expectations and the neutrality of money. *Journal of Economic Theory*, **4**(2), 103–24.

Lybek, T. and Morris, J. 2004, Central bank governance: A survey of boards and management, IMF Working Paper Series, no. 226.

Masciandaro, D. 1995, Designing a central bank: Social player, monetary agent or banking agent? *Open Economies Review*, **6**(4), 399–410.

Masciandaro, D. and Eijffinger, S. (eds) 2018, *Hawks and Doves: Deeds and Words. Economics and Politics of Monetary Policymaking*, London: CEPR Press.

Molnar, K. and Santoro, S. 2014, Optimal monetary policy when agents are learning. *European Economic Review*, **66**, 39–62.

Muth, J. 1961, Rational expectations and the theory of price movements. *Econometrica*, **29**(6), 315–35.

Neuenkirch, M. and Neumeier, F. 2013, Party affiliation rather than former occupation: The background of Central Bank governors and its effect on monetary policy, MAGKS Discussion Paper Series in Economics, no. 36.

Orphanides, A. 2015, Fear of liftoff: Uncertainty, rules, and discretion in monetary policy normalization. *Review*, **97**(3), 173–96.

Patra, M.D. and Samantaraya, A. 2007, Monetary policy committee: What works and where. *Reserve Bank of India Occasional Papers*, **28**(2).

Pollard, P. 2004, Monetary policymaking around the world, Presentation, Federal Reserve Bank of St Louis, 25 February.

Riboni, A. and Ruge-Murcia, F.J. 2010, Monetary policy by committee: Consensus, chairman dominance, or simple majority? *Quarterly Journal of Economics*, **125**(1), 363–416.

Rogoff, K. 1985, The optimal degree of commitment to an intermediate monetary target. *Quarterly Journal of Economics*, **100**(4), 1169–89.

Sargent, T.J. and Wallace, N. 1981, Some unpleasant monetarist arithmetic. *Quarterly Review*, Federal Reserve Bank of Minneapolis, Fall, pp. 1–17.

Wilson, L. 2014, A dove to hawk ranking of the Martin to Yellen Federal Reserves, Department of Finance, University of Louisiana at Lafayette, mimeo.

Woodford, M. 1999, Optimal monetary policy inertia, NBER Working Paper Series, no. 7261.

Woodford, M. 2003, Optimal interest rate smoothing. *Review of Economic Studies*, **70**(4), 861–86.

# 17. Trust the change? Trust and the impact of policy making: the case of the introduction of the MiFID II Directive in the financial advisory industry

**Caterina Cruciani, Gloria Gardenal and Ugo Rigoni**

## 1. A RADICAL CHANGE?

On 3 January 2018 the Markets in Financial Instruments Directive (MiFID II Directive) entered into force in the European Union. This Directive incorporates the response of the Union to the experience with the financial crisis, while at the same time trying to overcome the limits of the previous Directive regulating financial markets. The scope of the Directive is very broad and ranges across different financial institutions in order to strengthen investors' protection and increase transparency – two keywords of the Directive itself.

The MiFID II Directive introduces new normative requirements for the financial advisory sector, which are likely to have a profound effect on the nature and the practice of the services it offers to clients in the European Union. In particular, the Directive requires that the cost of financial advice becomes fully transparent and is kept separate from other management fees in the paperwork provided to clients. Following on its pursuit of increased transparency, the Directive describes the features of the independent advisors, qualifying them as fee-only financial professionals without any ties with other financial institutions.

While pursuing the objective of improving customer protection through increased transparency, these changes represent a very significant transformation of the way in which financial advisory services have been provided in many countries up to the time before the new Directive was introduced.

Being normative, the MiFID II Directive focuses on the objective features of the service provided (for example costs, information transmission and transparency), but is likely also to affect the relational components of financial advisory services. The idea that financial advisors may be more than simple money managers is consolidated in the financial literature, and implies that financial services span beyond the mere selection of financial assets. The financial advisor is very often a "money doctor" (Gennaioli et al., 2015) who manages stress and anxiety alongside money and who is trusted even in the presence of asymmetric qualities – clients rarely know more than financial advisors when it comes to financial matters.

This consideration suggests that understanding what drives trust in financial advisors may help shed some light on the secondary effects of the normative requirements introduced by MiFID II into the financial advisory sector. These secondary effects refer to the relational dimension of the service and stem from those directly deriving from the normative changes on the objective dimension. In the economic and financial literature, trust is a complex phenomenon that is rarely defined in the same way by different scholars. In the following, we posit that trust is defined along two co-existing dimensions, one based on objective considerations of value and trustworthiness and the other based on relational and emotional aspects.

Trust necessarily relies on both dimensions, which may be differently intertwined with each other. Studying the trust-formation processes can be used to possibly assess the complex impact of the new Directive, gauging its effects along both dimensions, even when only one is directly affected by the normative change.

## 2. MODELS OF TRUST IN FINANCIAL ADVISORY

The idea that trust is a crucial element in the provision of financial advisory services finds its scientific foundation in the assessment of the different roles that advisors can perform for their clients. As reviewed in Cruciani (2017), financial advisors may perform two different non-mutually exclusive roles, leading to two different types of benefits: they can help achieve superior financial performance (financial benefit) or they can provide other additional non-monetary benefits, such as better information and financial education, helping to deal with cognitive or behavioural biases (non-monetary benefit).

Interestingly, research finds that the ability to lead to superior financial performances is not a key feature of such services. In fact, using real performance data from managed and unmanaged accounts, the empirical evidence suggests that unmanaged investors' portfolios tend to have superior performances, mainly due to the lack of trading costs and commissions that erode returns (Bergstresser et al., 2009; Foerster et al., 2016; Hackethal et al., 2012).

This evidence brings further support to the idea that clients may indeed also be looking for the non-monetary benefit of financial advice – a topic that has not been neglected by scholars.

The added benefits of having an advisor seem to be perceived to a greater extent by more financially literate individuals (Calcagno and Monticone, 2015; Collins, 2012; Debbich, 2015). These individuals are better equipped to evaluate financial decisions, but are probably more aware of the risk of cognitive overload or value the extra non-monetary benefits that advisors bring more.

The literature converges on the idea that individuals are prone to a series of cognitive and behavioural biases (Kahneman, 2011), some of which have sound evolutionary roots and thus are difficult to correct (Santos and Rosati, 2015). Given the relevance of non-monetary benefits that financial advisors seem to bring, the possibility that they may help clients to deal effectively with such biases is an important issue. Despite some limited evidence on the lower propensity to some financially relevant biases (Shapira and Venezia, 2001), financial advisors may also cater to their clients' biases in order to reap further benefits, for instance by steering clients towards asset classes that generate higher commissions (Mullainathan et al., 2012).

Another important strand of literature that explicitly looks at the conditions that favour the production of these extra benefits is the one on trust in financial intermediation. Gennaioli et al. (2015) show that even the conflict of interest an advisor faces can ultimately be productive for clients who look for peace of mind by delegating a stressful choice. Investing can be a source of severe anxiety and individuals may prefer to rely on financial advisors to take care of their worries, just as they would rely on doctors to take care of their ailments. The trust clients place in advisors relieves them from having to deal directly with stressful choices and at the same time allows advisors to select the (often-riskier) assets that produce the highest commission. Nevertheless, the client is better off than he would be alone, as the presence of the financial advisor puts him, on average, in riskier asset classes, which produce higher average returns. For some clients having an advisor is the condition to invest in the financial market in the first place. A fairly recent study in the Italian context has shown that trust in the advisor is often higher than trust placed in the banking system and even in one's own bank (Monti et al., 2014). To what do advisors owe a higher degree of trust? This question has been only partially explored so far, but we believe it has acquired even more importance now, after the introduction of the new MiFID II Directive. As previously mentioned, the Directive focuses on the formal features of the provision of financial advisory services, translating its keywords – investor protection and transparency – into a set of rules that will affect the quantity and quality of information that advisors will need to provide to clients. This change is bound to affect also the perception of the financial advisor. This secondary effect is not absent in the spirit of the Directive, which was devised exactly to provide more solid foundations to financial institutions in order to restore confidence in financial intermediaries after the financial crisis. But how will this secondary effect deploy? We believe that trust-building processes may provide a suitable framework to address both direct and secondary effects, and propose a novel operational framework, developed from research on trust in an experimental context.

Trust has been studied at an experimental level using the well-known Trust Game (Berg et al., 1995), which uses a two-person set-up to test under which conditions trust and trustworthiness are present. The experimental literature (see Johnson and Mislin, 2011 for a review) agrees on the existence of two main motives for trust and trustworthiness: anticipated reciprocation and the adherence to a social norm of trust. We believe that this dichotomy applies well to the interaction between clients and financial advisors and may be used to describe their relationship. Anticipated reciprocation in this context translates into the desire to put in place actions that reinforce perceived professionalism of the advisor through measurable results and objective considerations. The social norm to trust and be trustworthy, instead, is more subtle and refers to the fact that the trust given to the advisor is inspired not just by measurable results, but by the reputation of the professional and his ability to take care of the client in a broader sense.

It is clear that the first paradigm suggests that trust can be earned by producing positive results in the financial domain. The direct effects of the new requirements introduced by MiFID II naturally apply in this context: through transmitting more detailed and more frequent information the client should be better able to assess how capable and successful an advisor is.

The second paradigm also shows that trust can simply be given thanks to other features of the relationship. Trust as a social norm is more akin to the idea of financial advisors as "money doctors", a paradigm introduced by the already mentioned paper by Gennaioli et al. (2015), but also present in the literature developed for expert practitioners like Statman (2005). The secondary effect of the MiFID II requirements are likely to take place within this definition of trust: by being better informed about financial products, the cost of advice and the financial results that accrue from them, clients may change their perception of the advisor. How do non-monetary benefits fare when judgement is based mainly on objective consideration? If the advisor was also perceived as a money doctor, how will the new information available change this perception?

We believe that both motives described above are present in the advisor–client relationship and that both should be assessed when analysing the dynamics of trust and their implications on the participation in the financial market and the taking up of financial advisory services. We have also already highlighted how useful the distinction between anticipated reciprocation and social norm is to gauge the direct and secondary effects of the MiFID II Directive on the industry.

Research conducted by members of this research team has shown that both motives are present (Cruciani et al., 2018) and that they depend on different factors in the relationship between advisors and clients. This suggests that normative developments that seemingly affect only some elements of the relationship may have unintended or unexpected effects on other domains of the relationship, both of which are crucial in determining client protection and satisfaction, alongside ensuring the correct functioning of the industry.

## 3.  A METHODOLOGICAL FRAMEWORK TO UNDERSTAND TRUST IN FINANCIAL ADVISORY

The previous section has shown that trust is a naturally multi-layered concept, characterized by very different co-existing elements. Building on Cruciani et al. (2018), we propose to study trust using a comprehensive framework to deal with both its domains, labelled "Exchange" to represent anticipated reciprocation, and "Relationship" to represent social norm. The model formalizes trust as the result of the interaction between these two elements in a structural equation model (SEM), formalizing Trust, Relationship and Exchange as latent processes. Latent processes cannot be observed directly and need to be observed through other indicators that theory suggests are linked to the latent process of interest. A structural equation model is composed of two elements: a measurement model and a structural model. The SEM specifies different elements underlying these latent processes and tests their relevance (measurement model), while at the same time testing the proposed relationship among latent variables (structural model).

Thus, the SEM allows two sets of claims to be validated: the first one is related to the ability of the indicators used to describe the latent process accurately. It is clear that in a context in rapid evolution, further validation of the theory underlying the latent process definition must be welcomed.

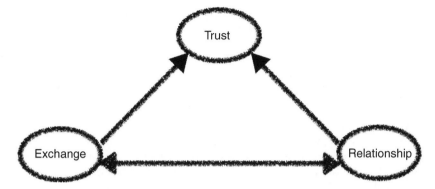

*Figure 17.1*    *The structural model of trust tested through a questionnaire to financial advisors*

Secondly, the SEM offers a framework to address if and how the posited relationship among latent processes is correct. To be more specific, is the idea that both Exchange and Relationship matter for Trust also confirmed in the advisory relationship? Do they matter in the same way? Do they interact or are they two separate avenues to Trust?

Figure 17.1 summarizes the structural model of Trust, describing it as a latent process determined by two other latent processes (Exchange and Relationship) that co-vary.

To give an example of how such a framework may be helpful to understand the direct and secondary effects of the MiFID II Directive, consider that its normative requirements are mainly targeted to increase transparency and foster further investor protection. For what concerns the financial advisory industry, these two goals are pursued through the complete disclosure regarding the cost structure of the financial advisory and through the introduction of the figure of the independent advisor, who will have to provide a further layer of information regarding professional ties and their performance.

Elements like the ones described, all belong to the domain of professional performance and, in the context of the SEM model described above, to the latent process labelled Exchange. Even before considering the secondary effect on the other latent variables, it is clear that different types of financial institutions that offer advisory services will be affected differentially depending on how much their trust-building process relies on this latent dimension.

Moreover, the increased reliance on documenting activity and performance and providing detailed information at every step of the way is likely to change the perception of the nature of the financial advisory services (as measured by the Relationship component), especially for those sectors of the industry that rely more explicitly on the "money doctor" component of the professional relationship.

The methodological framework described has been put to the test using a very large sample of financial advisors coming from three different Italian financial institutions. For each one, a set of voluntary financial advisors has participated in a survey devised by the research team to investigate the determinants of trust, looking both at Exchange-related and Relationship-related items. Importantly, these institutions differ in the tie that advisors have with it, ranging from tied agents to employees of the bank/financial institution. Moreover, one of the institutions is a new player in the financial advisory field, while the others can be considered incumbent in the sector.

The analysis allows support for the theory that different elements in the professional interactions with clients underlie the two latent processes of Exchange and Relationship. The model also confirms that the latent processes are correctly specified for the sample.

The most important result of the analysis is that the various institutions differ also in terms of the trust-building processes that emerge from the advisors' surveys. For the incumbent institution characterized by tied agents, the latent Relationship process is the only one significantly determining Trust, with no support for the existence of a significant covariance between Exchange and Relationship. For the other incumbent institution characterized by advisors that are bank employees, Trust depends significantly on both the Exchange and the Relationship component, but again no significant covariance between the two is found. Lastly, the new player institution, which is also characterized by employed financial advisors, is the only one for which the original structural model specified above is fully supported by the data.

The different trust-building processes that emerge across the different institutions involved in the study suggest that they may be differently vulnerable to normative or cultural modifications that affect one or all the elements that underlie trust building in the financial advisory.

## 4.   CONCLUDING REMARKS

Using a framework based on the underlying determinants in the trust-building process in the financial advisory, we have shown that just as there is no single definition of trust, there are different modalities in which trust can be built. The trust-building process is the result of formal and informal rules both within the institution an advisor works for and regarding the broader normative framework that regulates the sector. The framework proposed bypasses the need to understand how different business practices might have determined the trust-building process and focuses on its emerging features. By understanding what trust depends on, a financial institution may be better prepared to address both the direct and the secondary effects of the normative evolution brought about by the MiFID II Directive.

A financial institution that relies mostly on the Relationship component, which is not directly affected by MiFID II, but which is very likely to be the ground where several secondary adjustments will take place, will need to react differently to the change in order to strengthen its business model and continue fostering trust in the new environment.

The framework proposed fulfils a twofold purpose: on one side, it allows the understanding of trust, a theoretically elusive and complex concept, to be furthered. On the other side, it qualifies as a testing framework for the different roles that theory has found financial advisors play. By introducing the latent process Relationship next to the perhaps more obvious Exchange one, the model allows the testing of the relative importance of being not just a money manager, but also a money doctor.

The results discussed and the recommendations they may potentially provide to professionals and policy makers show that it would be worth extending the research along two different dimensions: first and more importantly, collecting further data from surveying professionals may provide further validation to the model and shed more light on the impact of different organizational structures. Secondly, so far the concept of trust has been assessed using only the perspective of the professionals, but it may be very interesting to also look at clients' perceptions.

# REFERENCES

Berg, Joyce, John Dickhaut and Kevin McCabe. 1995. "Trust Reciprocity and Social History". *Games and Economic Behavior* **10**: 122–42.

Bergstresser, Daniel, John M.R. Chalmers and Peter Tufano. 2009. "Assessing the Costs and Benefits of Brokers in the Mutual Fund Industry". *Review of Financial Studies* **22**(10): 4129–56.

Calcagno, Riccardo and Chiara Monticone. 2015. "Financial Literacy and the Demand for Financial Advice". *Journal of Banking and Finance* **50**: 363–80.

Collins, J. Michael. 2012. "Financial Advice: A Substitute for Financial Literacy?" *Financial Services Review* **21**: 307–22.

Cruciani, Caterina. 2017. *Investor Decision-Making and the Role of the Financial Advisor: A Behavioural Finance Approach.* Cham: Palgrave Macmillan.

Cruciani, Caterina, Gloria Gardenal and Ugo Rigoni. 2018. "Dinamiche Di Fiducia Nella Consulenza Finanziaria: Un' Analisi Empirica". *Bancaria* (1): 40–58.

Debbich, Majdi. 2015. "Why Financial Advice Cannot Substitute for Financial Literacy? Direction Générale Des Études et des Relations Internationales". (January). Accessed at http://ssrn.com/abstract=2552515.

Foerster, Stephen, Juhani T. Linnainmaa, Brian T. Melzer and Alessandro Previtero. 2016. "Retail Financial Advice: Does One Size Fit All?" *Journal of Finance* forthcoming. Accessed at http://www.nber.org/papers/w20712.

Gennaioli, Nicola, Andrei Shleifer and Robert Vishny. 2015. "Money Doctors". *The Journal of Finance* **LXX**(February): 1–40.

Hackethal, Andreas, Michael Haliassos and Tullio Jappelli. 2012. "Financial Advisors: A Case of Babysitters?" *Journal of Banking and Finance* **36**(2): 509–24.

Johnson, Noel D. and Alexandra A. Mislin. 2011. "Trust Games: A Meta-Analysis". *Journal of Economic Psychology* **32**(5): 865–89.

Kahneman, Daniel. 2011. *Thinking, Fast and Slow*. New York, NY: Farrar, Straus and Giroux.

Monti, Marco, Vittorio Pelligra, Laura Martignon and Nathan Berg. 2014. "Retail Investors and Financial Advisors: New Evidence on Trust and Advice Taking Heuristics". *Journal of Business Research* **67**(8): 1749–57.

Mullainathan, Sendhil, Markus Noeth and Antoinette Schoar. 2012. "The Market for Financial Advice: An Audit Study". *NBER Working Paper Series* 1–32. Accessed at http://www.nber.org/papers/w17929.

Santos, Laurie and Alexandra Rosati. 2015. "The Evolutionary Roots of Human Decision Making". *Annual Review of Psychology* **33**(4): 395–401.

Shapira, Zur and Itzhak Venezia. 2001. "Patterns of Behavior of Professionally Managed and Independent Investors". *Journal of Banking and Finance* **25**(8): 1573–87.

Statman, Meir. 2005. "Normal Investors, Then and Now". *Financial Analysts Journal* **61**(2): 31–8.

# 18. CMU and the role of institutional investors: investment behavior and governance of pension funds*

**Cristina Giorgiantonio and Zeno Rotondi**

## 1. INTRODUCTION

Small and medium-sized European businesses find it hard to raise capital, especially during their development phase. In 2016 the stock market capitalization to GDP ratio was equal to 65 percent in the Eurozone, against 100 percent in Japan and 147 percent in the US. In Italy the ratio was equal to only 31 percent, reflecting the relatively lower capitalization of Italian SMEs. Moreover, SMEs in Europe and even more in Italy face significant difficulties in identifying and accessing sources of funding due to the presence of an inconsistent trio (Rossi, 2015): an economic structure mostly requesting bank finance, regulators concerned with the risks posed by banks' activity, and banks consequently stepping back from ample parts of the credit markets. Therefore SME growth is firmly on the EU political agenda and has been heavily underscored in the European Commission's Capital Markets Union (CMU) action plan. In this perspective, institutional investors and in particular pension funds have been seen as a key source of "patient" capital, that is, of long-term financing for SMEs as the balance sheets of banks have become increasingly stretched.[1] Unfortunately, despite generally positive findings linking pension system development and economic growth, in too many European countries pension fund investments in equities remain low. In 2016 pension funds' assets represent 81 percent US GDP and 95 percent of UK GDP, against a mere 7 percent of both Italy and Germany's GDP (OECD, 2017a). The share of equities in investments of pension funds was 49 percent in the US, of which 70 percent are in domestic equities, and 47 percent in the UK, of which 40

\* The opinions expressed in this chapter remain, in all cases, the exclusive responsibility of the authors and do not reflect those of their respective institutions.

[1] In the present chapter the focus will be mainly on pension funds, but similar considerations can be developed for other institutional investors such as insurance companies.

percent are in domestic equities, while in Italy the figure was 16.3 percent, of which 1 percent was in domestic equities.[2] Moreover, in Italy the listed share of non-financial corporations subscribed by insurance companies and pension funds amounts to only 3.2 percent (2016, source: ECB). Hence pension funds contribute little to long-term funding for SMEs, as well as delivering disappointing investment returns and therefore pensions. In particular in Italy, as argued for instance recently by Botticini et al. (2017), pension funds, as well as other institutional investors, represent a negligible source of long-term, domestic capital for Italian SMEs. There are many causes behind the lack of diversification in investments of pension funds and indeed of other institutional investors. These causes may include adverse macro conditions,[3] distortions in asset management implied by regulation,[4] or structural features such as poor governance and lack of investment knowledge. Moreover, behavioral finance may play an important role in investment strategies of pension funds. The present chapter reviews the related literature and discusses policy proposals aimed at improving the role of pension funds in providing long-term finance for growth.

## 2.    GOVERNANCE

It should be stressed that strengthening the governance and management of pension funds is an important precondition for diversifying their portfolios. As institutional investors increase in size, they become more professional and may reduce the home bias in their investments. In Italy pension funds manage around €117 billion (2016, source: COVIP).[5] The market is very fragmented: 64 percent of pension funds have assets under management less than €100 million; 53 percent of pension funds have less than 1000 enrolled pensioners (2016, source: COVIP). The market share of

[2]    COVIP (2017a); Willis Towers Watson (2017). If we also include undertakings for collective investment in transferable securities (UCITS) for the case of Italy, the share of equity exposure increases to 24.8 percent.

[3]    For instance, in the past, high government bond rates disincentivizing diversification, although currently we are in a low interest rate environment.

[4]    An important factor in investment behavior is whether prudential regulations allow institutional investors to diversify across borders. Darvas and Schoenmaker (2017) have developed a new pension fund foreign investment restrictions index to control for the impact of prudential regulations on the ability of institutional investors to diversify geographically across borders. Their index suggests that most EU countries currently apply very limited, if any, restrictions on foreign investment.

[5]    Managed funds of social-security institutions (*casse previdenziali*) amount to €80 billion (2016, source: COVIP) of which 9.6 percent are investments in equities and 3.7 percent are in domestic equities.

assets managed by the first three pension funds is 22 percent (2015, source: EIOPA). In addition, they are characterized by very high administrative costs. In the long run Italian pension funds should increase their size in order to reach dimensions sufficient to guarantee economy of scale and adequate diversification. Improving their governance can facilitate this process.

Despite the recent reforms of the sector (in particular, Ministerial decree 166 of 2 September 2014), the governance of pension funds shows significant weaknesses (Bripi and Giorgiantonio, 2010). In view of this, Law 124 of 4 August 2017 provides for establishing a consultation table promoted by the Ministry of Labour, in agreement with the Ministries of Economy and Economic Development, *inter alia* in order to improve the governance of closed pension funds,[6] those with more members and assets in Italy (COVIP, 2017b),[7] and to promote initiatives for the aggregation of pension funds aimed at rationalizing the sector.

In particular, the current design of the governance of closed pension funds may not ensure proper composition of the trade-off between representation and competence inherent in the composition of boards of management and control of such investors.[8] Despite the fact that some reforms (in particular, Ministerial decree 79 of 15 May 2007) have introduced more stringent competence requirements and have raised the percentage of directors of closed pension funds that need to share them, their possession is still required for just half the members of the boards of

---

[6] Which have the legal status of association or foundation. Their boards of directors have the task of setting, according to regulatory guidelines, the strategic asset allocation and the duty to entrust the management of that property, known as tactical asset allocation, to external financial intermediaries (banks, management and insurance companies, which are selected via a competitive and regulated public procedure, and are tied to the mandate). Closed pension funds are also required to use an external custodian bank, which acts as treasurer and controller of compliance with the law, statutes and regulations.

[7] Besides this type of pension fund, there are the so-called *fondi pensione preesistenti*, that is, those that were already in place on 15 November 1992, which are subject to a specific discipline. However, Law 252 of 5 December 2005 provides for their progressive adaptation – with some exceptions – to the general provisions applied to closed pension funds (see Article 20 of Law 252/2005 and the related Ministerial Decree 62 of 10 May 2007). Moreover, there are the so-called open pension funds, which do not have an independent legal status from financial intermediaries that set them up and have the responsibility of managing their assets directly (they may also delegate one or more lines of investment to other entities). In fact, they consist of a segregated pool of assets, governed by the financial institution that has established them: this means that the boards and audit of these funds coincide with those of the subjects who have set them up. Finally, there are the so-called *piani individuali pensionistici*, similar to social security insurance policies (see Article 13 of Law 252/2005).

[8] It should be noted that Law 252/2005 provides – in general – the criterion of equal participation of representatives of workers and employers in the composition of boards of management and control of closed pension funds (see Article 5.1 of Law 252/2005).

directors.[9] Furthermore, the training initiatives designed to fill any skill gaps do not yet seem to have reached full development and effective dissemination. In line with international best practice, it could be appropriate to raise the overall skill level of the boards of directors, through the provision that a significant majority of directors gain adequate experience in the areas mentioned in Ministerial Decree 79/2007;[10] but – above all – by paying more attention to training and regular self-assessment, including the continued monitoring by the supervisory authority aimed at effectively verifying the adequacy of the skill level.[11]

Moreover, the relevant legislation does not adequately explain the tasks and responsibilities of the various executive and supervision bodies. In closed pension funds the tasks of the fund supervisor, the so-called *responsabile del fondo*,[12] overlap – in some cases – with those of the person responsible for the internal audit function,[13] with powers to monitor the adequacy and fairness of the management of the fund. In other cases, they overlap with those of the board of directors, especially with regard to the supervision of operations in conflicts of interest. In addition, since the law provides that the position of fund supervisor may be held by the general manager or a member of the board of directors, a serious conflict of interest may arise: in fact, the controller may be delegated to control himself.[14] To overcome these problems and remove – at least in part – the duplication of functions and possible conflicts of interest, a first step would be to allocate tasks of the fund supervisor to the person in charge of the internal audit function, for whom the possibility of conducting activities that are themselves subject to supervision is explicitly excluded.[15]

Finally, unlike the experience of other countries (particularly the United Kingdom, the Netherlands and the United States), self-regulation in Italy is not widely used for the regulation of pension fund governance; indeed, there is no self-regulatory code dedicated to the definition of the governance of pension funds and the regulation of pension fund conduct as institutional investors (Bripi and Giorgiantonio, 2010). It would help

---

[9]   See Article 2 of Ministerial Decree 79/2007.

[10]   See Article 2.1 (*a*) to (*f*), of Ministerial Decree 79/2007.

[11]   Note the English experience, where the Pensions Regulator promotes training and updating (see, in particular, the program named *trustee toolkit*), and conducts periodic audits of adequacy of the competence level shared by the Board of Directors, the results of which are also included in the assessment of pension funds (see Pensions Regulator, 2007).

[12]   Who has the role of verifying that the fund is managed according to the interests of members and beneficiaries and in compliance with legal and statutory provisions (investment rules, conflicts of interest rules, and so on).

[13]   COVIP Ruling of 4 December 2003.

[14]   Article 5.2 of Law 252/2005. See Messori (2007).

[15]   COVIP Ruling of 4 December 2003.

to regulate profiles that the law doesn't provide for and to organize the sector, given its need to grow and consolidate. These objectives may be more easily achieved in the presence of shared rules to define relationships within the sector.

Unfortunately, the implementation of these measures can also take a long time. However, in the short run, in order to counterbalance the negative effects associated with their small size, closed pension funds may participate together to form an investment consortium (*consorzio di investimento*) to collect and invest their funds according to the investment policies defined by the administrators of each pension fund, strictly linked to the life-cycle needs of their pensioners.

## 3.  ROLE OF BEHAVIORAL FINANCE

There is empirical evidence on herding behavior displayed by pension funds. For instance, Blake et al. (2016) show that pension funds in the UK tend to herd in subgroups, moving in and out of different asset classes following funds of similar size and sponsor type. Moreover, they systemically switch from equities to bonds as their liabilities mature, and mechanically rebalance their portfolios in the short term.

It has been argued that relative performance benchmarks encourage herding by fund managers as they are usually based on short-term measures. In the case of funds with pension schemes with minimum relative return guarantees, pension fund management companies are required to guarantee that the returns on their pension funds (over a certain period of time) do not deviate by more than a certain percentage from the average return of the industry. As pointed out by Randle and Rudolph (2014), while most of the literature highlights the herding effects of minimum guarantees, the problem is not one of herding but in the portfolio allocation resulting from the interactions in the market. Herding is in the nature of the fund management industry and having common portfolio benchmarks helps to ensure comparability among portfolios. The minimum relative return guarantees tend to drive investments into suboptimal portfolio allocations. Instead of optimizing the expected value of the pension fund at retirement age, pension funds focus their attention in maximizing short-term returns. Raddatz and Schmukler (2013) examine herding across asset classes and industry levels by focusing on pension funds' investment behavior. They study what incentives managers at various layers of the financial industry face when investing. Their results show that pension funds herd more in assets that have more risk and for which pension funds have less market information. Furthermore, their results show that herding is more prevalent for funds that narrowly compete with each other, namely, when comparing funds of the same type across pension fund administrators. There is much less herding across pension fund administrators as a whole and in individual pension funds within pension fund administrators. These herding patterns are consistent with incentives for managers to be close to industry benchmarks, and might also be driven by market forces and partly by regulation.

The global financial crisis caught many financial market participants by surprise and institutional investors were no exception. As the crisis intensified and concerns about capital loss arose, many investors abandoned long-term investment strategies. Exceptions certainly exist, but as a group, institutional investors tended to move with the rest of the market. This "institutional herding" is referred to in the literature as procyclical investment behavior. Papaioannou et al. (2013) argue that such procyclical investment behavior is understandable and may be considered rational from an individual institution's perspective. However, behaving in a manner consistent with long-term investing would lead to better long-term, risk-adjusted returns and, importantly, could lessen the potential adverse effects of the procyclical investment behavior of institutional investors on global financial stability. Broeders et al. (2016) distinguish between weak, semi-strong and strong herding behavior. Weak herding occurs if pension funds have similar rebalancing strategies. Semi-strong herding arises when pension funds react similarly to other external shocks, such as changes in regulation and exceptional monetary policy operations. Finally, strong herding means that pension funds intentionally replicate changes in the strategic asset allocation of other pension funds. While weak herding can contribute to financial stability, strong herding behavior is a risk to financial stability. Finally, Duijm and Steins Bisschop (2015) examine Dutch insurance company and pension funds equity and sovereign bond portfolios during the global financial crisis and the European sovereign debt crisis. In their paper, a first analysis shows that while insurance companies massively sold equities during the crisis, pension funds kept buying equities as markets tumbled. The behavior of insurance companies regarding investments in equities cannot be characterized immediately as 'strongly procyclical', since it may have structural causes. In anticipation of the new regulatory framework Solvency II, to be implemented from 2016 onwards, Dutch insurance companies have been replacing parts of their equity portfolio with less risky assets, such as government bonds. The increased pressure on their business model could also have initiated a shift away from equities. Results from regression analysis over a longer time horizon suggest procyclical behavior by insurance companies, while for pension funds they do not find evidence for procyclical or countercyclical investment behavior.

## 4. INVESTMENT RULES AND BEHAVIORAL POLICY RECOMMENDATIONS

The EU market in personal pensions is fragmented, with limited cross-border selling and portability. Developing a single market in personal pensions could offer economies of scale, better diversification of risk and more innovation. This could benefit those consumers who are looking to save in personal pensions to support their retirement but who have been dissatisfied with the options currently available. In addition, a better personal pension market could also help address a lack of investment on EU capital markets contributing to the completion of the CMU. To these ends, in 2017 the European Commission has proposed to introduce standardized pan-European personal pension products (PEPPs), which would be available in the accumulation phase, jointly with national personal pension plans. The intended standardization of the investment rules calls for the use of a limited number of default investment options and the presence of a de-risking strategy, at least for the default option. Consumer protection would be stimulated if the investment options that are offered and their labeling are comparable between different PEPPs in different countries. The choice to limit the number of investment options in PEPP products and to select one of them as the default seems to be well supported by the recent academic literature, which shows that consumers have difficulties in choosing from many alternatives (see for example Huberman and Jiang, 2006) and tend to select default strategies selected by trusted parties. Financial literacy rates differ enormously between the major advanced and emerging economies in the world. In 2014, on average 55 percent of adults in the major advanced economies – Canada, France, Germany, Italy, Japan, the United Kingdom and the United States – are financially literate (see Klapper et al., 2016). But even across these countries, financial literacy rates range widely, from 37 percent in Italy to 68 percent in Canada. Thus given the low level of financial education in Italy the introduction of PEPP products may help consumers to avoid being overwhelmed with too many investment choices.[16] However, limiting the

---

[16] On how communication can best be structured to reach out to the target audience of an educational program, see the analyses developed in Linciano and Soccorso (2017). In particular, with specific reference to retirement choices, Alemanni (2017) underlines that simplicity, reference to real and practical events, emotional connections, and proper goal framing are key to engage people in virtuous conducts. Moreover, to account for heterogeneity across individuals, communication cannot apply a one-size-fits-all approach, but needs to be attuned to the profile of the targeted audience. Once again, psychological and behavioral studies may provide important clues for the design of salient communication strategies, tailored to the characteristics of a specified target.

number of investment options too much may lead to a situation in which investment options will be very similar between providers, with little choice for consumers. Moreover, it has been argued by Laibson and List (2015), among others, that restricting people's choice and a paternalism that is too heavy handed have a bad track record. For this reason in recent years behavioral policy recommendations have tilted towards "nudges", which recommend or facilitate certain behavior without removing options or the freedom to choose (Thaler and Sunstein, 2008).

## 5.   CONCLUSIONS

At the European level, the capital market union should foster the creation of an effective European internal market for pension funds, promoting standardized rules for institutional investors to spur foreign investments and avoiding discriminatory taxation for cross-border invest-ments. National barriers are manifold and are related to restrictions to the investments of pension funds (for instance in different currencies), transferability of funds, and social, labor and contract law, but the most important barrier is tax legislation. These barriers imply that pension funds tend to remain small and that cross-border activity remains very low with limited competition among suppliers. Market fragmentation prevents pension providers from maximizing risk diversification, innovation and economies of scale. This reduces choice and attractiveness and leads to increased costs for pension savers. It also contributes to a lack of liquidity and depth in the capital markets compared with other advanced econo-mies where pension funds play a leading role as institutional investors. For creating a deeper EU internal market for pension products, in addition to the harmonization of national frameworks for pension products, another policy option is the creation of a parallel dedicated pan-European pension product.

At the national level, many national and international surveys have assessed that financial knowledge and competencies of Italian households are far from being satisfactory even at a basic level.[17] Moreover, it is important to improve Italian pension fund governance, which does not adequately guarantee the composition of the trade-off between compe-tence and representation and a clear definition of tasks and responsibilities among the various organs of the pension fund. It may be appropriate to raise the overall level of competence of the board of directors, with more

---

[17]   For empirical evidence see Montanaro and Romagnoli (2016), Linciano and Soccorso (2017), Klapper et al. (2016) and OECD (2017b).

attention to training and regular self-assessment, and to clarify the tasks of the board of directors, the fund supervisor and the person in charge of the internal audit function, eliminating the current duplication of functions and possible conflicts of interest. Some of these measures could be effectively implemented through the adoption of a self-regulatory code dedicated to the definition of pension fund governance, in line with the experience of other countries. Unfortunately, the implementation of these measures can also take a long time. However, in the short run, encouraging and incentivizing the creation of consortia of investment among pension funds could promote investments in SME equity, ensuring the support of "patient" capital to these enterprises. Pension funds may participate together in a consortium of investment in order to counterbalance the negative effects associated with their small size by improving their portfolio diversification, organizational framework and risk monitoring.

# REFERENCES

Alemanni, B. (2017), 'From nudging to engaging in pension', in Nadia Linciano and Paola Soccorso (eds), *Challenges in Ensuring Financial Competencies, Essays on How to Measure Financial Knowledge, Target Beneficiaries and Deliver Educational Programmes*, Consob, *Quaderni di Finanza*, No. 84, 119–30.

Blake, D., L. Sarno and G. Zinna (2016), 'The market for lemmings: the herding behavior of pension funds', Pensions Institute, Discussion Paper, No. 1408.

Botticini, A., Z. Rotondi and F. Sadun (2017), 'Accesso delle PMI alla finanza di mercato: come accelerare il processo di creazione di un mercato dei capitali pan-europeo?', *Rivista Bancaria Minerva Bancaria*, **73**(2–3), 135–56.

Bripi, F. and C. Giorgiantonio (2010), 'Governance of Italian pension funds: problems and solutions', Bank of Italy, Occasional Papers, No. 65.

Broeders, D., D. Chen, P. Minderhoud and W. Schudel (2016), 'Pension funds' herding', De Nederlandsche Bank, Working Paper No. 503.

COVIP (2017a), Annual Report for the Year 2016.

COVIP (2017b), Complementary Pension Schemes – Main Statistical Data, accessed 26 March 2018 at http://www.covip.it/wp-content/uploads/Agg_Stat-Dic2017.pdf.

Darvas, Z. and D. Schoenmaker (2017), 'Institutional investors and home bias in Europe's Capital Markets Union', Bruegel, Working Paper, No. 2.

Duijm, P. and S. Steins Bisschop (2015), 'Short-termism of long-term investors? The investment behavior of Dutch insurance companies and pension funds', De Nederlandsche Bank, Working Paper, No. 489.

Huberman, G. and W. Jiang (2006), 'Offering versus choice in 401(K) plans: equity exposure and number of funds', *Journal of Finance*, **61**(2), 763–801.

Klapper, L., A. Lusardi and P. van Oudheusden (2016), 'Financial literacy around the world: insights from the Standard & Poor's Ratings services Global Financial Literacy Survey', accessed 26 March 2018 at http://gflec.org/wp-content/uploads/2015/11/Finlit_paper_16_F2_singles.pdf.

Laibson, D. and J.A. List (2015), 'Behavioral economics in the classroom, principals of (behavioral) economics', *American Economic Review: Papers & Proceedings*, **105**(5), 385–90.

Linciano, Nadia and Soccorso, Paola (eds) (2017), *Challenges in Ensuring Financial Competencies, Essays on How to Measure Financial Knowledge, Target Beneficiaries and Deliver Educational Programmes*, Consob, *Quaderni di Finanza*, No. 84.

Messori, M. (2007), 'I problemi aperti nella previdenza complementare italiana', *Quaderni Europei sul Nuovo Welfare*, No. 7.

Montanaro, P. and A. Romagnoli (2016), 'Financial literacy of Italian teens and family's background: evidence from PISA 2012', Bank of Italy, Occasional Papers, No. 335.

OECD (2017a), Pension Funds in Figures, OECD.

OECD (2017b), PISA 2015 Results (Volume IV), Students' Financial Literacy.

Papaioannou, M.G., J. Park, J. Pihlman and H. van der Hoorn (2013), 'Procyclical behavior of institutional investors during the recent financial crisis: causes, impacts, and challenges', International Monetary Fund, Working Paper, No. 193.

Pensions Regulator (2007), 'The governance of work-based pension schemes', accessed at http://www.thepensionsregulator.gov.uk/docs/governance-discussion-paper.pdf.

Raddatz, C. and S. Schmukler (2013), 'Deconstructing herding: evidence from pension funds investment behavior', *Journal of Financial Services Research*, **43**(1), 99–126.

Randle, A. and H. Rudolph (2014), 'Pension risk and risk-based supervision in defined contribution pension funds', World Bank, Policy Research Working Paper, No. 6813.

Rossi, S. (2015), 'Finance for growth: a capital markets union', keynote by the senior deputy governor of the Bank of Italy, Rome Investment Forum 2015, Financing Long-Term Europe, Rome, 11 December.

Thaler, Richard H. and Cass R. Sunstein (2008), *Nudge: Improving Decisions About Health, Wealth, and Happiness*, New Haven, CT: Yale University Press.

Willis Towers Watson (2017), 'Global Pension Assets Study', accessed 26 March 2018 at https://www.willistowerswatson.com/en/insights/2017/01/global-pensions-asset-study-2017.

# 19. Italian households' wealth and their financial attitude: the new environment and a new approach

## Alessandro Varaldo and Lorenzo Portelli

The Italian Households financial portfolio (4 trillion euros) is allocated without considering the correct time horizon and the negative impact of inflation on liquidity (see Figure 19.1).

The actual and forward European interest rates environment is now vastly different from how it was 30 years ago and it is difficult to understand for private investors. The direct and indirect (insurance, pension and asset management solutions) portion of fixed income assets is extremely high and the equity component is very low. Global diversification is poor and it increases only through wealth management solutions, but only 22 percent of households have any assets apart from a current and deposit account (Assogestioni, 2017; Banca d'Italia, 2015; 2017).

In order to improve the value chain in time, it's necessary to reduce liquidity and enhance the financial asset allocation and education of the investors.

The new European Directive MiFID II (applicable from January 2018) has introduced a range of measures that enhance the protection of investors and force the wealth management industry to advise investors using a global and more efficient approach. The Italian banking system advises almost 90 percent of retail, private and HNWI (high net worth individuals) investors. The analysis of household behavior and the methodologies to suggest a better financial asset allocation according to different types of clients are a priority for the distribution system (banks, private banks, insurance companies, pension funds, asset managers, financial institutions).

There are three dimensions that need to be addressed properly:

1. understand, educate, correctly profile and support in time the investors, taking into account present and future scenarios and their radical changes;

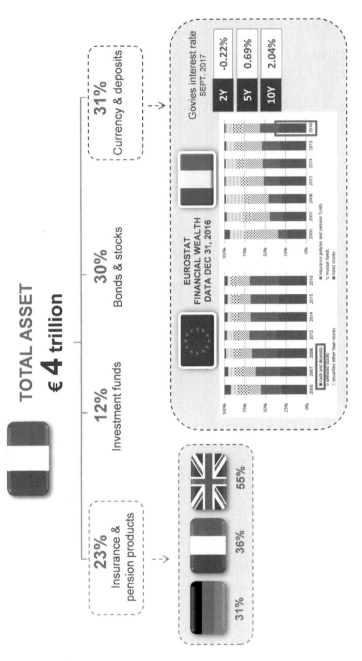

*Source:* Assogestioni (2017).

*Figure 19.1 Italian households' financial portfolio*

2. combine and optimize the investors' risk profile with their behaviors and needs within the proper time horizon;
3. enhance the wealth management solutions with dynamic risk-efficient embedded asset allocations and combine them with the matrix risk profile/behaviors/needs, to nudge (prompted choice) a more efficient asset diversification and create value in time.

The role of Behavioral Finance and its integration with the most efficient asset allocation theories in the new environment are key. In this chapter we provide a concrete example of the latest developed models.

## 1.   BEHAVIORAL FINANCE

The traditional financial paradigm seeks to understand investors' behavior in financial markets using theoretical models based on the assumption that agents are characterized by the infinite ability to make fully rational economic decisions. In this framework, individuals are consistent with Savage's notion of Subjective Expected Utility (SEU), in the sense that they always attempt to maximize their subjective utility function whenever asked to make economic decisions.

Unfortunately, the economic and financial literature is full of findings that demonstrate that theoretical predictions are not confirmed in empirical data. Behavioral economists and psychologists have demonstrated that humans are, in fact, not rational and that they tend to use heuristics to ease the cognitive burden associated with decision-making. *Overconfidence, optimism and wishful thinking, representativeness, conservatism* and *belief perseverance* are only some of the several biases highlighted in human decisions. In finance these decisions mainly relate to choices of individual portfolios and how these portfolios are recalibrated once new information is available. Despite the fact that experts in the field are expected to make fewer errors, there is still little evidence that they cancel them out altogether, which is why it is worth understanding agents' behavior.

This chapter focuses on one particular psychological bias: human risk aversion, first discovered by Kahneman and Tversky in their famous work "Prospect theory: An analysis of decision under risk" (1979). In particular, the aim of this work is to understand whether people's attitude regarding risk associated with gains proves to be different from that concerning losses and what can be done to limit the risk of wrong decision making.

## 2.   BEHAVIORAL FINANCE AND THE INVESTMENT PROCESS

The emotional and psychological sphere dramatically affects financial decisions, generating irrational behavior.

A responsible investment and advisory process has to assess and factorize irrational behavior by merging it with rationale and quantitative dimensions and framework. Briefly, the process should help to generate a proper preference architecture from a bottom-up and individual perspective.

In other words, it must help to reveal the "stream of consciousness" of investors' needs.

We identified two relevant factors in helping to generate a preference architecture:

- a scenario-based approach;
- a surveys set-up.

The scenario-based approach helps to describe financial assets behavior in different and specific regimes, or scenarios, and to assess the correct risk and rewards profile for all the financial assets; in other words it allows a relatively simple solution of a traditionally complex problem to be found, like returns expectations.

The survey set-up, above all when it is based on different scenarios, allows the individual behavioral attitudes of the investor to be evaluated when coping with financial choices. As a result, the survey helps to assess irrational behavior bias.

## 3.   HOW TO BUILD A PREFERENCE ARCHITECTURE IN PRACTICE

We developed a tool to allow the financial world to be divided into five economic phases of the global economic cycle based on the following four dimensions (see Table 19.1):

- growth: mainly earnings per share (EPS), GDP, unemployment;
- inflation: consumer price index (CPI), producer price index (PPI), unit labor cost (ULC);
- leverage: total debt non-financial;
- monetary policy: conventional/unconventional monetary policies.

*Table 19.1  The five economic phases and the drivers of the global cycle*

| | Growth | | | Monetary policy | | Inflation | Leverage |
|---|---|---|---|---|---|---|---|
| | GDP | Sales | EPS | Conventional | Unconventional | CPI-PPI-ULC | Credit leverage |
| Asset reflation | ↑ = | ↑ = | ↑ | ↓ | ↓ | ↑ | ↑ |
| Late cycle | ↓ | ↑ = | ↑ = | ↑ | ↑ | ↓ = | ↑ |
| Recovery | ↓ | ↓ | ↓ | ↑ | ↑ | ↓ | ↓ |
| Slowdown | ↑ | ↓ | ↑ | ↓ | ↑ | ↑ | ↓ |
| Contraction | ↑ | ↑ | ↑ | ↓ | ↓ | ↑ | ↓ |

*Note:*  Reference regions: US, Europe, Japan and EM countries.

*Source:*  Amundi Research, Amundi Asset Management.

*Table 19.2    US equities statistics (S&P 500)*

|  | Asset reflation (%) | Late (mature) financial cycle (%) | Recovery (%) | Slowdown (%) | Contraction (%) |
|---|---|---|---|---|---|
| Yearly avg. returns (all sample) | 11.9 | 15.7 | 13.1 | −4.0 | −13.1 |
| Yearly avg volatility (all sample) | 6.6 | 1545.0 | 12.1 | 16.4 | 27.3 |
| % of negative yearly returns | 3 | 14 | 8 | 59 | 69 |
| % of positive yearly returns | 97 | 86 | 92 | 41 | 31 |
| Avg yearly returns (subsample of negative returns periods) | −1.7 | −13.7 | −9.5 | −14.8 | −30.2 |
| Avg yearly returns (subsample in positive return periods) | 12.3 | 20.5 | 15.2 | 11.8 | 25.3 |

*Note:*   Sample: January 1989 to December 2017.

*Source:*   Amundi Research, Amundi Asset Management; Bloomberg.

For each of the five regimes the historical yearly returns with empirical distribution and volatilities are calculated for each asset class.

Taking US equities (S&P 500 Price Index) as a reference, the relevant statistics for the survey are the following (see Table 19.2):

1.  US equities average yearly return and volatility for each phase (mean-variance classic rational assessment);
2.  average negative and positive yearly returns with the probabilities of these events for US equities in each of the five regimes.

We then formulate a survey based on the five US equities scenarios in order to assess and map individuals in a two-dimensional diagram with flexibility and "emotionality" axes.

The survey asks the investors about the optimal US equities exposure for each of the five regimes, providing the same information in two different ways:

1. information in terms of expected return and volatility;
2. information in terms of expected loss and expected profits with the probability of the two events occurring in the five regimes.

The assumption is that if the individual is rational he/she must select the same equity exposure in both, regardless of their attitude to risk.

Four kinds of investor are identified in the survey (Figure 19.2):

1. *Up to seventies*: an investor with high emotional and low flexible components typical of investors up to the 1970s.
2. *Eighties*: an investor with high rational and low flexible components typical of the 1980s during the benchmark-like funds boom.
3. *Nineties*: an investor with high rational and flexible components typical of quantitative investment or trend following the strategies and product diffusion in the 1990s.
4. *Millennials*: an investor with high emotional and flexible components

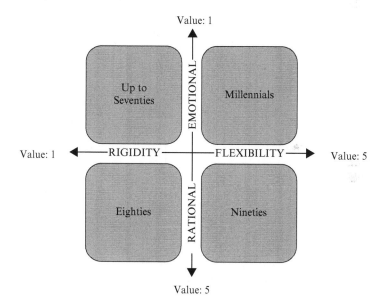

*Note:*   Survey results are classified and rescaled from 1 to 5 in order to quantify the degree of flexibility and rationality (X and Y Cartesian axes): 1 = minimum; 5 = maximum.

*Source:*   Amundi Research, Amundi Asset Management.

*Figure 19.2   Behavioral chart*

typical of dynamic and asymmetric pay-off products actively managed mitigating drawdowns while seeking profitable opportunities.

## 4.  SURVEY RESULTS: MAIN FINDINGS

The empirical results confirm that the presence of behavioral bias is significant when investors build their preferences.

Despite the limited sample size, the empirical evidence suggests the following (see Box 19.1):

---

### BOX 19.1  SURVEY RESULTS AND STATISTICS TO QUANTIFY AND EVALUATE THE DEGREE OF RATIONALITY AND FLEXIBILITY OF THE INDIVIDUALS

Sample: 30 respondents for a total of 300 questions

| Answers | Rational | Behavioral biased |
|---|---|---|
| *Obs.* | 78 | 72 |
| *% of total* | 52% | 48% |
| *direction of bias (2)* | pro risk | |
| *avg degree of bias (3)* | 9% | |

| Individual assessment | | |
|---|---|---|
| | Rational | Flexible |
| *Avg. ex ante (self-assessment) (4)* | 3.8 | 3.7 |
| *Avg. ex post (answer results) (5)* | 2.6 | 2.7 |

| Self overestimation | | |
|---|---|---|
| | Rational | Flexible |
| *Delta average (6)* | 1.2 | 1 |

*Notes:*
1.  Number of questions framed in two different ways for a total of 300 questions.
2.  Direction of bias: if the behavioral equity exposure is higher than the rational one the bias is pro-risk; if the behavioral equity exposure is lower than the rational one the bias is against risk.
3.  Average delta equity exposure between behavioral and rational.
4.  Individual self-assessment of degree of flexibility and rationality (1 = min.; 5 = max.).
5.  Degree of flexibility and rationality (1 = min.; 5 = max.) derived from the answers.
6.  Delta *ex ante* and *ex post* assessment.

1. 48 percent of the total answers have a behavioral bias. That means that 48 percent of the times splitting the returns in losses and profits the optimal equities exposure is different from the one based on the total average (even if in both cases it is the same).
2. The answers tend to have an irrational slight bias toward risk seeking as they are based more on potential profit opportunities than potential losses.
3. The results confirm that individuals have a significant preference for flexibility (average 2.7), which means a not negligible min/max equities range along different phases.
4. Although individuals tend to overestimate their rational and flexible attitude, rationality looks less easy to self-evaluate.

## CONCLUSIONS

The empirical evidence confirms that investors are influenced by their emotional bias when they formulate investment decisions deviating from the rational framework. Furthermore, they tend to overestimate their rationality and flexible attitudes, generating suboptimal asset allocation decisions without a comprehensive preference-generating process. In order to smooth this attitude, the following three strategies are necessary:

1. Greatly increase the training and the education of investors. The last Einaudi report on 1500 households showed that only 1.5 percent of them attended a financial course and only 22 percent of them understood the meaning of "negative interest rates".
2. Combine the traditional investors' analysis based on generic and pure financials (holdings and portfolio allocation) with global (assets-liabilities management on real and financial assets) and behavioral-financial (needs, behaviors and asset allocation combined optimization) (see Figure 19.3).
3. Accelerate the Financial Industry evolution to provide investors with more efficient solutions in term of cost, risk and return and continue to change the fiscal rules to facilitate and make more attractive the long-term investments in: financial assets related to the real economy (i.e. piani individuali di iisparmio (individual saving plans) – PIR), mid- to long-term dynamic wrapper solutions, complementary pension funds and social and ethical investments.

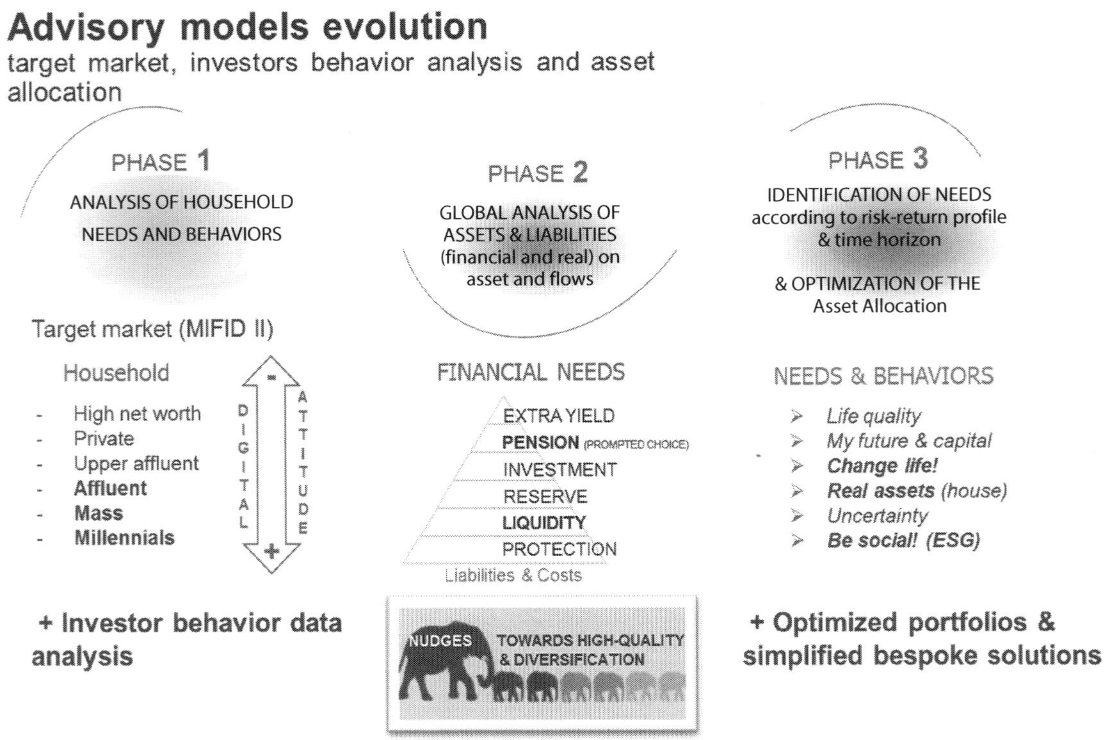

## Advisory models evolution
target market, investors behavior analysis and asset allocation

### PHASE 1
ANALYSIS OF HOUSEHOLD NEEDS AND BEHAVIORS

### PHASE 2
GLOBAL ANALYSIS OF ASSETS & LIABILITIES (financial and real) on asset and flows

### PHASE 3
IDENTIFICATION OF NEEDS according to risk-return profile & time horizon

& OPTIMIZATION OF THE Asset Allocation

Target market (MIFID II)

Household
- High net worth
- Private
- Upper affluent
- **Affluent**
- **Mass**
- **Millennials**

- DIGITAL
+ ATTITUDE

FINANCIAL NEEDS
- EXTRA YIELD
- **PENSION** (PROMPTED CHOICE)
- INVESTMENT
- RESERVE
- **LIQUIDITY**
- PROTECTION

Liabilities & Costs

NUDGES TOWARDS HIGH-QUALITY & DIVERSIFICATION

NEEDS & BEHAVIORS
- Life quality
- My future & capital
- **Change life!**
- **Real assets** (house)
- Uncertainty
- **Be social!** (ESG)

**+ Investor behavior data analysis**

**+ Optimized portfolios & simplified bespoke solutions**

*Source:* Thaler and Sunstein (2008), Thaler (2015), Bodie et al. (2010) and the models used from the most important Italian financial distributors and wealth management companies.

*Figure 19.3 Advisory models evolution: target market, investor behavior analysis and asset allocation*

# REFERENCES

Assogestioni (2017). The Italian asset management market. Key figures.

Banca d'Italia (2015). La ricchezza delle famiglie Italiane.

Banca d'Italia (2017). Gli investimenti delle famiglie attraverso i prodotti del risparmio gestito. Occasional paper, November.

Bodie, Z., Kane, A. and Marcus, A.J. (2010). *Investments and Portfolio Management*. Maidenhead: McGraw-Hill Europe.

Kahneman, D. and Tversky, A. (1979). Prospect theory: An analysis of decision under risk. *Econometrica*, **47**(2), 263–91.

Thaler, Richard H. (2015). *Misbehaving: The Making of Behavioural Economics*. New York, NY: Penguin Books.

Thaler, Richard H. and Sunstein, Cass R. (2008). *Nudge: Improving Decisions About Health, Wealth, and Happiness*. New Haven, CT: Yale University Press.

# Index